From Seed to Table

From Seed to Table

A Practical Guide to Eating and Growing Green

Janette Haase

INSOMNIAC PRESS

Library and Archives Canada Cataloguing in Publication

Haase, Janette, 1958-
   From seed to table : a practical guide to eating and growing green / Janette Haase.

ISBN 978-1-897178-75-1

1. Vegetable gardening--Handbooks, manuals, etc. 2. Organic gardening--Handbooks, manuals, etc. I. Title.

SB324.3.H38 2009   635   C2008-908157-9

The publisher gratefully acknowledges the support of the Department of Canadian Heritage through the Book Publishing Industry Development Program.

Printed and bound in Canada

Insomniac Press
520 Princess Avenue
London, Ontario, Canada, N6B 2B8
www.insomniacpress.com

To Mother Earth
and to all those who rejoice in her beauty and her bounty

With special thanks to my family and friends
for years of support, friendship, and fun.

Contents

Recipe Index

Thai Noodle Salad
Spanish Endive Salad
Cobb Salad
Beet Sandwiches
Sugar Snap and Snow Pea or Mushroom Salad
Chicken with Dill Sauce
Strawberry Shortcake
Strawberry Nut Torte

July   184–187

Beet and Potato or Pasta Salad
Potato Salad with Green Onions and Dill
    Pickles
Greek Pasta Salad with Fresh Herbs
Beet and Parsley Salad with Goat Cheese
Salade Nicoise
Tomato and Cucumber Salad
Cucumbers with Yogurt or Sour Cream
Spicy Chicken and Cucumber Salad
Chilled Cucumber Soup
Marinated Green Bean Salad
Sautéed Zucchini with Garlic, Onions, and
    Tomatoes
Black Beans and Rice
Fresh Coriander and Lemon Sauce

August & September   203–206

Fresh Tomato Salsa
Gazpacho
Sliced Tomatoes with Fresh Garlic
Roasted Tomatoes
Fresh Tomato Soup
Chicken Soup with Tomatoes, Peppers,
    and Corn
Potato and Green Bean Salad
Tomato and Corn Salad
Corn Pancakes
Broccoli and Carrot Salad
Danish Cucumber Salad
Grilled Roasted Vegetable and Cheese
    Sandwiches
Sautéed Swiss Chard with Onions, Garlic,
    and Tomatoes
Summer Salad with Arugula, Tomatoes,
    and Cucumber
Tabouleh
Poached Pears with Ginger and Lemon

October & November   224–230

Carrot, Beet, and Apple Salad
Carrot and Parsley Salad
Sunflower Seed Spread with Kale and Parsley
Beet Borscht
Mixed Vegetable Borscht
Fried Green Tomatoes
Swiss Chard and Rice Casserole
Spanakopita
Steamed Kale with Balsamic Vinegar
Kale and Potato Soup
Creamed Kale
Leek and Potato Soup
Mustard and Leek Sauce
Mushroom and Leek Quiche
Leek and Mushroom Casserole
Baked Spaghetti Squash
Spaghetti Squash with Onions, Garlic, and
    Tomatoes
Garlic Mashed Potatoes
Oven Roasted Potatoes
Pumpkin Soup
Pumpkin Pie
Pumpkin Muffins
Pumpkin Purée

December   238–240

Roasted Vegetables
Scalloped Potatoes
Potato and Leek Pie
Baked Squash, Onions, and Apples
Wild Rice, Cranberry, and Hazelnut Stuffing
Cranberry Apple Strudel
Cranberry Muffins
Cranberry Upside-down Cake

Introduction

Whatever you can do, or dream you can, begin it,
boldness has genius, power, and magic in it.
    –Johann Wolfgang van Goethe

As we make our way into this first decade of the twenty-first century, it is becoming increasingly evident that Canadians view climate change and environmental degradation as two of the most important issues facing our society today. But Canadians have the unfortunate reputation of having the third largest ecological footprint in the world. We consume far more than our share of fossil fuels, water, and electricity. Many of the efforts at addressing this problem have focused on encouraging energy conservation in our homes and in the cars we drive. Recently, there has been an increasing awareness that the food we consume is also highly energy intensive. A 2001 British study estimated that the average family of four emits approximately 4.4 tonnes of carbon dioxide while driving their car in a year, while an astonishing eight tonnes of carbon dioxide are emitted as a result of the production, processing, packaging, and distribution of the food they eat in that same year. The average kilogram of food travels some 3000 kilometres from producer to consumer. Our food systems expend an average of ten calories of energy to produce one calorie of food. Compare this to the half calorie of energy that so-called 'traditional agriculture' uses to produce one calorie of food. We seem to have a few problems with efficiency.

Planting a garden is an important and enjoyable way of significantly reducing greenhouse gas emissions, but it can also be about much more than that. Growing one's own food can be a highly political choice, the first step on an exciting and educational journey to ecological awareness. When we grow our own food, we are transformed from passive to active consumers. We feel the soil in our hands; we take pride in what we are growing, and we enjoy our harvest. But perhaps most important, we have time to think about and to question the dynamics of our lives and the implications of our lifestyles for the environment.

Wangari Maathai is a Kenyan environmentalist who was awarded the Nobel Peace Prize in 2004. There are those who questioned the choice of an environmentalist for a prize that honours peace work. But, in a recent article, Frances Moore Lappé, author of *Diet for a Small Planet*, argues that the genius of Wangari Maathai is that she recognizes the direct connections between environmentalism, equality, democracy, and peace. Maathai began her work in 1977 when she planted seven trees to honour Kenyan women who were environmental leaders. She went on to found the Green Belt Movement through which Kenyan women have planted more than 30 million trees and established some 6000 tree nurseries. Lappé suggests that Maathai envisioned the planting of trees as both a good in itself and as an entry point, a way in which women could find courage to act and to change their lives. Her vision was true. Through the planting of trees, the women of the Green Belt Movement gained greater control over their own firewood; this not only gave them power in their communities, it also freed up their time for other issues. Through education programs, organic methods of farming for kitchen gardens were developed and indigenous crops were reintroduced. This went against government and International Monetary Fund (IMF) policies of export oriented agriculture. Each of these actions brought greater self-sufficiency and independence as Kenyan women gained control of both their food and their cooking fuel. By the late 1990s, the Green Belt Movement had become a major pro-democracy force in Kenya, and in 2002 Maathai was elected to Parliament. By honouring the work of Wangari Maathai, the Nobel committee gave its support to the idea that global peace lies not only with individual leaders, but also with ordinary citizens who, by becoming active participants in the life of their communities, can change their world.

In Canada, our problems differ from those in Kenya, but the underlying need to address them is the same. Canadians face problems of environmental degradation, air and water pollution, global warming, and alarmingly high rates of cancer and other diseases. Many of us feel disconnected from our environment and powerless to stop the dehumanizing forces of globalization that often seem to make little sense and that undermine the health of our communities and our ecosystems. As consumers, we can begin to make active choices. By finding a place from which to enter the environmental arena, by educating ourselves, and by changing the ways in which we interact with each other and with our environment, we can embark on the same kind of journey that Wangari Maathai envisioned. Food touches all aspects of life; eating is a simple act but it is one that can bring about fundamental shifts in our society.

It is clear that Canada has had little success in reducing its greenhouse gas emissions. In 2004 our emissions totalled one third more than the Kyoto target levels; if we continue as we are, we will be at double the target levels by 2012. As a society we must change the way we think about the environment and about our use of energy. Every one of us can find simple and positive ways to lessen our impact on the environment. Try planting a garden and eating food that you have grown yourself—food that is unpackaged and unprocessed and that has travelled only a few metres from producer to consumer. Get outside, taste those first tomatoes, share your seeds and your stories with your neighbours, and see where the journey takes you.

Sources:

Lappé, F.M. and Lappé, A., "The Genius of Wangari Maathai," in *Alternatives Magazine,* University of Waterloo Press, Waterloo, Ontario, Nov./Dec. 2004, page 30.

From the Author

I planted my first garden in 1984, the same year that I was pregnant with my eldest son. My husband and I were living in Newfoundland and we had made friends with a couple who were 'living off the land'—goats, chickens, a root cellar, and a very large garden. Concerned about the new life inside of me, my friends filled my fridge with fresh goat's milk and produce from their garden. They had built a root cellar into a hill beside their house and I will never forget the quality and taste of their produce—carrots that were still crisp and sweet in April and most amazingly, apples that had been stored all winter in wooden drawers, still crunchy and far better than anything the grocery store had to offer. For the first time I began to wonder why there was such a huge difference between food from the grocery store and food from the garden.

Growing up in Montreal and attending Queen's University in Kingston, most of my education had happened in the classroom. I knew very little about farming, the term 'organic,' or the ins and outs of environmental issues. That summer I planted a small kitchen garden and, as I had always been interested in food, I grew Butterhead lettuces, Sugar Snap peas, and tiny French beans. I found that I loved the whole experience of working outside, planting, weeding, harvesting, and best of all, eating.

In 1986, my husband and I moved back to Ontario and we bought a fifty-acre farm north east of Kingston. I was expecting my second son and we had vague ideas of selling specialty vegetables and herbs to restaurants. As luck would have it, a year and a half later I landed a job as a waitress at a Kingston restaurant that was also interested in buying seasonal organic vegetables. So began twelve years of hard work, in which our family grew to five and our garden grew to two acres. Our clients included the National Arts Centre and Chateau Laurier in Ottawa and Chez Piggy in Kingston. We began growing all of the vegetables for our family; we raised chickens and pigs, made maple syrup, cut our own firewood, and generally immersed ourselves in farm life. I was fortunate to be invited to join a food buying club and began ordering organic food in bulk. Living in the country, we had to bring our own garbage to the dump. Watching the site fill had a profound effect on me and I began to work seriously towards reducing the amount of garbage

that our family generated.

When my marriage ended in 1994, I continued to run the market garden. However, raising three children and running a farm on one's own is exhausting work and in 1998 we moved to a village north of Kingston. A small village is a good place to be a single parent—people are really supportive and schools, shops, and friends are all within walking distance. But living without a garden was not a pleasant thought and so it wasn't long before I began digging up my lawn. I was amazed at the quantity of vegetables I could produce in a small garden of about 300 square feet. I grew peas, lettuces, salad greens, tomatoes, cucumbers, and much more. In fact, from May to November I bought very little from the store, only staples such as carrots, onions, and potatoes. That fall I went to a local organic farmer and bought my winter supply of storage vegetables. One Saturday afternoon I insulated the old cistern in my basement and made a very respectable root cellar.

Leaving a fifty-acre farm and moving to a postage stamp-sized lot without even a backyard has certainly been a challenge. The past years have been ones of change and of re-examining my life. But they have also been years of growth. I have found new ways to nurture my interests in organic agriculture, sustainability, and food. Living close to a university is always a blessing and I took courses in Women's Studies, Environmental Studies, Introductory Ethics, and Development Studies. I also began mulling over the idea for this book, compiling recipes, documenting the work in my garden, and organizing my research notes. I believe from my own experience that the act of planting one's own food is not just about the produce, it is also about a very different way of approaching the world. As I have spent time in my garden, my understanding of the environment, my relationship with nature, my definitions of value and social justice, my approach to waste disposal, and much more have changed significantly. What would our world look like if we each grew and ate some of our own foods? After reading an article tying individual food consumption to astonishingly high levels of carbon dioxide emissions, the impetus to start writing this book took on a whole new relevance.

Anyone with a small backyard can grow a significant amount of food. We can all learn to incorporate seasonal and local foods into our diets. These kinds of small individual actions are not only personal, they also strengthen our communities and benefit our environment. I hope that you find the information in this book practical, interesting, and challenging. May the hours you spend in your garden provide fertile ground for your own journey in life and may this work contribute in a positive way to environmental change in our society.

About the Book

When I first envisioned this project, I knew that I wanted to write about more than the practical details of growing vegetables in a small backyard garden. I wanted to use the garden as inspiration for menu ideas and recipes while exploring what it means to eat seasonally and locally in a northern climate. I also wanted to include a discussion of some of the issues that surround food production because they contribute to many of our current environmental, social, and health problems.

I wrote the gardening section so that it would work for someone who has never bought a package of seeds before, but who nevertheless would like to grow a successful garden and eat well from that garden. Many gardening books offer a wealth of useful information, but using that information can be challenging because it does not always come in an orderly or sequential form. I wanted to walk you, the reader, through a year of gardening, so information about planting, harvesting, and eating is presented at the times it is needed. To do this, *From Seed to Table* is organized on a month-by-month basis, so the work that needs to be done is explained when it needs doing. In January, I talk about ordering seed catalogues; in February, I present several different garden plans and describe how to place a seed order; and in March, there is a discussion of why and how to make transplants. I then go on to talk about things such as planting methods, mulching, composting, winter storage, and garden clean up.

In each section there is information on what foods are considered seasonal in my area (southeastern Ontario) as well as harvesting and storage information for those foods. Winter storage is covered in the fall and includes a section on building and stocking a simple cold room. There are menu ideas and recipes designed to help you enjoy both local produce and the fruits (vegetables) of your labour!

Finally, in each chapter I also present material about environmental, social, and political issues that I feel are relevant to the whole discussion. Growing your own food, buying locally, and eating seasonally have the potential to bring about some very fundamental shifts in our society. It is my hope that these discussions will contribute to an understanding of how our food systems work.

The gardening information in *From Seed to Table* is based upon the premise that there is a limited amount of growing space. Even when a large garden is possible, I would strongly recommend that you start small and concentrate on growing and harvesting efficiently. I have watched several people in my area struggle with gardens that are far too big and that produce far too much food. Their desire to grow their own food and their enthusiasm for the process does not seem to survive the discouragement of overwhelming weeds or of twenty-five feet of lettuce that matures in the same week!

In the February chapter, you will see that I have given detailed plans for a number of small gardens. There are three 'summer garden' plans, designed to provide fresh vegetables from early May to late November. The first summer garden is about 350 square feet and should easily feed two people; the second is 500 square feet and is designed for a family of four or five. Both of these gardens concentrate on growing what I call summer vegetables—greens, tomatoes,

beans, and peas—but they are too small for things like onions or carrots. There is also a small plan with two extra beds for growing some carrots, onions, potatoes, and squash. If you have space, these two beds can be added to either of the summer garden plans. Finally there is a 750-square-foot 'winter storage garden' plan that should provide a family of four with enough produce to see them through the winter, as long as they have some sort of cold storage area. The instructions and timelines for planting and harvesting in the book are based upon these four garden designs. The plans are quite detailed because it took me many years of trial and error to grow a really productive and efficient garden and I want to share what I learned. Growing on a commercial scale required an attention to timing and detail that has been invaluable in my own small garden where there is very little wasted effort and very little wasted space—I have grown an incredible amount of food in about 300 square feet of garden for the past ten years.

I realize that gardening is a creative and personal endeavour and many of you will want to adapt my plans or make something entirely your own. To help with this, I have discussed some basic principles, including planting requirements and seeding dates for the vegetables that are not in my garden plans. I encourage you to make your own plans and to keep a notebook with your own schedules and notes. What I really want to convey in the gardening section is the idea of small, successive plantings over the whole summer and the efficient use of time and space.

There is a great deal of information in this book and it is not meant to be read all at once. Try to work your way through each chapter and let each new section build on the previous one. Before you know it you will be an expert gardener, have a whole new repertoire of cooking ideas, and be looking forward to a new year. It is my wish that *From Seed to Table* helps you to enjoy and eat well from a really productive garden, that you learn something about food issues, and that your time in the garden nourishes your soul and brings you peace and much satisfaction.

On Eating Seasonally

Creating a diet that includes locally grown and seasonal food does require some work and patience. If you also want this food to be organic, the process is somewhat more involved, but not impossible. The way by which you accomplish your goals very much depends upon your circumstances, the amount of garden space and time that you have, and to some extent, the openness of your family to the project. Much of my own success started with a decision not to go to the grocery store for vegetables unless absolutely necessary and a willingness to be creative with what I had. I am a great believer in the idea that necessity is the mother of invention.

Eating seasonal produce means choosing foods that are currently being harvested or that have been stored in your area. One article I read on the subject was fairly pessimistic—essentially saying that eating local foods in a northern climate was an all right idea if you liked rutabagas. This has not been my experience. For me, the summer months are filled with a wide variety of wonderful fruits and vegetables. The winter months offer just as many delicious and satisfying foods especially if one has some sort of cold storage area and some basic freezing and canning skills.

When I first started growing my own food, I spent a great deal of time filling my freezer with peas, beans, corn, peppers, and so on during the summer months. Each winter we would eat these vegetables, along with some storage vegetables but by spring I always felt as though I had some sort of nutrient deficiency. As I pondered this, I began to wonder if perhaps this was because the summer vegetables that I had frozen did not contain the vitamins and minerals needed to get me through a northern winter. Was it possible that I should be eating far more winter storage vegetables? Many of these vegetables extract a significant amount of nutrients from the ground (i.e. they are heavy feeders); others have roots that extend deep into the soil, and others still are important sources of beta-carotene. As well, vegetables such as carrots, cabbage, and beats can be eaten fresh throughout the winter months. I decided to spend a lot less time freezing and a lot more time growing an adequate supply of leeks, onions, garlic, carrots, beets, cabbage, turnip, squash, and potatoes to get me through the winter. When I did this I found that I felt much healthier, though by March and April I had cravings for something green. The final answers to my pondering came from a friend who encouraged me to grow sunflower seed, mung bean, and alfalfa sprouts in a fairly serious way, and from another friend who introduced me to the idea of drinking herbal tonics, particularly nettle tea during those last months of winter. The sprouts added something fresh and vigorous to my diet and the herbal tonics provided me with chlorophyll and extra vitamins and minerals.

If I look at this in a more holistic way, I would say that in the summer my energy comes primarily from the sun and the foods that I eat embody this energy—they are primarily green; they tend to have shallow root systems; and they are best eaten immediately after picking. In the winter, my energy comes mainly from the earth. The plants that I eat have used the sun and their roots to draw in and store the earth's energy, producing foods that remain fresh throughout the winter and retaining their nutrients through storage. There is some overlap and I do supplement my winter diet with frozen, home canned, and dried fruits and vegetables but I have moved away from that initial reliance on my freezer. In this book I present an almost journal-like look at what I do, but I really believe that food is an intensely personal thing and each of us must find our own balance. I would also say that I have given suggestions on canning but have avoided any kinds of detailed instructions—this is beyond the scope of this book and there are many good books on the subject available through libraries and bookstores.

Eating seasonally involves a much different approach to eating. Some foods, such as onions and garlic are available almost all year round; carrots and salad greens are available for six to eight months of the year; and peas, beans, and radishes are in the garden for only six to eight weeks. Our diet has a rhythm and a cyclical nature about it that begins to feel quite natural. In the spring, we eat very little other than salads. In early June we move on to peas, beets, and endive and by August it's cucumbers, tomatoes, beans, corn, and basil. The early fall brings a feast of cold weather greens as well as carrots, leeks, and potatoes. After Christmas, we focus on the cabbage, onions, squash, and turnip in the root cellar. For me, there is a feeling of anticipation as I await my first salad of the year. Those first peas taste absolutely wonderful; we enjoy them to their fullest and then they are gone until the next year. I look forward to each of the vegetables in my garden in ways that I wouldn't have had I been eating them throughout the year. It is also my belief that the nutrients in each vegetable are suited to the needs of your body at that time of year: salads to nourish in the spring, cool cucumbers in the heat of summer, and in the cold of winter warm stews whose ingredients have gathered nutrients from deep within the soil.

The beauty of homegrown vegetables is that they really do taste so much better than commercially grown produce. It is easy to serve simple meals and salads; the flavour of each vegetable stands on its own. I can remember going to the garden and picking a zucchini to slice up and cook for supper. I snuck a few slices to munch on before cooking them and was absolutely struck by the sweetness and creaminess of what I was eating—these qualities are lost within a few hours of picking and are missing in store-bought vegetables. Refrigeration affects the taste and quality of vegetables and as a result, many people never experience the real potential for flavour in the vegetables that they eat. For those who are committed to eating organic produce, gardening allows one to enjoy large quantities of vegetables at a fraction of the cost of purchased produce. This was brought home to me in the fall of 2008 when I was away from my garden for two months. I was doing my own cooking and found myself spending from $20-25 per week just for organic vegetables at a local farm stand.

Eating seasonal fruits is much more difficult in northern climates, though our great-grandparents managed it by having a good root cellar for apples and by canning and drying berries, apples, peaches, pears, cherries, grapes, and plums. I do rely on my freezer to store strawberries, raspberries, blueberries, cranberries, and rhubarb. I also like to do some preserving and I purchase some dried fruits. In summer we enjoy local strawberries and raspberries, as well as pears, peaches, plums, cherries, and cantaloupe. Every fall, I buy several bushels of local apples, which stay fresh and crispy in my root cellar and fridge until sometime in January. During the winter months and in early spring, we eat a lot of cooked fruit, including pies, crisps, compotes of apples, frozen berries, and rhubarb, as well as stewed prunes. My children enjoy these dishes but in all honesty, it has been a process of gradual adjustment and I often buy some imported fruit in late winter and early spring. Perhaps because they are getting used to me or perhaps because of the success of my writing, this year (2008) is the first year that we have bought only a very small amount of imported fruit.

I do think that there is potential for growing or scrounging some of your own small fruits. I have always been somewhat of a hunter/gatherer and I like to pick wild blackberries, strawberries, grapes, and apples wherever I can find them. This summer I hit the jackpot when I found an abandoned house with raspberries growing all along its north wall. I harvested about twenty litres of berries from this patch and I realized that a patch like this could easily be incorporated into one's landscaping. I was also pleasantly surprised one summer when the two plum trees that I had planted six years before on my tiny front lawn exploded with fruit. They were smaller than commercial plums but the branches were literally drooping to the ground under the weight of the fruit. I gave away bushels of fruit and still had enough to fill my freezer with a two-year supply of stewed plums that I used in juices, compotes, custards, and cheesecakes—I am not a fan of jam. The amazing thing is that both the plums and the raspberries did well with little or no care. I think I pruned the plum trees twice in six years and one spring I had to burn off some tent caterpillars. The raspberries were full of weeds and old canes that should have been cut out but they were

One of my plum trees in the summer of 2006. I noticed that the tree was really drooping when the plums were still small and green. At first I thought it was dying but when I looked closely I saw that it was absolutely laden with plums! (In hindsight I probably should have removed some of the fruit because several branches broke under the weight).

still loaded with berries. When we begin to look for different ways of doing things, it is my belief that the universe will do its best to provide.

On Buying Locally

In the last few years, the idea of buying local foods has received a great deal of media attention. As public awareness and interest grows, many feel that this issue is one place where, as consumers, they can find a meaningful expression for their social and environmental convictions. For those who feel that the organic industry has abandoned its grassroots principles and sold out to big business, 'local has become the new organic.'

As you work your way through this book, I hope you will learn how to incor-porate local and seasonal foods into your diet. Perhaps the first step should be to decide what you can grow for yourself and what you prefer to buy. I try to grow a large portion of my own vegetables but I can't grow everything in my small garden so I buy such things as local asparagus, corn, and storage vegetables. I also try to support local producers of fruit, maple syrup, honey, eggs, grains, and meat.

Perhaps the easiest places to find local produce are farmers' markets, small independent grocery stores, and health food stores. I live near Kingston, Ontario, and there are several organic growers at the local market as well as many conventional growers who do not use a lot of chemicals. It is a good idea to find out exactly where a vendor's produce has come from because many farmers' markets allow vendors to buy wholesale produce from a distributor and then resell it.

Farmers' markets and small local grocery stores are the best places to buy local fruit, though it is my experience that fruit that is both local and organic is seldom available commercially. Often the exceptions to this are pick-your-own strawberry and raspberry operations, as well as small apple orchards that do not use a lot of chemical sprays. Many health food stores will sell organic fruit in bulk. Though usually not local, the bulk price is often not much different from what one would pay for conventional produce that is bought in small quantities. For the most part, it does seem that one must choose between eating local fruit that is not organic or eating organic fruit that is not local. Cost and the environmental implications of importing food may influence your decisions. Unfortunately, there are many things to consider and few easy answers.

Local organic growers will often sell vegetables through a sort of buying club, something that has been called 'Community Supported Agriculture' or CSA. Generally, a CSA scheme operates with an arrangement between you and the grower whereby you agree to accept a certain amount of produce every week. It is based on the idea that you take a share of what is grown and thereby guarantee the farmer a steady customer. Generally the produce is delivered to your door or to a central drop-off point. Produce is either supplied only during the growing season or throughout the year if the farmer has cold storage facilities. CSAs often work to foster a feeling of community among their members and many require that you spend some time working on the farm. There are also organic growers who supplement their own vegetables with commercial organic produce and offer a home delivery service for which you place an order every week.

Finding some sort of producers list can be very helpful when you first start to look for sources of local produce. Canadian Organic Growers (COG) publishes a quarterly magazine, *Eco-Farm & Garden*, and many of COG's local chapters compile lists of both certified and non-certified organic producers of vegetables, fruits, meat, eggs, herbs, and honey. These lists are available on the *Eco-Farm & Garden* Web site (*www.cog.ca*). Look under your local chapter for details.

There are numerous campaigns throughout North America that focus on promoting local agriculture. In 2007, the Kingston chapter of the National Farmers Union launched its own local food campaign called Food Down the Road. The campaign generated a huge amount of interest and momentum through educational and promotional materials, a local food logo, a speaker series, and a two day conference. Its Web site, *www.fooddowntheroad.ca* has an excellent farm product guide.

Another Canadian initiative is Toronto's Local Food Plus (LFP). LFP promotes local products with an added emphasis on environmentally and socially responsible practices. In order to use the LFP logo, producers must undergo an inspection and certification process in which they meet standards that include: the reduction or elimination of chemical fertilizers and pesticides; safe and fair working conditions; the humane treatment of animals; and a reduced use of fossil fuels.

In return, Local Food Plus connects farmers with consumers and institutions. In 2006, it negotiated a much coveted local purchase agreement with the University of Toronto.

In the United States, western Massachusetts has one of the most successful local food initiatives in North America. "Be a Local Hero, Buy Locally Grown" is a marketing and awareness campaign that focuses on supporting local farmers through a wide range of community programs and activities. These include farm tours, product guides, a farm share program for seniors, a farm to school program, the promotion of city market and institutional sales, and a very visible logo wherever local products are sold. Interestingly enough, their market research found that it is the public's desire to support and maintain a strong local community (rather than environmental issues) that is the driving force behind the success of their campaign.

The demand for local products is increasing steadily and with it comes more and more growers and retailers. Our support for them is so important if we want to ensure a dependable food supply and a vibrant agricultural community.

Getting Started

Before I go into the monthly sections, there are a few things that you should think about if you are going to try a garden out for yourself.

Gardening Books

We'll start with the one that involves the least amount of work and that is the purchase of one or two good gardening books. These books should serve as a reference as well as provide enjoyable reading and inspiration in the winter months. They should offer basic advice on soil fertility, composting, planting, and harvesting techniques, give a detailed description of each vegetable, and have a section on common garden pests. My favourite gardening book is called *Joy of Gardening* by Dick Raymond. It is one of the most comprehensive books I have seen and is full of interesting ideas. There are instructions for organic and conventional methods of gardening; perhaps because the book was written quite a while ago, wherever he calls for 'fertilizer' I read 'compost.' I was not able to find this book in stores in my area, but sales personnel indicated that it can easily be ordered. Other books I have found useful include *The New Organic Grower* and *Four-Season Harvest* by Eliot Coleman and *Square Foot Gardening* by Mel Bartholomew. If you enjoy salad vegetables, *The Fine Art of Salad Gardening* by Annie Proulx (the author of *The Shipping News)* is an interesting and enjoyable read. Unfortunately, it's out of print but you may be able to find it in a good second-hand book store or online.

If you are interested in gardening and/or farming issues, Canadian Organic Growers (*www.cog.ca*) and the National Farmers Union (*www.nfu.ca*) both publish quarterly magazines, have local chapters, and host a variety of events throughout Canada. Canadian Organic Growers also has an extensive lending library that is free to members.

Composting Facilities

If there is one aspect of organic gardening that seems to create a great deal of uncertainty, it is composting. Perhaps this is because the quality of your compost and the speed at which it is produced is directly tied to the amount of effort that you put into turning and watering it. I have found that two compost bins and a single turning with Mother Nature doing the watering produces a reasonable quality of compost in two years. For me, this is good enough.

Composting is covered in detail in the October/November section. For now it is a good idea to think about locating and building two compost bins. If possible, place the bins against a natural boundary such as a cedar rail fence or a line of trees, so that this can form the back 'wall' of the bins. My two enclosures are about three feet by five feet in size. The first I built by stacking some used concrete blocks on top of each other, forming a wall about 30" high against a cedar rail fence. I tend to be a fairly lazy handyperson (much to the frustration of my very handy son) and there is no cement holding the blocks together, but the design seems to work well. The second bin is parallel to the first one and its outside wall is made from three straw bales, two on the bottom and one on top. They do eventually start to decompose, at which time I add them to my compost and/or use them to mulch my garden. Then I buy another three bales and rebuild the wall.

Wooden pallets, and/or wire fencing can also be used to form walls. If you don't want to build, the large plastic barrels that many communities sell will also work— you will probably need at least two. I have never had any problems with pests such as raccoons and skunks, perhaps because we have a dog. If you do have problems you may need to build something more substantial with solid sides, a removable front wall, and a lid.

I begin each fall with one empty compost bin, filling it with garden and kitchen waste throughout the next year. It is not a good idea to put any kind of meat products such as bones or fat on your compost as this may attract animals. I also avoid grass clippings if they have come from a gas-powered lawn mower or a chemically sprayed lawn. If you have a wood stove you must add the ashes very sparingly as they will affect the pH of your soil. About two to three gallons of ashes per 1000 square feet of garden per year is tolerable. The second compost bin contains material from the previous year that has been turned and layered with straw and manure.

Some Basic Equipment

Gardening is a fairly simple exercise and does not require many special tools. My most valued tool is a traditional, four-tined garden fork, available at most hardware stores for about $30.00. Look for one where the tines are strong and large—smaller forks have 8" tines, larger ones have 10" tines. A bigger fork makes for easier digging. A round ended shovel is also useful for scooping compost or manure, but the fork is far more efficient when it comes to digging.

Other useful items include:

- Seven or eight second-hand five- and seven-gallon food grade pails to carry water, manure, compost, and weeds.
- A wheelbarrow to move compost and weeds. (A wheelbarrow is not essential and it is expensive for some.)
- A decent set of hand tools, including a small trowel, a hand fork, and a small hoe.
- A four-foot stick marked at one-foot intervals to mark your beds and space your plants.

❧ A pair of shoes that can get wet and muddy.

For watering you will need:

❧ Some garden hose.

❧ A gentle sprinkler (you do not want anything that blasts your plants with a hard spray of water.)

❧ A watering wand with a soft spray.

❧ A timer that automatically shuts off the water to your sprinkler. I find these really worthwhile because you can water at night or turn the water on and go away. Also you don't have to worry about forgetting to turn off the sprinkler and possibly running your well dry (don't ask me how I know this!).

To Till Or Not To Till: Many people ask me if they should purchase a small tiller. For the most part I would say no. A small garden is easy to work by hand – the hardest job is the initial digging but even this is quite manageable if you first kill the top growth (see later in this chapter). If you are planning a larger garden it is often enough to rent a tiller for a day. The main reason I do not like a tiller is that it is not very manoeuvrable in a small space - one must till a large area at once and have clear access to that area. A fork allows for far greater flexibility because you can dig small sections at a time, even if they are surrounded by other vegetables that are still growing. A fork is also far easier to start, needs no gas or oil, requires minimal maintenance, and takes up very little space in the shed!

The Garden

If possible, it is preferable to dig your garden in the fall, once the weather has cooled down but before the ground freezes. If this can't be done, start in April and dig, fertilize, and plant as you go. I do recommend that you start with a small garden—a large garden requires more compost, more weeding, more watering, and generally a lot more work. Nothing is more discouraging than looking at a field full of weeds and a small garden will grow an enormous amount of food. So start small, get good at what you are doing, and then, if you still feel ambitious, expand slowly.

If you only have a small backyard, you probably don't have too many choices as to where you can put your garden. Many people ask me if a garden can be near or on their septic bed. I called the Ministry of the Environment and they assured me that there is no danger of pathogen contamination if your septic is functioning properly. If you are using a Rototiller, you may want to be careful that this activity does not cause any damage. You should also consider issues of drainage, shade, soil depth, and wind protection. Avoid areas that are very wet in the spring or that are heavily shaded, though a small amount of shade is not a bad thing, especially when it gets really hot. If there is bare rock exposed on your lawn you will have to find the area where the soil is deepest and you may want to increase your soil depth with additional organic material. Avoid wide open spaces without wind protection as it only takes one very windy day to wreak havoc on a garden.

I have a very small lot and so I actually have several different gardens. There is a small area on my patio that is very well protected and warms up quickly in the spring as well as a few beds on the south side of my house where I plant my tomatoes and peppers. Then there is the main garden where I do the bulk of my planting. This arrangement has some advantages but it does make watering more complicated, as I cannot water everything at once.

I prefer to dig my garden by hand. The easiest way to do this is to cause the top growth to decompose before you dig. This can be done by covering the area for four to six weeks with some sort of tarp, scrap wood, or other material that will block the light. When you lift the covering, much or all of the sod will have decomposed and become organic matter and a part of your soil. Turn the soil over using a garden fork—it penetrates the ground and lifts the soil far easier than a shovel can. As you dig you should remove and compost any remaining roots. You may see some small white grubs; these are June bug larvae and should be killed, as they will eat the roots of your plants. If you decide to dig through the sod, shake off as much soil as possible and put the remaining grass and roots on the compost. If you decide to Rototill your new garden it should be done several times, preferably in the fall so that the grass and roots have time to decompose.

Don't be discouraged if your soil isn't perfect – my lot is tiny and the only logical place for my garden was an area that was once an old gravel road. I dug off the weeds and grass. There was some soil but also an awful lot of rocks and gravel so I decided to get a truckload of soil and composted cow manure from a farmer. My garden isn't perfect and the lack of soil depth means that it dries out very quickly in hot weather. Each year as I add more compost and dig out a good supply of stones, the soil gets deeper and richer, and with regular watering it grows a great deal of food.

Fertility

A garden needs yearly applications of organic matter to do well. Soil fertility and ongoing soil care are discussed in detail in the April section but, in the short term, I would encourage you to think about finding a good source of manure. I don't think that one can make enough compost to keep a garden going, especially if you are doing a winter storage garden and/or are also using compost on your flower beds. The best solution I have found is to get well composted horse manure from a nearby riding stable, which I transport home in my large plastic pails. I find I need about one to two dozen pails a year— my Honda Civic holds six to eight pails at a time so I do have to make a few trips. You can also buy commercially bagged manure or perhaps you know a small farmer who has extra.

Climate

As you work your way through this book, you will see that I have provided schedules for seeding vegetables indoors as well as for planting them in your garden. These schedules work for me, living in Southeastern Ontario at about 45° latitude. But not all of us live in an area with a similar climate so the next question is— how can one use the information in this book and apply it to other parts of Canada and the United States? My first thought is that the basic premises of this book—a small and efficient garden, many successive plantings, and eating what you are growing—all still apply. However, you must have some idea about the suitability of different vegetables to your region as well as how to adapt the planting and transplanting schedules.

I would suggest that you begin by looking at frost dates for your area, both the average last frost in the spring and the average first frost in the fall. This information can easily be obtained by talking with an experienced local gardener. Failing that, it is also available online: visit *The Old Farmer's Almanac—frost dates for Canada* or *for the United States* (www.almanac.com). These dates will give you a sense of when you can start planting in the spring and when (or if) you will have to start protecting your garden in the fall. The number of days in between these dates will give you your growing season.

Frost occurs when the temperature at ground level dips below 0°C (32°F). In the spring, one generally waits until after the last spring frost to plant frost sensitive crops such as tomatoes, peppers, eggplant, and basil. Keep in mind that these are only average dates, so pay attention to your local weather forecast; if it predicts frost, you will have to cover your plants. Late spring frosts are generally not severe, so a light sheet or a layer of floating row cover is usually sufficient. (See February section for information on floating row covers.)

In my experience fall frosts are far more variable.

For the most part, the first fall frost is a light frost, with the temperature falling to between 0 to -4°C (32° to 25°F) and again, a length of floating row cover may well protect your whole garden.

The next grade of frost is called a hard frost. This is when the temperature falls between -4° and -8°C (25° to 20°F). Frost-hardy crops will survive with some protection but frost-sensitive crops usually do not.

Finally, there is the killing frost when the temperature dips below -10° to -12°C (15° to 10°F). This frost damages all but the hardiest vegetables, but plants such as kale, Swiss chard, and spinach will often survive if they are covered with sheets, blankets, straw, and/or cold frames.

I went online and looked at frost dates for North America. For the purposes of this section, I divided the data into three general areas for which I think the information in this book can apply. These areas are general because frost dates are greatly affected by altitude (the higher up you are the colder it will be) and by proximity to water. Gardeners in Kingston, which is on Lake Ontario, will often still have tomatoes and basil in late October several weeks after my garden, which is 20 minutes north of the city, has been hit by a hard frost. So before you decide which area you fall into, get an accurate sense of your climate.

Area 1 is warmer than where I live in Southern Ontario, with last spring frosts in April and first fall frosts in late October or early November. This area includes the

Eastern Seaboard and the mid-western states as well as Southern British Columbia.

Area 2 has its last spring frosts in May and first fall frosts in late September or early October. It includes my home north of Kingston, Ontario as well as most of southern Canada, from the Prairies to the Maritimes. In the U.S., it includes the New England States as well as states that border Canada to the south, east of the Rocky Mountains.

Area 3 is for those really tough gardeners who live where the last spring frost is in June and the first fall frost is in early September. This area encompasses pretty well all of northern Canada, from B.C., through the Prairies, into Northern Ontario and Quebec and all the way to Newfoundland and Labrador. I cannot profess to give advice on the Far North or the Far South as I would imagine that both experience very different growing conditions.

Also for the purposes of this section, I have divided vegetables into those that do best in cool weather, those that do well in almost all types of weather, and those that need really hot weather to produce.

Cool weather crops include endive, green garlic, kohlrabi, lettuce, peas, radishes, spinach, and spring turnips. These plants will all tolerate many frosts and even a light snow. When the weather gets really hot, they will either start to go to seed, stop producing, or get tough.

All weather crops include basil, beans, beets, broccoli, Brussels sprouts, cabbage, carrots, cauliflower, celery, corn, cucumbers, green onions, kale, leeks, onions, parsley, parsnips, potatoes, rutabaga, salad greens, Swiss chard, winter squash, zucchini, and most herbs. Most of these plants will produce well in all of the zones but keep in mind that corn and members of the squash family like some heat and are frost sensitive.

Hot weather crops include tomatoes, peppers, melons, and eggplant. These plants need heat to produce well and are definitely frost sensitive.

If you live in Area 1

You enjoy early springs and late falls, but summers will vary from hot to temperate depending on whether or not you live near a major body of water. **Cool weather crops** should be planted as early as possible, as soon as the soil is no longer frozen. In areas where spring turns almost instantly into summer it may be difficult to grow these crops. Try to create garden areas that receive some shade for at least part of the day. You can also buy something called a shade cloth—vegetables grow underneath it and it blocks some of the sunlight. Most cool weather crops can be planted again in late summer for a fall garden and should survive well into December. In areas with mild winters it may well be possible to eat frost hardy vegetables such as green onions, salad greens, spinach, kale, and Swiss chard right through the winter, especially if you have some frost protection. You will have to experiment with the timing of your fall plantings as they are greatly affected by rapidly diminishing light levels, which results in a much slower growth rate.

You will probably enjoy many months of warm weather and will not have to work hard to grow any of the **all weather crops**. Similarly, it should not be necessary to trap heat for **hot weather vegetables** such as peppers, melons, or eggplant. In hot, dry areas it may be a challenge to maintain adequate moisture in the garden. Try to incorporate rain barrels under your eavestrough wherever possible and mulch your garden to prevent moisture from evaporating (see the June section).

If you work through my planting and transplanting schedules you can probably move all the dates ahead by two to four weeks, depending upon how mild your climate is.

If you live in Area 2
My planting and transplanting schedules are based upon a last spring frost date of May 21. You may have to adjust them by one or two weeks, either earlier or later, but for the most part, they should work for you. **Cool weather crops** should be planted as early as possible, most **all weather crops** will be easy to grow, and **hot weather crops** will do well with some extra heat. Don't underestimate the effect of little micro climates. I have a stone patio with a small terraced bed that gets lots of sun and grows excellent cucumbers and peppers. I also have a south sloping garden that borders my driveway and the road and I do not grow good peas

there. They do well for a few weeks and then the plants start to dry up because the area traps heat. My neighbour down the road (literally six houses away) has some shade on the west side of her garden and was bringing me peas for about a month after mine were finished. So take advantage of hot, sheltered areas and of areas with some shade protection.

If you live in Area 3
My first years of gardening took place in Newfoundland so I have some experience with short season gardening. On the bright side, **cool weather vegetables** flourished and I remember absolutely beautiful Butterhead lettuces, spinach, and Sugar Snap peas all summer long. I did not grow a fall garden but I imagine it is possible to plant frost hardy vegetables, but again you will have to experiment with last planting dates.

It was also easy to grow **all weather vegetables**, especially things like carrots, beets, cabbage, and potatoes. Those that require some extra heat such as zucchini and cucumbers benefit from the use of cold frames or the floating row cover. The biggest disadvantage here is that the season is short, so vegetables such as corn, beans, and zucchini that cannot tolerate frost are only available for a very short period of time.

The challenges, of course, come with **hot weather crops** like tomatoes and peppers. As the growing season is very short, these depend on growing really good transplants and providing extra heat. Seed catalogues and gardening stores offer a variety of heat trapping products, from black plastic mulches to row tunnels supported with wire hoops. There is a compostable bio-film mulch but more often these methods involve a great deal of non-biodegradable materials. One really successful northern gardener I knew grew all of his hot weather crops under an open ended greenhouse made from recycled windows. Another friend built something called a "hot bed." This is essentially a very large cold frame that has 6-10 "of fresh manure under a layer of soil. The manure provides heat to the plants that grow in the soil.

When it comes to my planting and transplanting schedules I would recommend that you make as many transplants as possible. Transplanting is described in detail in the March chapter. For a northern gardener, making transplants allows you to have plants growing inside for several weeks before they can go in the garden, which essentially allows you to extend your season considerably. You can delay both my transplanting and planting schedules by one or two weeks, depending on your last spring frost date. Alternatively you can leave the transplant schedules as they are but delay the planting schedules by two to three weeks. This will mean that your transplants are several weeks older and bigger before they go in the garden but as long as their containers are big enough to accommodate them it should be fine.

JANUARY

Those who dwell among the beauties
And the mysteries of the earth
Are never really alone
Or weary of life

— Rachel Carson (1907 – 1964), *American biologist and
environmental activist, author of* Silent Spring.

In the Garden
Getting Ready for Spring

For those who garden, January does not mark the dead of winter but rather the beginning of another year of possibility. It is a time to do some reading, to decide what projects are on the agenda for the spring, and to order your seed catalogues. It is possible to buy all of your seeds from gardening and hardware stores; however, seed companies tend to offer a far greater variety of both vegetables and package size.

Canadian seed companies come in several different sizes, with each offering a very different selection of products. Larger companies tend to carry a far greater variety of vegetables as well as gardening products and accessories. They tend to give a good description of both the vegetables and the different varieties of those vegetables in terms of growing requirements, days to maturity, disease resistance, nature of the plant, and so on. Most vegetables are sold in a variety of package sizes, from five grams to five kilograms; the larger sizes are often far more economical than individual packets. They offer some older varieties of vegetables but the majority of their seeds are hybrids (see Seed Types and Definitions below). Their seeds are often treated with a fungicide to prevent the seed from rotting before it germinates and only a small portion of their seeds, if any, are organically grown.

Among the smaller companies, there are an increasing number that specialize in organically grown, open-pollinated, and heritage varieties of seeds (again, see Seed Types and Definitions). They offer most of the common vegetables but usually only a few varieties of each. Their biggest disadvantage is that they give very limited descriptions of the varieties that they do sell and their seeds usually come only in small package sizes. They also do not sell gardening products and accessories.

On the following pages you will find some definitions to help you sort out seed terminology. There is also a list of some of the many Canadian seed companies. I have included one American company that has an impressive selection of untreated, organically grown seeds of excellent quality—it also has a wonderful catalogue full of growing and harvesting information for each vegetable, which, in itself, is a valuable reference. It is a good idea to order two or three catalogues from the larger companies as well as several from some of the smaller operations and then decide on one or two from which to order. William Dam Seeds in Dundas, Ontario, Stokes Seeds in St. Catharines, Ontario, and Veseys Seeds in Charlottetown, P.E.I. are perhaps some of the better known Canadian seed companies. Of the three, William Dam Seeds has had a reputation for being a fairly 'ecological' seed company because it has made a commitment to selling untreated seeds and it does offer some organically grown seeds. Experimenting with many different kinds of seeds is fun but it also takes more time; finding a happy medium can be a challenge.

Keep in mind that seeds grown in your area will generally be more suitable for your climate. It is best to order your catalogues as soon as possible so that you can order seeds in early February. In this way the seeds should arrive in March when it is time to begin your transplants. (Note— if you want to grow leeks and onions from transplants that you start yourself, they must be started around the beginning of March, so order early.)

Seed Types and Definitions

Heritage or Heirloom Seeds
Generally accepted as seed varieties that have been around for at least 75 years.

Open-pollinated Seeds
These are seeds that have been saved from a vegetable that has been pollinated with

other vegetables of the same variety. Pollination occurs naturally and the seed produces vegetables with the same traits as the parent vegetable. Often seeds are selected from plants that are bigger, more disease resistant, matured earlier, and/or tasted better than their rowmates. Not to be confused with . . .

Cross-pollinated Seeds

Cross-pollination occurs when two different varieties of a plant, for example a pumpkin and an acorn squash are grown in close proximity to each other. Insects often take pollen from the acorn squash and use it to pollinate the pumpkin. The pumpkin plant will produce pumpkins but the following year the seed from one of those pumpkins will probably produce 'squmpkins'! Cross-pollination will also occur if you plant two varieties of, say, beans in the same area; each plant will produce true to its variety but the next year the seed will produce a bean that has aspects of both varieties. This is a random process that can produce interesting results.

Hybrid Seeds

These are seeds of mixed parentage that have been developed by breeders and for which breeders control the line. They are developed by mechanically pollinating one variety of vegetable with pollen from another variety of that vegetable, thereby creating a new variety. Hybrids are bred for productivity, taste, disease resistance, and heat tolerance, among other things. I do not believe that hybrid seeds are incompatible with organic gardening;

many hybrid varieties are wonderful and far better than their old-fashioned parents, while others are definitely bred for their 'shipability' and uniform looks. Over time, the seeds from a hybrid vegetable will always revert to one of the parent varieties. It is possible to produce stable, reproducible hybrid seeds however plant breeders do not do this as it would allow people to save their own hybrid seeds.

Genetically Modified (GM) Seeds

These are seeds in which the DNA of another organism (including plant, animal, and bacteria) has been inserted into the seed. The DNA is engineered into the seed through a genetic manipulation. The seeds are patented and are the property of the multinational corporations that developed them. GM seeds are purportedly engineered for productivity and pest and disease resistance. In fact, this often means that the plant is able to withstand very high doses of pesticides, fungicides, and herbicides. Most GM seeds are grown by large producers and are not offered for sale in small seed catalogues. There are ten GM crops approved for sale in Canada—these include alfalfa, canola, corn, cotton, flax, tomatoes, potatoes, rice, soybeans, and squash. In fact we only grow three of these in Canada—canola, corn, and soybeans.

Saving your own seeds:

Over the past few decades there has been a growing interest in saving seeds. With annual vegetables this can be as easy as letting a pea pod mature and dry on the vine or allowing a spinach plant to flower and produce seed pods. Biennial vegetables such as carrots, beets, onions, and leeks are trickier because they only produce seeds in their second year of growth. There are several organizations devoted to saving seeds. In Canada we have **Seeds of Diversity** (www.seeds.ca), which publishes an annual Seed Exchange Directory. In the United States **The Seed Savers Exchange** (www.seedsavers.org) publishes a book called **Seed to Seed** by Suzanne Ashworth ($24.95). They can be reached at: R.R.3, Box 239, Decorah, Iowa, U.S.A. 52101

Some Larger Seed Companies

Dominion Seed House,
P.O. Box 2500,
Georgetown, Ont., L7G 5L6
www.dominion-seed-house.com
1-905-873-3037

Johnny's Selected Seeds,
184 Foss Hill Road,
Albion, ME, 04910-9731,
www.johnnyseeds.com
1-207-437-2675

Ontario Seed Company
P.O. Box 7, 330 Phillip St.,
Waterloo, Ont., N2J 3Z6
www.oscseeds.com
1-519-886-0557

Stokes Seeds Limited
P. O. Box 10,
St. Catharines, Ont., L2R 6R6
www.stokeseeds.com
1-800-396-9238

Veseys Seeds,
P.O. Box 9000,
Charlottetown, P.E.I., C1A 8K6
www.veseys.com, 1-800-363-7333

William Dam Seeds,
R.R. #1, Box 2580,
Dundas, Ont.,
L9H 6M1
www.damseeds.com
1-905-628-6641

Some Smaller Seed Companies

Aimers Seeds
126 Catherine St. N.,
Hamilton, Ont., L8R 1J4
www.aimers.seed@sympatico.ca
1-905-841-6226

Alberta Nurseries and Seeds,
P.O. Box 20,
Bowden, Alta., T0M 0K0
1-403-224-3544

Greta's Organic Gardens
399 River Road,
Gloucester, Ont., K1V 1C9
www.seeds-organic.com
1-613-521-8648

Prairie Grown Seeds,
P.O. Box 118,
Cochin, Sask., S0M 0L0
www.prairieseeds@sk.sympatico.ca

Salt Spring Seeds
P.O. Box 444,
Ganges, B.C., V8K 2W1
www.saltspring.com
1-250-537-5269

Terra Edibles
P. O. Box 164,
Foxboro, Ont., K0K 2B0
www.terraedibles.ca
1-613-961-0454

West Coast Seeds,
3925 64th St., RR #1
Delta, B.C., V4K 3N2
www.westcoastseeds.com
1-604-952-8820

Winter Eating

Throughout this book, I try to give menu ideas and recipes using available seasonal produce. To show what kinds of produce are available I decided to compile a table for each chapter, which I have called **Available Foods.** Each month I went to our local IGA (which, at one time, won an award for the largest selection of local produce) and made a list of all produce from Ontario. Initially, I made a few trips to other grocery stores in the Kingston area but they had essentially the same selection so I did not go back. I also compiled lists of what produce I had in my garden (a small summer garden), my freezer, and my root cellar (purchased from a local organic farmer in the fall). If this is your first foray into gardening and

vegetable storage, you will probably be restricted to what local groceries offer. As you begin to grow, preserve, and store your own foods, the options will increase. Whatever your situation, try to use what local vegetables are available to you and begin to replace some of those January Caesar salads with a more seasonal menu.

In the fruit department, you may initially find yourself restricted to local apples from the grocery store and perhaps some frozen berries. I make a lot of stewed fruit—usually some combination of apples, rhubarb, and frozen berries, as well as pies and crisps. Dried fruits are another option—they may not be local but they are far more efficient to ship than fresh fruit. Stewed prunes are great with oatmeal; dried apples and apricots make good nutritious snacks; and dried cranberries are wonderful in stuffing and salads. My daughter loves to make blueberry, strawberry, or raspberry smoothies and this often satisfies her winter cravings for something fruity.

The recipes in this book are ones that I have developed and adapted over the years, along with some that friends have given to me. Once I made a commitment to eating seasonally, I did my best to avoid the grocery store and to be creative with whatever I had available. Recipes that called for things like red peppers or celery I either made without these ingredients or tried to find a suitable replacement. Most of the recipes are for vegetable dishes that accompany a main meal; sometimes they are for a stew or a stir-fry. When this is the case, you are welcome to use whatever source of protein you prefer—whether it's chicken, tofu, chickpeas, or beef—it's the use of seasonal vegetables that is important. Bookstores offer a number of good seasonal cookbooks that usually arrange recipes by both the vegetable and the season. *The Garden Fresh Vegetable Cookbook* by Andrea Chesman, *Simply in Season* by Mary Beth Lind and Cathleen Hockman-Wert, and *Nourishing Traditions* by Sally Fallon all come highly recommended. The secret is to be creative and to try to keep things simple. Our ancestors knew how to live lightly—we can too.

Recipe Ingredients and Terms: I hope most of my recipes are straightforward and easy to follow. There are a few ingredients and terms of which you may be unsure. These include:

- A small bunch: the stems fit easily in one hand, about 1-2" in diameter.
- A large bunch: the stems take up all of your hand, 4-6" in diameter.
- Bulgur: a quick cooking form of cracked wheat.
- Coriander: fresh, the leaves of the coriander plant (also called Cilantro).
- Coriander: ground, the dried and ground seeds of the coriander plant.
- Feta cheese: a soft, white, Middle Eastern cheese usually packed in brine.
- Fish Sauce: a strong smelling extract made from dried anchovies and shrimp. Available from Asian food stores.
- Flour: I use a mixture of spelt and white flours.
- Oil: I generally use olive oil because I like the taste. I also buy some organic canola and sunflower oil.
- Phyllo pastry: very thin sheets of wheat pastry used to make strudels and other flaky pastries. Available frozen in most groceries and Mediterranean food stores.
- Quinoa: a nutty tasting South American grain with a high protein content
- Red Curry Paste: a spicy paste sold in Asian food stores.
- Soba noodles: a Japanese noodle made with buckwheat flour.
- Stock: I buy organic chicken and vegetable stock cubes from my local health food store, I cube to 2 cups boiling water. Sometimes I use my own homemade chicken stock.
- Sugar: I try to use organic cane sugar or honey.
- Tamari sauce: a Japanese fermented bean sauce, similar to soy sauce. It is stronger in taste than soy sauce and it does not contain wheat, sugar, colouring, or chemical preservatives.
- Tofu: fresh soybean curd available in most groceries and health food stores.
- ♥—denotes recipes with difficult to like vegetables that kids seem to like as well as recipes that we really like.

Available Foods

In My Freezer	In My Root Cellar	At the Grocery*
Tomatoes	Carrots	Carrots
Corn	Cabbage	Cabbage
Swiss Chard	Onions	Onions
Pesto	Turnip	Turnip
Rhubarb	Potatoes	Potatoes
Strawberries	Garlic	Parsnips
Raspberries	Leeks	Sprouts
Blueberries	Squash (in a closet)	Squash
Cranberries	Apples	Mushrooms
	Dried fruit	Apples

* *from the Sydenham, Ontario IGA*

Menu Ideas for January include:

Fresh Carrots
Coleslaw (x2)
Red Cabbage Salad (x2)
Steamed Carrots
Puréed Carrots with Ginger
Puréed Turnip and Carrot
Creamy Scalloped Turnip
Turnip and Apple Casserole
Mashed Turnip
Baked Delicata Squash
Maple Whipped Squash
Winter Squash Gratin
Squash and Apple Soup
Curried Squash Soup
Danish Red Cabbage

Creamy Cabbage with Leeks and Noodles
Sautéed Cabbage with Onions and
    Mushrooms
Cabbage and Rice Casserole
Tomato Lentil Soup
Any kind of soup, stew, or curry with
    onions, carrots, potatoes, turnip,
    cabbage, and/or leeks
Stir-Fry or Fried Rice with onions, carrots,
    cabbage, and/or leeks
Fruit Crisps and Pies
Apple, Strawberry, and/or Rhubarb
    Compote
Strawberry, Blueberry, and/or Raspberry
    Smoothies
Fruit Tapioca

Recipe Information: When I wrote this section I had a difficult time deciding whether to spread my winter recipes over the first three chapters or put most of them in this chapter. The selection of winter vegetables remains fairly constant from November to March so there really wasn't one logical answer. In the end I decided to put the bulk of my winter recipes in this chapter because I refer to them in the menu ideas and it seemed silly for you to have to flip to another chapter. There are other recipes for winter vegetables in the February, March, October/November, and December chapters.

A Few Recipes

Coleslaw

6-8 carrots
1/3 medium green cabbage
Salt and pepper

Peel and grate the carrots. Trim cabbage and either slice very thinly or grate. Toss with carrots, salt, and pepper. Dress with olive oil and lemon juice or cider vinegar to taste. Another good dressing uses 1/2 cup mayonnaise, 1/4 cup ketchup, 1 tbsp Worcestershire sauce, and 3 tbsp lemon juice. Serves 4-6.

Another Coleslaw

2 cups shredded green cabbage
1 cup shredded carrots
1 cup shredded red cabbage
1/3 cup mayonnaise
1/3 cup yogurt
1 tbsp prepared mustard
2 tbsp vinegar
1 tsp honey or sugar
Salt and pepper

Combine the shredded cabbage and carrots in a bowl. In a bowl or measuring cup combine the remaining ingredients and mix well. Add the dressing to the salad and mix well. Serves 4-6.

Red Cabbage Salad

1/3 medium red cabbage
1/2 cup raisins
1/3 cup cider vinegar and/or lemon juice
1/3 cup oil
Salt and pepper

Trim and coarsely grate the cabbage. Place all the ingredients in a bowl and toss gently. This salad should sit for several hours so that the raisins can soften. Serves 6.

Another Red Cabbage Salad

2 cups shredded red cabbage
1 apple, peeled, cored and sliced
1 onion, finely chopped
1 tsp ground cumin
1 tbsp poppy seeds
1/2 cup sour cream
2 tsp Dijon mustard
1 tbsp lemon juice
2 tsp sugar or honey
Salt and pepper

In a large bowl combine the cabbage, apple, onion, cumin, and poppy seeds. Toss to mix well. In a measuring cup, combine the remaining ingredients and then add to the bowl, mixing thoroughly. (You can also add raisins to this salad). Serves 4.

Puréed Carrots with Ginger

6-8 carrots
2-4 tbsp butter
1 tsp ground ginger
Salt and pepper

Peel and slice the carrots and put them in a pot with water. Bring to a boil and simmer until soft, about 15-20 minutes. Remove from the heat and drain the water. Add butter, ginger, salt, and pepper and blend until smooth using a potato masher, hand blender, or food processor. Serves 4.

♥ Puréed Carrot and Turnip

4-6 carrots
1/4 medium turnip
2-4 tbsp butter
2-3 tbsp maple syrup
Salt and pepper

Peel the carrot and the turnip. Cut into 1/2-inch cubes and put them in a pot with water. Bring to a boil and cook until soft, about 20-25 minutes. Remove from the heat and drain most of the water. Add butter, maple syrup, salt, and pepper and blend until smooth using a potato masher, hand blender, or food processor. Serves 4-6.

Turnip and Apple Casserole

1 onion
2 tbsp butter
2 cups cubed turnip
2 apples (peeled or unpeeled)
3 eggs
1 1/2 cup fine bread crumbs
4 tsp sugar
Salt and pepper
Dash cayenne

Preheat oven to 350°F (175°C). Chop the onion and sauté in butter until soft. Cook the turnip in water until soft, drain and mash. Dice the apples. Combine onions, turnip, apples, eggs, 3/4 cup of bread crumbs, sugar, and spices. Pour into greased baking dish and top with remaining bread crumbs. Dot with melted butter. Bake for 45 minutes. Serves 4-6.

Creamy Scalloped Turnip

4 cups cubed turnip
2 tbsp butter
2 tbsp flour
1 cup milk, warmed
1/4 tsp nutmeg
1/3 cup bread crumbs
2 tbsp melted butter
Salt and pepper

Preheat oven to 350°F (175°C). Cook the turnips in salted water until soft, drain and mash. Melt 2 tbsp butter in a medium saucepan. Add the flour and stir, then slowly add the milk, stirring constantly. Cook until thick. Season with nutmeg, salt, and pepper. Add turnip and spoon into buttered casserole dish. Combine bread crumbs with melted butter and sprinkle on top of casserole. Bake for 20 minutes. Serves 6. (From the *Harrowsmith Cookbook*)

♥ Baked Delicata Squash

3 Delicata or other small squash
Maple syrup
Grated cheese

Even my children like squash this way! Cut the squash in half lengthways and scoop out the seeds. Place the squash, cut side down on a cookie tray and bake at 350°F (175°C) until soft, about 25 minutes. When soft, drizzle maple syrup in the hollow of the squash and top with grated cheese. Serves 4-6.

♥ Maple Whipped Squash

3 cups cooked squash
3 tbsp butter
3 tbsp maple syrup
1/3 cup light cream

This is a quick way to serve leftover squash. Place the squash in a medium saucepan with a small amount of water. Gently heat the squash, using a spoon to mash it so that it is smooth. When hot, add the remaining ingredients and mix thoroughly. Heat through and serve. Serves 4.

Winter Squash Gratin or Lasagne

1/2 medium Butternut squash
2 tbsp oil
1 jar tomato sauce—homemade or
    store-bought
2-3 cups grated cheese
9 cooked lasagne noodles

Cut the squash in half, remove the seeds and peel and cut into 1/4" slices, about 2" long. In a cast-iron pan, sauté the squash in oil over low heat for about 15 minutes. Stir often so it does not burn. Preheat oven to 350°F (175°C). Grease a 9x13" baking pan. If you are making lasagne, place a layer of noodles in the bottom of the pan. Then add a layer of squash, some spaghetti sauce, and then some grated cheese. Repeat another one or two times. If you want to make the gratin, omit the lasagne noodles. Bake for about 40 minutes. Serves 6.

Squash and Apple Bake

1/2 medium Butternut squash
6 tart apples
1/4 cup brown sugar
3 tbsp butter
Salt and pepper

Preheat oven to 350°F (175°C). Cut the squash in half, remove the seeds and the peel, and cut into 1-2" chunks. Cut the apples into quarters and remove the cores. Combine in a buttered casserole dish. Toss with brown sugar and dot with butter. Bake for about 1 hour or until the squash is tender. Serves 6.

Squash and Apple Soup

1/2 medium winter squash
3 medium apples
2 onions, chopped
3 tbsp butter
6 cups stock
1/4 tsp dried rosemary
1/4 tsp curry powder
1/2 tsp salt
Pepper

Cut the squash in half, remove the seeds and peel and cut into 1" cubes—you should have about 4 cups. Peel, core, and dice the apples. In a large soup pot, melt the butter and sauté the squash, apples, and onion for about 10 minutes. Add the spices and the stock and simmer for about 45 minutes. Purée the soup using a potato masher, hand blender, or food processor. This soup is also nice made with equal parts stock and light cream. Serves 4-6.

Curried Squash or Pumpkin Soup

2 onions
4 cloves garlic
2 tbsp oil
2-3 tbsp prepared curry paste (such as
     Patak's)
4 medium potatoes, peeled and cubed
2-3 cups squash or pumpkin, cubed
6 cups stock
1 tbsp curry powder
1 tsp cumin
Salt and pepper
1/2 cup dried red lentils

Finely chop the onions and garlic. In a large pot, sauté the onions and garlic in oil. Add the curry paste and mix well. Add the potatoes, squash, and stock and simmer for about 20 minutes or until the vegetables are soft. In another pot, cook the red lentils in water until just soft, about 10 minutes. Drain. Purée the soup using a potato masher, hand blender, or food processor. Add the curry powder, cumin, salt, pepper, and red lentils and simmer for another 10 minutes, stirring often so soup does not stick. This soup is also good made with equal parts stock and light cream. Serves 6.

Danish Red Cabbage

1/3 medium red cabbage
4 tbsp butter
1/2 cup water
1 apple, pared and grated
1-2 tbsp cider vinegar
1/2 tsp salt
1/2 cup red currant jelly or honey
1 tsp caraway seed (optional)

Peel and core the cabbage, then slice finely. In a large pot combine the butter, water, grated apple, cider vinegar, caraway seeds, and salt. Place over medium heat and let this mixture come to a boil, then stir in the red cabbage and toss thoroughly. This dish can either be simmered on the stove until the cabbage is well cooked, adding more water if necessary, or it can be braised in the oven for about 2 hours at 350°F (175°C), again adding water if necessary. During the last 15 minutes of cooking, add the red currant jelly or honey. This dish is much better if allowed to rest for a day in the fridge and then reheated. Serves 4-6.

♥ Creamy Cabbage with Leeks and Noodles

1/4 cup butter
1/3 medium cabbage, shredded
4-6 medium leeks (or onions), chopped
1 lb cooked noodles
1 cup yogurt
1/2 cup sour cream
1 tsp dried dill
Salt and pepper

In a large saucepan, melt the butter over medium heat and add the leeks and cabbage. Cook about 15-20 minutes, stirring often, until the cabbage is soft and tender. Add the noodles, yogurt, sour cream, and dill to the cabbage mixture and stir until well mixed. Season with salt and pepper. Serves 4. This is also nice topped with feta cheese.

Sautéed Cabbage with Onions and Mushrooms

1/3 medium green cabbage, chopped
2 medium onions, chopped
1 pound mushrooms, sliced
2-3 tbsp butter
1 tsp basil
1 tsp dill
1 tsp tarragon
Salt and pepper

In a cast-iron pan, melt the butter over medium heat. Add the onion and sauté for 3 or 4 minutes, and then add the mushrooms and the cabbage. Sauté over low heat, stirring often, until the vegetables are soft. You can add a little bit of water if necessary. Add the herbs and the salt and pepper and cook a few more minutes. This dish is nice served with cooked barley and sour cream. You can also combine it with cottage cheese and eggs and make a strudel with phyllo pastry. Serves 4-6.

♥ Cabbage and Rice Casserole

1/3 medium green cabbage, shredded
1 large onion, chopped
2 large carrots, grated
1 cup sliced mushrooms
2 tbsp butter
1 cup uncooked rice
1 lb tofu or ground beef
3 cups boiling water or stock
1 tsp each parsley, oregano, thyme
Grated Cheddar or Parmesan cheese
Salt and pepper

Preheat oven to 375°F (190°C). In a large pot with a lid, sauté the vegetables over medium heat until soft, 5-10 minutes. Add the rice and cook another few minutes, stirring often. Crumble the ground beef or tofu and add to the pot, along with the boiling water or stock, and the herbs. Place the covered pot in the oven and bake for about 45 minutes. You may have to add a bit more water in the last 15 minutes of cooking. Season with salt and pepper and pass the cheese. Serves 4-6.

Tomato-Lentil Soup

2 cups green lentils
7 cups water
1 tsp salt
4-6 cloves garlic, chopped
2 onions, chopped
2-4 carrots, peeled and chopped
2 tbsp oil
2 cups stewed tomatoes
2 tbsp red wine vinegar
2 tbsp brown sugar or honey
4 Italian sausages (optional)
1 tsp each oregano, basil, and parsley
Salt and pepper

Simmer the lentils in salted water until soft. In a large pot, sauté the onions, garlic, and carrots in oil for about 10 minutes, stirring often. Add the tomatoes, the cooked lentils and most of their cooking liquid, vinegar, sugar, spices, salt, and pepper. If you are adding Italian sausage, break it into small pieces and add to the soup. Simmer for about 30 minutes, stirring occasionally so the soup doesn't stick. For a spicier soup, add some prepared hot sauce or some hot salsa. Serves 6-8.

Apple Pie

Pastry for 9" double crust
8 cups apples, cored and sliced, and
    peeled if you wish
1/3 cup brown sugar
1 tbsp flour
2 tsp cinnamon
1/2 tsp nutmeg
2 tbsp butter
Water or milk

Preheat oven to 425°F (220°C). Combine the apples, sugar, flour, and spices in a large bowl. Line a pie plate with pastry and put the apple mixture into it. Dot apples with butter and cover with the top layer of pastry. Seal the edges of the pastry by running a bit of milk or water along the bottom edge and pressing the top edge down with your finger. Brush the top of the pastry with a little milk or water. Bake for 10 minutes at 425°F (220°C), then turn the oven down to 325°F (160°C) and bake for a further 30 – 35 minutes. Serves 6-8.

Winter Fruit Compote

1 quart frozen rhubarb
2 quarts frozen berries
4-6 apples, peeled, cored and sliced
1/4 - 3/4 cup sugar
4-6 tbsp cornstarch
1/3 cup cold water

Place the frozen fruit in a large pot and let it defrost. When soft add the apples, bring to a boil and simmer until everything has sort of mushed together. Sometimes I use a potato masher to get a smoother consistency. Add sugar to taste (white sugar seems to taste the best in this). Dissolve cornstarch in cold water and slowly add about half of it to the boiling fruit. Stir until thickened; add more cornstarch and water until the fruit is the consistency of thick custard. The amount of cornstarch you need will also depend upon the fruit that you use. Cook another 5 minutes and let cool. Serve with milk, yogurt, or cream. Serves 4-6.

Winter Fruit Crisp

3-4 cups frozen berries, strawberries,
    raspberries, or cranberries or a mix-
    ture of the three
6 – 8 apples
Sugar to taste
1 tsp cinnamon
4 cups rolled oats or 2 cups flour and 2
    cups oats
1/2 - 3/4 cup brown sugar or honey
2/3 cup melted butter
1/4 cup water

Preheat oven to 350°F (175°C). Place the berries in a 9" x 13" baking dish and let them defrost. Core and slice the apples, peel them if you wish. Mix the apples with the cinnamon and add sugar if you wish. Then add the apples to the baking dish, stirring to mix with the berries. In a bowl, combine the oats and/or flour, brown sugar or honey, melted butter, and water. Spread on top of the fruit mixture and bake for 35-40 minutes. Serves 6-8.

Winter Fruit: Cranberry Apple Crisp; Frozen Strawberry Ice; Apple, Strawberry, and Rhubarb Compote with Yogurt

Frozen Berry Ice

A total of 2 cups frozen strawberries, raspberries, cranberries, and/or blueberries
1/2 - 3/4 cup milk or soymilk
1 - 2 tbsp maple syrup

Place the berries in a food processor. Let them sit for about 15 minutes so that they soften slightly and can be puréed. Add the milk or soymilk a little bit at a time and purée, adding more liquid until you get something with a soft consistency—similar to frozen yogurt. A little bit of lemon juice is nice if you use blueberries. Serves 2-3.

♥Tapioca with Berries

2 cups milk
2 eggs, beaten
1/3 cup quick cooking tapioca
1/4 - 1/3 cup sugar
1 tsp vanilla
2 cups frozen berries

In a medium saucepan, mix the milk, beaten eggs, tapioca, sugar, and vanilla. Cook over low heat for 10-15 minutes, stirring often. Fold in the berries. This simple dessert is great in winter lunches and I am always surprised by how much my children love it.
Serves 4.

Food for Thought
Food Production and Our Environment

About fifteen years ago I attended a weekend conference on organic farming. I was a budding organic grower, excited about what I was doing and about the issues that organic farming was trying to address. There was one speaker who left me with three pieces of information that have really shaped my thinking about the way our food systems work.

I learned that:

- Modern agriculture requires an average of ten calories of energy to produce one calorie of food. So-called 'traditional agriculture' or 'subsistence agriculture' requires half a calorie of energy to produce one calorie of food.
- The average pound of Canadian food travels about 3000 kilometres from producer to consumer.
- In the early 1900s, most farmers sold relatively simple foods to local markets and received about 95 cents of every food dollar spent. Today, farmers who are part of our conventional food systems receive about seven cents of every food dollar spent.

At the time, this information seemed important because of its implications for the success of grassroots organic agriculture, which largely depended upon selling unprocessed foods directly to consumers. It also said a great deal about political and economic policies that allow and encourage such inefficiencies. In a society that constantly argues for competitiveness and efficiency in order to ensure a healthy economy, we really do spend a great deal of energy running in circles.

Today, these figures are about much more than the inefficiency and economics of conventional farming. They are about the very significant contribution that farming makes to global warming and to the potential destruction of our planet. Those 10 calories of energy that are required to produce one calorie of food represent processes of animal husbandry, cultivation, fertilization, irrigation, processing, packaging, storage, and distribution that are completely reliant on the burning of fossil fuels. The industrial food supply system is one of the biggest producers of greenhouse gases. A 2001 British survey estimated that "the CO_2 emissions attributable to producing, processing, packaging, and distributing the food consumed by a British family of four are about eight tonnes per year."[1] These emissions are almost double the CO_2 emissions that this same family emits through driving their car for a year. Moreover, farmers who produce simple food for local consumption often receive very little monetary compensation for their efforts and find themselves forced into industrial agriculture and unsustainable market structures.

I have encountered many knowledgeable people who are quite sceptical about numbers that put CO_2 emissions for food production at double those for personal vehicle use. Certainly, these are British figures and perhaps the British import significantly more food than Canadians do. They may also drive less and use more fuel-efficient cars than we do here in North America. But a trip to my local grocery store confirms my belief that we are very much a part of this global food system. I am writing this section sometime around the middle of July. My garden is overflowing with vegetables, yet there is a very limited amount of produce from Ontario at the local supermarket. There are snow peas from China, asparagus from Peru, green onions, radishes, herbs, salad mix, peppers, leeks, celery, corn, broccoli, red cabbage, potatoes, onions, and carrots from the U.S., squash from Mexico, and lettuce, zucchini, peppers, and potatoes from other parts of Canada. And this is only the vegetable section.

By understanding the link between food production and greenhouse gas emissions, one can transform some interesting agricultural information into something that has real relevance when it comes to lessening one's impact on the environment. There are a number of studies that have tried to put real numbers on the energy used in food production. It is estimated that U.S. agriculture uses 1000 litres of oil per hectare of land.[2] A Waterloo, Ontario study looked at a total of fifty-eight imported foods and found that they each travelled an average of 4800 kilometres, creating more than their own weight in greenhouse gas emissions during transportation.[3] The study estimated that 94% of these GHG emissions could be eliminated if these foods were replaced with local ones that travelled less than 250 kilometres. Another British

study estimates that 127 calories of aviation fuel are required to transport 1 calorie of lettuce from the U.S. to Britain, 97 calories of transport energy are needed to import 1 calorie of asparagus by plane from Chile, and 66 calories of energy are used when flying 1 calorie of carrots from South Africa.[4] These numbers are astounding. They are for relatively unprocessed vegetables that have been shipped long distances. When we look at processed foods, the system is equally as inefficient—one study involving Swedish tomato ketchup found that its production involved more than fifty-two transport and process stages.[5]

Organic farming, i.e. farming without the use of chemical fertilizers, pesticides, and herbicides and with a greater reliance on human labour, uses about half the energy that conventional farming does when it comes to the processes of cultivation, irrigation, and harvesting. Organic systems of raising livestock are almost five times more energy efficient than conventional systems, primarily because they rely more on grass than grain for feed.[6] However, increasingly the energy inputs of organic products are only slightly less than their conventional counterparts. This is because the organic industry has moved away from producing unprocessed foods for local consumption and has embraced processed and packaged foods that are shipped all over the world. The actual production of a food on the farm accounts for only about a tenth of its total energy input or about 1 calorie of energy per calorie of food produced. The remaining nine calories are the same for both organic and conventional foods because these calories are consumed in the processing, packaging, distribution, and storage of that food.

How is it that we have become so enmeshed in such an unhealthy and inefficient food system, seemingly without any understanding of its ramifications? The short answer to this question would be the low price of oil, and the possibilities for agricultural chemicals and global trade that this has enabled. A longer answer would have to include a serious look at our part in the exploitation of those less fortunate than ourselves and in the degradation of our environment. Our food systems contribute to a world in which there is a very unequal distribution of resources and where many of those who grow the foods that we eat do so under environmentally dangerous conditions and receive wages that are nothing less than shameful. Millions of Third World subsistence farmers have been denied access to land and water so that we can enjoy corporate-farmed exports of foods such as coffee, sugar, and bananas. We must also look at the lack of any kind of serious accounting for the real costs of agricultural and environmental degradation.

Where do we, as environmentally conscious citizens, fit into this complicated and bewildering scenario? Our patterns of food consumption have changed drastically over the past 100 years. My great-grandparents would not recognize our modern diet, nor would my children recognize my parents' diet. As a child in the 1960s, I remember going to the local Steinberg's grocery store with my mother. The store was small by today's standards; it did not carry a large selection of imported vegetables or exotic fruit and there was very little packaging other than paper bags. I remember that my school lunches were fairly simple, usually a sandwich and an apple, and I know that I did not feel in any way deprived or unhappy because of my seemingly limited (by today's standards) food choices.

As consumers, it is time we looked honestly at the impact of our food choices on our environment and on our society. Does this vast array of products meaningfully contribute to our quality of life; is it part of a just and fair global society; does it result in a clean environment? To return to a more efficient, ecological, and equitable food system we must once again choose foods that are simple and in season, that provide a fair income to farmers, and that are grown in an environmentally sustainable manner. We can all benefit from this kind of food system, through strong and stable rural economies, healthier and more nutritious food, a cleaner environment, and a decreased reliance on fossil fuels. There are many who would suggest that this last benefit is the most important and that if we do not become far more self-sufficient in our food production, we are going to have a very rude awakening as our supply of fossil fuels decreases and the price increases.

This book is about the very real power of individual action and personal choice. For the vast majority – living, working, and raising families —public political activism takes more time than we have in our day-to-day lives. Yet there are many concerned Canadians who want to do their part to reduce greenhouse gas emissions and to live in a more ecologically sustainable manner. As consumers, we make food choices every day. These choices are about much more than a bag of apples or a head of lettuce. They are about the very real human and environmental parameters that govern food production. They are about teaching our children that we are not helpless in the face of seemingly overwhelming global problems. They are about respecting our boundaries within nature and recognizing our connections to those who feed us. Ultimately they reflect our respect for each other and for the world in which we live.

Sources and Further Information

Pfeiffer, Dale Allan, *Eating Fossil Fuels*,
    New Society Publishers, Gabriola
    Island, B.C., 2006.
www.Powerswitch.org.uk (UK)
Thought for Food, in Alternatives Magazine, University of Waterloo Department of Environmental Studies,
    Waterloo, Volume 32, #3, Fall 2006.
The Oil in Your Oatmeal,
    www.sfgate.com
The Oil We Eat,
    www.harpers.org/TheOilWeEat.html

Endnotes

1 Church, N., *Why Our Food is So Dependent on Oil,* Powerswitch (UK), April, 2005, p. 3.
2 Pfeiffer, Dale Allen, *Eating Fossil Fuels,* New Society Publishers, Gabriola Island, B.C., 2006, page 19.
3 Xuereb, Marc, *Home Grown Hurrah,* in Alternatives Magazine, University of Waterloo Department of Environmental Studies, Waterloo, Ontario, Volume 32, #3, 2006, page 20.
4 Church, N., *Why Our Food is So Dependent on Oil,* Powerswitch (UK), April, 2005, p.2.
5 Ibid., p. 2
6 Ibid, p. 4.

FEBRUARY

Even if I knew that tomorrow
the world would go to pieces,
I would still plant my apple tree.

— Martin Luther King, Jr. (1929 – 1968), *American pastor and civil rights activist*

In the Garden
Making Plans

February is the time to decide on a garden plan and to order seeds. Ideally, the catalogues you sent for in January have arrived and you can curl up on a wintry Saturday afternoon and start browsing and garden dreaming. It is best to order seeds in early February so that they arrive in time to start your March transplants. But before you do a seed order you must have some idea of what vegetables you would like to plant.

In this chapter, I provide plans for the two summer gardens as well as for the winter storage garden. I also discuss a few useful perennials, some of which I incorporate into my flower beds and others that I plant on the edge of my vegetable garden. Finally, there is a very long table which lists all of the common vegetables I could think of, their spacing requirements, planting times, and some general comments to assist you in making your own garden plans.

The Summer Gardens

When I designed the summer gardens I decided to work within several different size constraints. The 350- and 500-square-foot gardens are designed to keep two and four people in fresh vegetables from May to November. There is also a small plan with two extra beds for growing some carrots, onions, potatoes, and squash. If you have the space, these beds can be added to either of the summer gardens. As much as possible I concentrate on growing vegetables that are relatively trouble free and productive in a small space. Many summer vegetables mature in about four to eight weeks and the area they occupy can be dug and replanted later in the season. Most of the vegetables that I grow do not take up a lot of room, have significant pest problems, or require a heavy concentration of nutrients (a heavy feeder, in gardening terms). My summer gardens include:

- Baby salad greens were the backbone of my organic market garden and they are wonderful in a small garden. These tender and delicious greens are ready three to four weeks after plant-

ing. My own salad greens mix consists of arugula, kyona (also called mizuna), tatsoi, red mustard, red kale, and lettuce. Other possibilities include green mustard, garden cress, corn salad, endive, and chicory. It is possible to buy pre-mixed seed packages (called mesclun mix) but they often contain a lot of lettuce and endive. I prefer the sharp and tangy taste of the arugula and mustard greens. I also prefer to buy each variety separately rather than to buy a mix as they each have a different growth rate. When a mixed seed is planted, the faster maturing plants tend to crowd out the slower growing varieties.

- Lettuce is a wonderful salad vegetable but it is not always easy to grow a proper head that is sweet and tender. Of all the lettuces I grew in the market garden I preferred varieties belonging to the Crisphead (also called Batavian) family. They tasted wonderful, almost always formed a proper head, and did well through the heat of the summer.
- Spinach is easy to grow and does well in both the spring and fall.
- Endive is not that common a vegetable in North America. It is a member of the dandelion family, as is lettuce, and it forms a rosette of slightly bitter tasting leaves. There are a number of different types of endive, from coarse leaved to finely toothed. The finer varieties are referred to as 'Frisee' or 'Tres Fin'—these are the ones I grow because they have a delicious creamy white centre when mature that is relatively mild and good in salads.
- Green onions are great in cooking and in a variety of salads. They grow quickly and take up very little space.

- An easy and delicious spring crop is the young shoots of garlic cloves—I call them green garlic.
- Radishes are quick and easy to grow and there are many beautiful varieties.
- Shell peas are always a favourite. Dwarf varieties of snow peas (the flat ones) and sugar snap peas (both the shell and the peas are edible) are easy to grow in a small space.
- Beets are perhaps not everyone's favourite vegetable but our family loves them. The greens are a nutritious bonus if you like them.
- Tomatoes, cucumbers, and zucchini are standard summer vegetables, being both dependable and productive. They do take up more room but one can buy space saving bush varieties.
- Sweet peppers are perhaps a labour of love as they require a great deal of heat to really produce. I find that the smaller, hotter peppers are far more productive and ripen easily in our climate. I like Hungarian Hot Wax, which is only moderately hot.
- Beans are both prolific and easy to grow. Pole beans require more work because they grow tall and need to be staked but a lot of people love their flavour and they produce over a longer period of time than bush beans do.
- Swiss chard and kale are easy to grow and very productive. They survive hard freezes and can often be harvested right into December. They do have a strong taste but we have found ways to enjoy them in our cooking.
- Small plantings of parsley, coriander, dill, and basil add flavour to our meals.
- If you have the space, small sections of onions, carrots, potatoes, and winter squash round out a summer garden.

There are some common vegetables that I do not grow in my summer garden because they take up a lot of room, take a long time to mature, and/or they have a lot of pest problems. These include most members of the *brassica* family (cabbage, broccoli, Brussels sprouts, and cauliflower) as well as corn, celery, and eggplant. I prefer to buy these vegetables locally when they are in season. If you have a large garden and wish to grow any of these vegetables you must allocate space for them and then order the required seeds.

The Winter Storage Garden

The winter storage garden is designed to provide a family of four with enough onions, leeks, garlic, carrots, parsnip, beets, rutabagas*, cabbage, winter squash, and potatoes to last from sometime in October to the following May. There is also enough space to grow some paste-type tomatoes to either freeze or can for the winter. The garden is about 29' x 25' in size and is considerably more work than the summer garden. However, the taste of homegrown winter vegetables and the feeling of pride one gets from filling a root cellar with one's own produce make it all very worthwhile. To store vegetables successfully you do need some sort of cold storage area—we cover this subject in August/September.

*generally rutabaga stores better than turnip.

The Perennial Garden

If space permits, a few perennials can provide some interesting additions, especially to the early spring diet. Where possible I incorporate smaller perennials into my flower beds.

- Perennial herbs such as thyme, oregano, mint, and tarragon are all easy to grow. Mint is very invasive so find a spot where it can spread.
- Chives and garlic chives are trouble free and they make a welcome addition to early spring meals—I grow large clumps of them in a shady section of my flower beds.
- Perennial onions are also called multiplier onions and can be found in the William Dam catalogue "Onion Sets." They grow much like a large bunch of green onions, dividing continuously over the summer, and eventually forming a large clump from which you can pull individual sections the next spring.

Larger perennials can be incorporated into your landscaping or you can dig a small perennial bed specifically for them.

- Sorrel produces a tangy, lemony leaf in early May that is good with eggs, fish, or potatoes. It is easily grown from seed and is available from most seed catalogues.
- Rhubarb is usually purchased as a root from a nursery or obtained from a friend.
- Jerusalem artichokes, also called sunchokes, are the tuberous roots of a type of sunflower plant that is indigenous to North America. They have a mild taste and an easy to digest starch that is safe for diabetics; some people say they remind them of water chestnuts. They are extremely prolific and a few plants will provide many pounds of tubers in early April. The tubers can be hard to find, I got mine from a friend, and the only seed catalogue I found them in was Johnny's Selected Seeds in Albion, Maine.
- Asparagus is both delicious and beautiful. It is easy to grow in fertile soil but it does take a few years to begin producing well. Buy one-year-old plants, called crowns, from a nursery or seed catalogue and plant them with a good supply of compost.

Wide Beds

All the gardens are designed around four-foot beds with one-foot walkways. You can easily reach each half of the bed from the adjacent walkway. Within the bed, the plants are spaced far enough apart that they have room to mature, but they are close enough together that they shade the soil underneath them, keeping it cool, conserving moisture, and blocking weeds. Shell peas are the only plants that I do not grow in a wide bed as they grow tall and need to be staked. I prefer to grow them in two parallel rows that are spaced about eight inches apart.

This wide bed system is based upon an intensive method of planting developed in Europe where it is common to find small commercial gardens (less than five acres) that rely on small tillers and hand labour. Many North American gardens are planted with a single row of plants separated by a three- or four-foot-wide walkway. This type of spacing was originally designed for mechanical planting, weeding, and harvesting so the area between the rows had to be wide enough to accommodate the wheels of a tractor. There is no reason to give vegetables that much space. For the backyard gardener, this method of planting results in a great deal of unproductive space that must be dug, weeded, and watered along with the productive part of your garden. By using the wide bed method, the harvest is much greater because almost the entire garden is planted in vegetables.

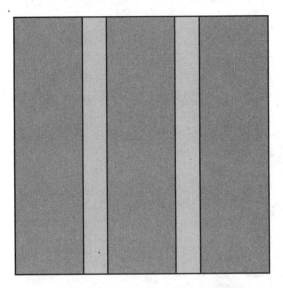

Wide Bed Design with four-foot beds and one-foot walkways — 80% of the garden is planted.

Narrow Bed Design with one-foot beds and four-foot walkways — 20% of the garden is planted.

Within these wide beds there are two ways that I plant my vegetables.

🌿Seeds can be directly sown into the ground and then thinned as necessary.
🌿Vegetables can be started indoors as transplants and later planted in the garden as individual plants that do not require thinning.

Some vegetables such as tomatoes or peppers must be started indoors as transplants in order to produce in our climate—you can buy transplants if you do not wish to start them yourself. Others such as lettuce, spinach, or beets do well either way—there are advantages to both methods. Transplanting is discussed in detail in the March chapter. Vegetables such as carrots, radishes, and salad greens are not suitable for transplants and must be seeded directly into the garden. When I direct seed vegetables, I either plant them in distinct rows in my garden (i.e. carrots) or I broadcast the seed in a small area (i.e. salad greens). If this sounds confusing—I hope the following diagrams will help.

PLANT SPACINGS WITHIN FOUR-FOOT-WIDE BEDS
* denotes multi-plant transplants which are explained in the March section.

6-8" spacing – rows 6-8" apart and plants 6-8" apart within the rows.
This spacing is suitable for basil, beets, carrots, garlic, green garlic, green onions*, kohlrabi, onion sets, parsnip, radishes, spinach, and spring turnip.

```
o o o o o o o o o o o o o
o o o o o o o o o o o o o
o o o o o o o o o o o o o
o o o o o o o o o o o o o
o o o o o o o o o o o o o
o o o o o o o o o o o o o
```

1 foot spacing – rows 1' apart and plants 1' apart within the rows.
This spacing is suitable for beets*, celery, celery root, chives, corn, endive, fennel, garlic chives, Jerusalem artichokes, kale, leeks*, lettuce, onions*, parsley, potatoes, perennial onions, rutabaga, sorrel, and Swiss chard.

```
O   O   O   O   O   O   O
O   O   O   O   O   O   O
O   O   O   O   O   O   O
O   O   O   O   O   O   O
```

18-24" spacing – rows 18-24" apart with plants 18-24" apart in the rows and staggered within the bed.
This spacing is suitable for broccoli, Brussels sprouts, cauliflower, Chinese cabbage, cucumber, eggplant, melons, peppers, and sweet potatoes.
Note - winter squash is planted in a single line down the center of the bed

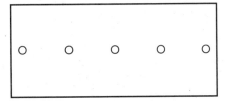

30-36" spacing – rows 30-36" apart with plants 30-36" apart in the rows and staggered within the bed.
This spacing is suitable for cabbage, rhubarb, tomatoes, and zucchini.

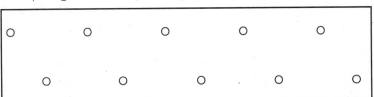

Broadcast seeds

Seeds about 1" apart
This spacing is suitable for coriander, dill, green onions, and salad greens.

Seeds 2-3" apart
This spacing is suitable for dwarf peas and bush beans.

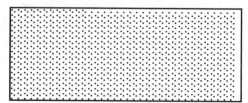

Designing a Garden

If you look at the summer garden plans at the end of this section you will see that there is a continuous planting of some vegetables from April to August. Other vegetables, such as carrots, tomatoes, or zucchini are only planted once in the year as they require a full growing season to mature. Garden plans are made by deciding how many plants of a specific vegetable you want in a month or a season, then multiplying that number by the spacing requirement. So for example, if you think you can eat eight heads of lettuce in a month and lettuce requires one square foot of garden space per plant, each month that you plant lettuce you will need eight square feet of garden for that lettuce. This translates into two feet of a four-foot-wide bed, which is not a large area. Tomato plants need to be three feet apart. If you look in the spacing diagram you will see that they are staggered across the bed and they require about six square feet of garden per plant. Six plants will take up about nine feet of a wide bed.

In the winter storage garden I had to decide how much of each vegetable was needed to feed a family of four. So, for example, I tried to estimate how many onions this family might use in a year. I decided on one onion per day. This allowed for days when they used several onions and days in which they used none, as well as for losses, both in the garden and in storage. Onions require a 6" spacing; if you draw this out you will see that you can get four onion plants per square foot of garden, so 365 onion plants will require about 91 square feet of garden or a four-foot bed that is about 23' long. You can use this same system for any vegetable that you want to plant.

Planning Your Own Garden

If you decide to make your own garden plan, I really encourage you spend some time planning what you want to grow and also to draw your plan out on paper. Begin by making a list of all of the vegetables that you want to grow. At the end of this section there are several pages of charts with details on garden spacing, approximate planting dates, the amount of seed to order, storage amounts for a family of four, and some relevant comments for all of the vegetables that I could think of. Use these charts along with your seed catalogues and a good gardening book to make notes on the planting requirements for each vegetable, including fertility and water requirements, which month(s) it can be planted in, days to maturity, whether it must be started as a transplant, and spacing requirements.

Once you have done this, you must then figure out how much garden space each vegetable is going to need and how often you are going to plant it. To do this, decide on how many of each vegetable you and your family will realistically eat from a planting and how many plantings of that vegetable you want in your garden. Generally vegetables such as lettuce, beets, spinach, green onions, and other similar crops take from five to eight weeks to mature and can be planted several times over the summer. Other vegetables such as tomatoes or cucumbers ripen over a long period but are usually only planted once, or perhaps twice, in a season. Finally things like carrots, onions, and potatoes can be planted once or twice, in May and/or June, mature sometime in late summer, and are then available for as long as you can store them.

Once you have decided what you want to plant, use the spacing diagrams to figure out how much space each vegetable will take up and what month(s) it must be planted in. Use this information to draw a garden plan—I have included two pages of graph paper with my garden plans. I hope this process will let you know if your dreams fit into the space that is available to you!

Preparing a Seed Order

Once you have decided what you want to grow, you must make a list of the seeds that you will need and then compile a seed order. To do this, go through your seed catalogues and decide on some varieties that sound interesting and dependable. Look for varieties that have good flavour, are resistant to disease, yield well, mature early, and/or that don't take up too much space. Many seeds can be bought in larger quantities, as they will last several years stored in a dry area such as a cupboard or drawer—certainly if you enjoy salad greens single packets can become very expensive. The main exception to this is seeds in the onion family, which only last for one year.

Growing Onions: Onions take a long time to mature and in our climate they must either be planted as onion sets or started early from seeds.

- Onion sets are onions that were planted from seed the year before, grown for about two months, and then stored for the winter. They look just like small (1″ or so) onions. You plant them and they grow to maturity in their second summer. They can be ordered from a seed catalogue or purchased in the spring from a garden centre. They are easy to plant, but you are limited as to what varieties you can buy and I find they do not always grow as big as I would like them to.

- Onion seeds must be started indoors in February or March so that they can mature the same year. They are easy to grow but you must do the work. Generally there are many more varieties of onion seeds available and they seem to grow bigger than onion sets do.

Floating Row Covers

Along with your seeds, it is a good idea to order something called a 'floating row cover.' This is an extremely lightweight blanket made of spun polypropylene, a bit like a light fabric interfacing. It comes in four- to five-foot widths, is placed directly over the garden bed, and is held down along the edges—I use small rocks. The row cover is lightweight enough that plants grow easily underneath it, it lets 80% of the light through and 100% of the rain, and is one of the most effective and non-toxic methods of pest control that I have found. It traps warmth in the spring to speed up growth and gives some protection against frost in both the spring and fall. If cared for properly it should last five or six years. I use the floating row cover to protect salad greens and cucum-

bers from insects, as well as to help along my April crops. This cover is available through some seed catalogues (Stokes sells it) and this year I noticed it at our local Home Hardware.

FEBRUARY GARDEN SUMMARY

☐ Decide what vegetables you want to grow.

☐ Use the planting guidelines at the end of this chapter to decide when and how often you want to plant each vegetable.

☐ Decide how much of each vegetable you can eat in a given time.

☐ Use the planting guideline to figure out how much garden space each vegetable will require.

☐ Make a garden plan.

☐ Prepare a seed order or wait until spring and buy seeds from a garden center.

Garden Plans
350-SQUARE-FOOT SUMMER GARDEN

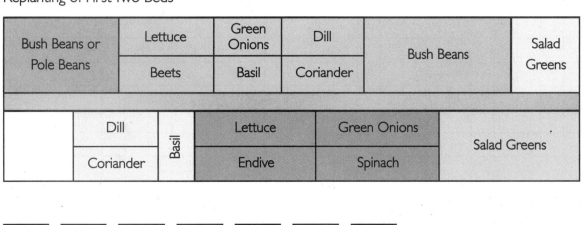

0'　　　　5'　　　　10'　　　　15'　　　　20'　　　24'

| Salad Greens | Snow Peas or Sugar Snap Peas | Green Onions | Radish | Lettuce |
| | | | Green Garlic | Spinach |

| Swiss Chard | Parsley | Lettuce | Beets | Green Onions | Dill | Salad Greens | Shell Peas |
| | | Spinach | Endive | Green Garlic | Coriander | | |

| Tomatoes | Peppers | Zucchini |
| | Cucumbers | |

Replanting of First Two Beds

| Bush Beans or Pole Beans | Lettuce | Green Onions | Dill | Bush Beans | Salad Greens |
| | Beets | Basil | Coriander | | |

| | Dill | Basil | Lettuce | Green Onions | Salad Greens |
| | Coriander | | Endive | Spinach | |

April　May　June　July　Aug.　Sept.　Oct.

Your Own Garden Plan

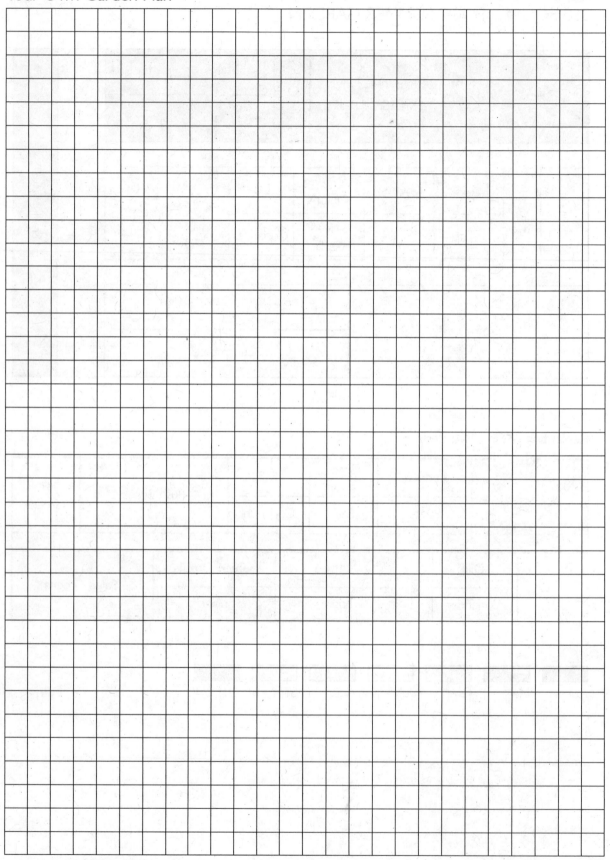

Garden Plans
500-SQUARE-FOOT SUMMER GARDEN

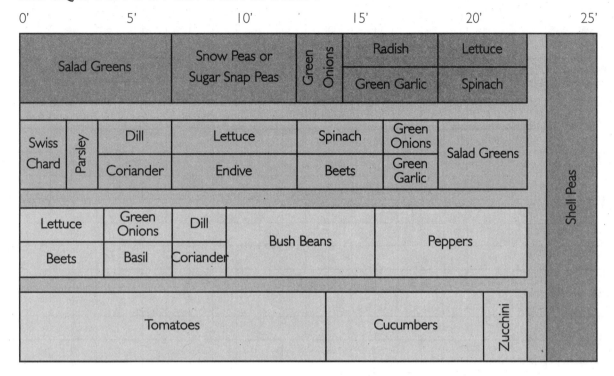

| 0' | 5' | 10' | 15' | 20' | 25' |

Salad Greens | Snow Peas or Sugar Snap Peas | Green Onions | Radish / Green Garlic | Lettuce / Spinach | Shell Peas

Swiss Chard | Parsley | Dill / Coriander | Lettuce / Endive | Spinach / Beets | Green Onions / Green Garlic | Salad Greens

Lettuce / Beets | Green Onions / Basil | Dill / Coriander | Bush Beans | Peppers

Tomatoes | Cucumbers | Zucchini

Replanting of First Two Beds

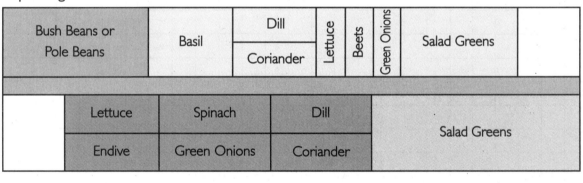

Bush Beans or Pole Beans | Basil | Dill / Coriander | Lettuce | Beets | Green Onions | Salad Greens

Lettuce / Endive | Spinach / Green Onions | Dill / Coriander | Salad Greens

April May June July Aug. Sept. Oct.

Your Own Garden Plan

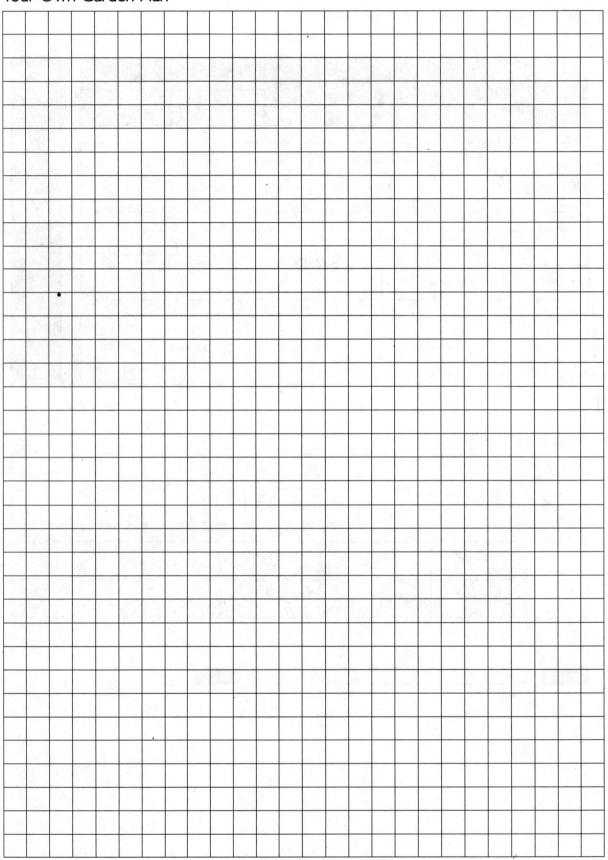

Garden Plans
TWO EXTRA BEDS FOR SOME STORAGE VEGETABLES

0'	5'	10'	15'	20'	25'

Onions	Carrots

Potatoes	Winter Squash

750-SQUARE-FOOT WINTER STORAGE GARDEN

0'	5'	10'	15'	20'	25'

Onions	Leeks

Carrots

Parsnips	Early Potatoes	Beets	Rutabaga

Tomatoes	Cabbage

Potatoes

Winter Squash	Garlic

April   May   June   July   Aug.   Sept.   Oct.

Your Own Garden Plan

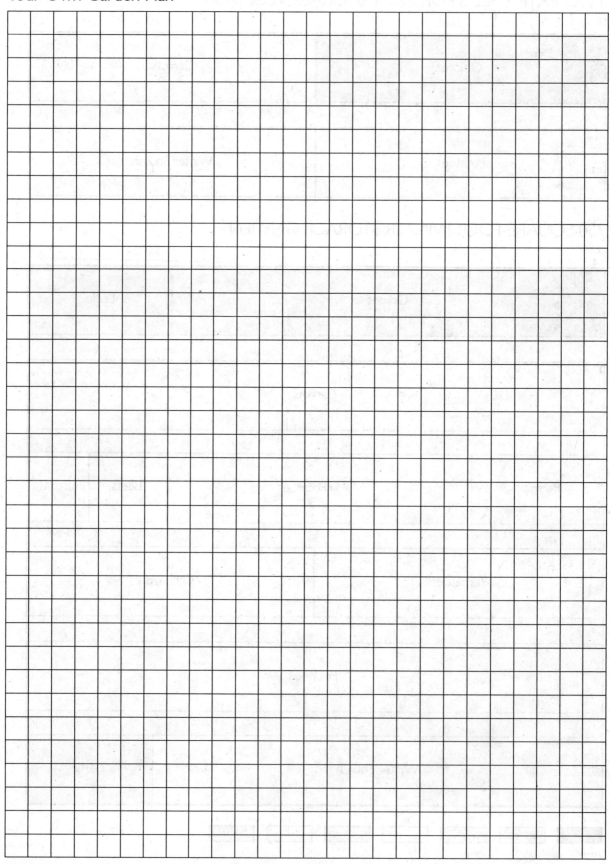

GUIDELINES FOR PLANTING VEGETABLES

	Direct Seeding	Transplanting	Comments
Asparagus	-buy one-year-old roots (called crowns) -plant in April at 2'spacing	-start seeds in February -plant in late May at 2' spacing	-requires fertile soil -wait one to two years before harvesting -buy 8-10 crowns in the spring
Basil	-plant in June and July -rows 6-8" apart -seeds 2- 3" apart in rows, thin to 6"	-start transplants in May & June, -plant in June & July at 6-8" spacing	-easy to grow -order 1 pkt or up to 5 g -Genovese basil is popular -many interesting varieties
Bush Beans	-plant in late May and June -broadcast seeds at 2-3" spacing, about 10 seeds/square foot		-easy to grow -requires warm soil
Dry Beans	-plant in late May -broadcast seeds at 2-3" spacing, about 10 seeds/square foot		-easy to grow -allow bean pods to fully mature and begin to dry before harvest -many heirloom varieties including Jacob's Cattle, Agate Pinto, Swedish Brown
Pole Beans	-plant in late May -double rows 8" apart -seeds 2-3" apart in rows and 2-4" deep		-requires staking -productive over a long period -many heirloom varieties
Beets	-plant in May and June -rows 6" apart -seeds 2-3" apart in rows, thin to 6"	-start transplants from April to June -plant from May to July at 1' spacing	-easy to grow -order 1 pkt or up to 25g -many heirloom varieties -look for both summer and storage varieties
Broccoli	-plant in May and June -rows 18-24" apart -seeds 4-6" apart in rows, thin to 18-24"	-start 4-6 transplants in early May and 6-8 in early June -plant in May and June at 18 – 24" spacing	-order 1 pkt -needs fertile soil -flea beetles and cabbage worms are a problem

	Direct Seeding	Transplanting	Comments
Brussels Sprouts		-start in early May -plant in late May at 24" spacing	-same as for broccoli -requires a long growing season, harvest in October
Cabbage	-plant in May -rows 24-30" apart -seeds 4-6" apart in rows, thin to 24-30"	-start transplants in May -plant 9-15 for storage -plant in early June at 24"-30" spacing	-same as for broccoli -look for storage varieties -try some of each red, green, summer, and/or Savoy
Carrots	-direct seed in May -plant in rows 6" apart -seeds 1-2" apart in rows, thin to 3-4" -yields 6-8 carrots per sq.ft.		-order 1 pkt – 1 ounce -need 60-80 square feet for winter storage, look for storage varieties -can buy pelleted seeds—the seeds are coated with clay and are larger and easier to plant
Cauliflower		-start 3-6 transplants in May -plant in June at 18"-24" spacing	-same as for broccoli
Celery		-start 6-12 transplants in early March -plant in late May at 1' spacing	-order 1 pkt -requires fertile soil and regular watering
Celery Root		-start 10-12 transplants in early March -plant in late May at 1' spacing	-order 1 pkt -requires fertile soil and regular watering -stores well in a cold room
Chinese Cabbage	-can direct seed but tends to be badly damaged by insects -plant in June and July -rows 1' apart -seeds 3-4" apart in rows, thin to 18"	-start 2-4 transplants mid June & mid July -plant in July and early August at 18"-24" spacing	-order 1 pkt -much easier to grow as a fall crop as there is less insect damage -use floating row cover
Chives		-plant in April or May at 1' spacing	-plant in partial shade -buy 2-3 plants from a nursery

	Direct Seeding	Transplanting	Comments
Coriander	-plant from April to August -broadcast seeds at 1" spacing		-easy to grow -also called Cilantro, order pkt or up to 25 g
Corn	-plant in warm soil, mid May and June -rows 1' apart -seeds 6" apart in rows, thin to 1' apart		-need 2 seeds per foot, so order by amount of seeds you need -yields 1-2 cobs per plant -about 150 seeds/ounce -needs fertile soil
Cucumber	-plant in late May -rows 18" apart -plant several seeds at every 18" interval -thin to one plant every 18"	-start transplants in early May -plant in June at 18" spacing	-order 1 or 2 pkts -Middle Eastern varieties are excellent -can be trellised to save space
Daikon Radish	-plant in May -plant as you do carrots		-store like you do carrots
Dill	-plant from April to August -broadcast seeds at 1" spacing		-easy to grow, will reseed itself -order 1 pkt
Eggplant		-start 6-8 transplants in March -plant in June at 18" spacing	-look for early varieties -benefits from extra warmth -order 1 pkt
Endive	-plant from April to June -rows 6" apart -seeds 1-2" apart in rows, thin to 1'apart	-start transplants from April to June -plant from May to July at 1' spacing	-order 1 pkt -I grow a variety called Rhodos
Fennel	-plant in May and June -rows 1' apart -seeds 4" apart in rows, thin to 1' apart	-start transplants in May and June -plant at 1' spacing	-easy to grow and delicious -order 1 pkt

	Direct Seeding	Transplanting	Comments
Garlic	-plant in October for next year's harvest -rows 6" apart -individual cloves 6" apart in rows		-buy bulbs from a local grower if possible -need about 50-60 bulbs for summer eating, winter storage and for planting
Garlic Chives		-plant in April or May at 1'spacing	-plant in partial shade -buy 2-3 plants from a nursery
Green Garlic	-plant cloves in October, April & May -rows 6" apart -cloves 3-4" apart in rows		-buy 4 or 5 bulbs from grocery store and break into cloves for planting
Green Onions	-plant from April to July -broadcast seed at 1" spacing	-start transplants from March to July -plant at 10 seedlings per 8" spacing	-green onions are the same as scallions -buy 1-2 pkts, seed only lasts one year -I never had any luck with red varieties
Jerusalem Artichoke	-plant 16-20 tubers in April -rows 1' apart -tubers 1' apart in rows		-need about 20 tubers -hard to find—try Johnny's Selected Seeds, Albion, Maine
Kale-	plant in June and July -rows 1' apart -seeds 2-3" apart in rows, thin to 1'apart	-start transplants in June and July -plant at 1' spacing	-pests same as for broccoli -Red Russian Kale seems to have fewer pest problems
Kohlrabi	-plant in April and May -rows 6" apart -seeds 6" apart in rows		-order 1 pkt -needs fertile soil and regular watering
Leeks		-start 100-120 leeks in late Feb or early March -seed 6 leeks per cell and thin to 4 -plant in mid April at 1' spacing	-look for storage varieties with longer days to maturity -order 1 pkt, seed does not keep for more than one year

	Direct Seeding	Transplanting	Comments
Lettuce	-plant in April and May and again in late July -rows 1' apart -seeds 1-2" apart in rows, thin to 1.	-start transplants from March to July -plant from April to August at 1' spacing	-order pkt or up to 5g -Summer Crisphead (also called Batavian) are the most dependable for all seasons -Butterheads are delicious but need cool temperatures so plant in April & May only
Melons		-start 6-12 transplants in early May -plant in early June at 18" spacing	-look for early varieties -order 1 pkt of 1-2 varieties -requires extra heat -use row cover
Onions	-plant onion sets in April -rows 6" apart -bulbs 6" apart in rows	-start transplants in late Feb or early March -seed 6 onions per cell and thin to 4 -plant in Mid April at 1' spacing	-for winter storage need 300-400 onions, either from sets or from transplants -order sets (bulbs) from a seed company or buy them at gardening stores in the spring -order pkts of red and/or white storage onions -seed does not keep more than one year
Parsley		-plant in May at 1' spacing	-hard to start indoors, must be started in February and then takes weeks to germinate -buy 2-3 plants from a nursery
Parsnip	-plant in May -rows 6" apart -seeds 1-2" apart in rows, thin to 4-5"		-order 1 pkt -plant 20-30 square feet for winter storage -plant as you do carrots
Tall Peas — shell, snow or Sugar Snap	-plant in April -double rows 8" apart -seeds 2-3" apart and 2-4" deep		-must be staked -order 1 pkt or up to 125 g
Dwarf Peas — Shell, Snow or Sugar Snap	-plant in April & May -broadcast seeds at 2-3" spacing, about 10 seeds/square foot		-order up to 125 g -do well in cooler weather -dwarf varieties don't need staking

	Direct Seeding	Transplanting	Comments
Peppers		-start transplants in early March -plant in June at 18" spacing	-order 1-2 pkts, look for early varieties -sweet varieties prefer extra warmth, hotter varieties seem to produce well without it
Perennial Onions		-plant in April or May -2-3 plants about 1' apart	-William Dam Seeds carries them under Onion Sets, are called Multipliers
Potatoes	-plant in May and June -plant eyes 1' apart in rows that are 1' apart		-need 100-200 square feet for winter storage -average yield is 3-6 potatoes per plant; estimate 2 plants per meal for a family of 4 -order from seed catalogues or buy from a gardening store
Radishes	-plant in April and May -rows 6" apart -seeds 1-2" apart in rows, thin to 2-4"		-order 1 or 2 pkts -many heirloom varieties -flea beetles are a problem
Rhubarb		-plant in April or May -2-3 crowns, 3' apart	-buy from a nursery in spring or get from a friend
Rutabaga	-plant in May -rows 1' apart -seeds 2-3" apart in rows, thin to 1'	-start 12-18 transplants in mid May -plant in early June at 1' spacing	-order 1 pkt -generally rutabaga are for storage, turnips are for fresh eating -flea beetles are a problem
Sorrel	-plant in April -rows 1' apart -seeds 2-3" apart in rows, thin to 1'	-start 2-3 transplants in April -plant in May at 1' spacing	-buy 1 pkt
Salad Greens	-plant from April to September -broadcast seed at about 1 tsp of seed per 4 square ft of garden, larger seed such as Red Kale 2 tsp seed per 4 sq. ft or garden		-order up to 25 g of seeds, it keeps and is far cheaper -I order mizuna, arugula, tatsoi, red and green mustard, red Russian kale, and a red oak leaf lettuce -cover after planting with floating row cover

	Direct Seeding	Transplanting	Comments
Spinach	-plant in April, May and August -rows 6" apart, seeds 1" apart, thin to 3-4"	-start transplants in March, April and July -plant in April, May and August at 6" spacing	-order 1 pkt or up to 5 g -easy to grow in cool weather
Swiss Chard	-plant in May -rows 1' apart -seeds 3-4" apart in rows, thin to 1'	-start 3-4 transplants in April -plant in May at 1' spacing	-order 1 pkt of seed -many beautiful varieties
Tomatoes		-start transplants in March -plant in June at 3' spacing	-order several pkts -huge variety of heirloom seeds -paste varieties good for cooking, canning, and freezing -determinate varieties have a finite size and are usually more manageable -indeterminate varieties should be staked and can grow 10-12 feet tall
Turnip	-plant in April, May and August -rows 8" apart -seeds 2-3" apart in rows, thin to 8"		-order 1 pkt -cover as soon as they are planted with floating row cover to protect against flea beetles and root maggots
Winter Squash	-plant in late May or early June -1 row in center of wide bed -plant 3-4 seeds at each 2' interval, thin to 1 plant every 2'	-start 12-18 transplants in early May -plant in June, 1 row down center of wide bed, plants at 2' spacing	-order 1 pkt each of several varieties, long and short term storage -Buttercup, Butternut, Delicata, Spaghetti and Pie Pumpkin all nice
Zucchini	-plant in late May -rows 3' apart, 3-4 seeds 3' apart, thin to 1 plant per 3' spacing	-start 2-3 transplants in May -plant in June at 3' spacing	-easy to grow -only need 1 or 2 plants -look for more compact varieties

Winter Eating Continued!

Our February menu is essentially the same as our January menu with the addition of some homemade sprouts. Whatever apples I have in the root cellar are losing quality quickly so I bring what is left upstairs and put them into my refrigerator. If they are no longer suitable for fresh eating, I try to cook some big batches of applesauce, which I then freeze. If necessary, I order a case of organic apples from our local health food store; when ordered by the case they are usually about the same price as conventional apples bought in small quantities from the grocery store. Having a friend to share the case with makes it easier, both in terms of cost and space in the fridge.

Making Sprouts

Sometime around the middle of the month I start making a variety of sprouts, primarily mung bean, lentil, and alfalfa. The mung bean sprouts are good eaten fresh, in salads, and cooked in stir-fries. The lentil and alfalfa sprouts are nice in salads, sandwiches, wraps, and tortillas. There are many other interesting types of seeds suitable for sprouting, including radish, clover, and fenugreek. You can buy sprouting seeds at health food stores or order them by mail from the following companies:

Sprout Master
1-888-333-4456

Mumm's Sprouting Seeds
P.O. Box 80
Parkside, Sask., S0J 2A0
www.sprouting.com
1-306-747-2935

Sprouts can be grown in Mason jars or in a commercially purchased sprouter, available at health food stores and through some seed catalogues.

- In a Mason jar, place about 2 tablespoons of seeds in the jar and cover with water. Cover the mouth of the jar with cheesecloth or some sort of screening and secure with an elastic band. Soak the seeds overnight, and then drain the water, leaving the jar upside down and on a slight angle in the sink or in a bowl. Continue to rinse and drain the sprouts one to two times a day for three to five days.
- Commercial sprouters have five plastic layers that nest on top of each other, with a drain in the top four and a solid bottom section. The seeds must be soaked overnight, then drained and spread evenly over the middle three sections of the sprouter. If you want, you can put a different kind of sprout on each layer. Once per day, water is poured onto the top layer; it slowly makes its way to the bottom layer where you empty it out. Because the plastic layers nest on top of each other they must be watched to make sure that they are getting enough air circulation, otherwise the sprouts can start to get mouldy. If it looks like this is going to happen, separate the trays for the day and restack them in the evening.

In February I also start making a herbal tea or infusion from dried stinging nettles. Nettles are a good source of chlorophyll, calcium, magnesium, iron, and Vitamins A and C. I place about 1/3 cup of dried nettles in a one-litre Mason jar and cover it with boiling water, then let it stand several hours or overnight before pouring the liquid through a sieve. The flavour is not to everyone's taste, but I don't mind it—I tell my kids that it makes me feel like Popeye! I try to make a batch one or two times a week until my garden starts producing again. I have not ventured much further into the world of dried herbs but if you are interested in making herbal tonics, there are many good books on the subject—try *www.susunweed.com* for information. A word of caution—herbs can have strong medicinal effects and should not be used without some research.

Blanching Mung Bean Sprouts: For a lighter flavour, mung bean sprouts can be cooked in boiling water for about one minute and then quickly cooled in cold water. This is called blanching and with mung bean sprouts it also works to separate the green outer hulls from the sprout. Remove as many of the hulls as you can and then drain the sprouts and use in any of the February recipes.

Available Foods

Fresh Eating	In My Freezer	In My Root Cellar	At the Grocery
Alfalfa sprouts	Tomatoes	Carrots	Carrots
Lentil sprouts	Corn	Cabbage	Cabbage
Mung bean sprouts	Swiss chard	Onions	Onions
	Pesto	Garlic	Parsnips
	Rhubarb	Turnip	Mushrooms
	Strawberries	Potatoes	Sprouts
	Blueberries	Squash (in a closet)	Apples
	Cranberries	Apples	
	Applesauce		

Menu Ideas for February

Much the same as for January but add sprouts wherever you can and go for the applesauce!

Soba Noodles with Mung Bean Sprouts
Spicy Cabbage with Sprouts
Hot and Sour Soup

Grated Carrot and Sprout Salad
Spicy Korean Pickled Cabbage
Danish Apple Cake
Carrot Applesauce Cake
Applesauce Bread Pudding

A Few Recipes

♥ Soba Noodles with Mung Bean Sprouts

1 pound soba (buckwheat) noodles, cooked
2 tbsp oil
4 cloves garlic, minced
1 medium onion, chopped
1/3 cup tamari
1/4 cup fresh lime juice
1 tsp sugar
1/4 tsp dried chili flakes
2 cups mung bean sprouts
1/2 cup sunflower seeds or peanuts

Sauté onion and garlic in oil over medium heat for 2 or 3 minutes. Add the tamari, lime juice, sugar, chili flakes, and mung bean sprouts and cook 1 minute longer. Pour over the noodles, garnish with toasted sunflower seeds or chopped nuts. Serves 4.

Spicy Cabbage, Carrots, and Sprouts

2 tbsp oil
1/4 tsp chili flakes
2 cups shredded cabbage
1 onion, thinly sliced
1-2 carrots, grated
2 cups mung bean sprouts
1 tbsp fish sauce
1 tbsp rice vinegar

Heat the oil in a wok or a cast-iron pan. Add the chili flakes, shredded cabbage, and onion and cook for several minutes. Add the remaining ingredients and cook another minute; the vegetables should be hot but crunchy. This recipe goes well with rice or rice noodles, and either tofu or meat. Also great with black bean sauce or my friend Carlina's wonderful concoction of 2 tbsp sesame oil, 2 tbsp tamari, 1 tsp balsamic vinegar, 1 tsp brown sugar, 1 tsp grated ginger, and 2 cloves of garlic, grated. Serves 4.

Hot and Sour Soup

6 cups stock
1 tbsp grated ginger
2 cloves garlic, grated
2 carrots
2 cups sliced mushrooms
1-3 tsp red curry paste
1-2 cups mung bean sprouts
1/4 cup tamari
1/2 cup white vinegar
2 tbsp cornstarch in 4 tbsp water
2 cups rice noodles

Dice the carrots into 1/4" pieces (small). In a large pot bring the stock to a boil and add the ginger, garlic, carrots, and mushrooms. Simmer for 15 minutes. Add the curry paste, mung bean sprouts, tamari sauce, and vinegar and return to a boil. Slowly add the cornstarch and water and stir to thicken soup. Add the rice noodles; simmer 2-3 minutes until they are soft. You can add protein to this soup by adding leftover chicken, cubed tofu, or 3 well-beaten eggs which you slowly stir into the boiling soup. Serves 6.

Grated Carrot and Sprout Salad

4 large carrots, peeled and grated
1 to 1 1/2 cups lentil or mung bean sprouts
1/4 cup cider vinegar
1/3 cup oil
Salt and pepper

Combine all the ingredients in a bowl.
Mix well. Serves 4.

Spicy Korean Pickled Cabbage or Kimchi

6-8 cups coarsely chopped or grated cab-
    bage
2-3 cups grated carrots
2 onions or leeks, finely sliced
1 tbsp grated ginger
4-6 cloves garlic, finely chopped
1 medium hot pepper, chopped or 1/8-1/2
    tsp chili flakes
2 tbsp salt

Combine all the ingredients in a bowl.
Using your hands, knead the vegetables
until the juices are released. This takes a
few minutes, but once it happens you will
see that the vegetables begin to shrink
considerably. Pack into two 1 litre mason
jars (or other jars with lids) and press the
vegetables in firmly so that there is some
liquid on top. The vegetables should be a
few inches below the top of the jar. Cover
tightly and keep at room temperature for
4-6 days, then store in the fridge for 1-2
weeks before eating. It will keep for several months..

(Adapted from *Nourishing Traditions* by
Sally Fallon, If you are interested in naturally fermented vegetables, her book
devotes a whole chapter to the subject.)

Danish Apple Cake

4 tbsp butter
3 cups fine bread crumbs
3 tbsp sugar
3 cups applesauce
1 cup whipping cream
2 tbsp grated chocolate (optional)

In a cast-iron pan, melt the butter over
medium heat and cook the bread crumbs
until just brown, stirring often to avoid
burning. Remove from the heat. In a
large bowl, layer the bread crumbs with
the applesauce, making three layers of
each. Pumpernickel or dark rye bread
makes excellent bread crumbs for this
dessert. Danish Apple Cake can be eaten
right away but it is much better if it stands
for several hours or overnight in the
fridge. Top with whipped cream and
grated chocolate. Serves 4-6.

Carrot Applesauce Cake

2 1/2 cups flour
3 tsp baking powder
1 tbsp cinnamon
1 tsp nutmeg
1 cup sunflower seeds (optional)
4 eggs
1/2 cup oil or melted butter
1/2 cup honey or brown sugar
1 tsp vanilla extract
1 1/2 cups applesauce
3 cups grated carrots

Preheat oven to 350°F (175°C). In a large bowl, combine the dry ingredients. In another bowl, whisk the eggs. Then add the remaining ingredients and mix well. Add to dry ingredients and stir until just mixed. Baked in a greased 9 x 13" pan for about 45 minutes. Serves 6-8.

Applesauce Bread Pudding

8 slices dry bread, cut in cubes
3 cups applesauce
1/2 cup raisins
1 tsp cinnamon
1/4 tsp nutmeg
2 eggs
2 cups milk
1/2 cup brown sugar
sprinkle of cinnamon and sugar

Preheat oven to 350°F (175°C). Arrange the bread in a greased 9" square baking pan. Combine 2 cups of the applesauce, raisins, and spices and spoon over the bread, mixing it up a bit. In a bowl, beat together the eggs, milk, and brown sugar and pour over the bread mixture. Top with the remaining applesauce and a sprinkling of cinnamon and sugar. Bake for about 45 minutes. Serves 6-8.

Food for Thought

Seeds Have Issues Too

The saving and selecting of seeds is as old as agriculture itself. For many, agricultural seeds are an expression of the living history and traditions of a society, a product of thousands of years of agricultural knowledge. Until the last century, seeds have represented the co-operative labour of communities, shared collectively for the benefit of all. Sometime in the mid-nineteenth century the Western World saw the emergence of small, family owned seed companies. For the first time, farmers had a source from which to buy seeds as well as access to a greater variety of seeds. By the mid-twentieth century plant breeders were an integral part of the seed industry, actively developing and patenting new seed varieties, first hybrids and then genetically modified seeds.

As we enter the twenty-first century we find that only ten corporations control 30% of the world's commercial seed market. The basic premise that a culture has a right to benefit from its agricultural heritage is being threatened by multinational manipulation and patenting of all aspects of agriculture. Corporations are racing to patent seeds and agricultural products that have been part of traditional knowledge for centuries.[1] This has occurred because in 1980 the U.S. Supreme Court, under pressure from multinational corporations, overturned laws banning the patenting of living organisms. There are many who oppose this patenting of life forms, most notably Costa Rica and the European Union. Citizens groups around the world are lobbying for a Treaty to Share the Genetic Commons and Costa Rica has banned all patenting and profiting from the genes of native plant and animal species.[2]

As agriculture has become increasingly industrialized, seed companies have concentrated on growing only a small number of commercially viable fruits and vegetables. As a result we have lost thousands of traditional varieties of grains, vegetables, and fruits. Modern agricultural production relies on only a handful of varieties for most types of foods. For example, two varieties of peas account for 96% of North American consumption and 86% of known apple varieties have become extinct since 1900.[3] As we lose this genetic diversity, our food supply becomes increasingly vulnerable to corporate control and to unexpected conditions of weather, pests, and disease.

Often we do not understand the seriousness of this loss of diversity until disaster strikes. In 2001-2002, there was widespread drought in the Indian state of Andhra Pradesh. The one district that did not require assistance was one of the poorest districts in India, with a large population of members of the 'untouchable' or Dalit caste.[4] These people had not been able to afford modern varieties of grains and pulses and still relied on traditional varieties of foods that had been grown in the area for centuries. The crops they planted produced food in the drought because they had been adapted over centuries to flourish in a dry climate without irrigation or chemical inputs.

In addition to preserving traditional seeds and growing them ecologically, the people of this area ensure their own food security by preserving, lending, borrowing, and exchanging all the seeds they use in their fields. In their community, women are valued as they are recognized as seed keepers and the ones who share the seeds for the collective benefit of the community.

As awareness of this loss of seed diversity has grown, there have been many efforts around the world to catalogue, store, and save traditional seeds in seed banks. In Canada we have Seeds of Diversity Canada (formerly the Heritage Seed Program) that has catalogued over 19,000 seed varieties. The program also publishes a newsletter and offers a seed exchange to members. As well, many small seed companies have worked to preserve older varieties of seeds by offering them for sale in their catalogues. Buying open-pollinated and/or heritage seeds is an interesting way to support their efforts and to discover the seed heritage in your area. There are many beautiful and flavourful varieties of vegetables that have lost favour simply because they don't ship well or are not uniform in shape. When I had my market garden, I became very interested in growing my own dried beans and was once given some beautiful white and red speckled beans that were of Iroquois heritage. Holding these seeds in my hands and trying to imagine their connection to people who lived over a century ago was a very powerful and moving experience.

Genetically modified (GM) seeds are in the forefront of today's battle for control of our food choices. Five major corporations produce and therefore control all of the genetically modified seeds. When these corporations also control the processing and distributing facilities, they begin to control our whole food system. Multinational corporations are perfectly candid in admitting that this is their goal—as one Monsanto co-president stated, the introduction of genetically modified seeds is "not just about a consolidation of seed companies, it's really about a consolidation of the entire food chain."

There are about 114 million hectares (1.14 million square miles) of genetically modified crops grown in 23 countries throughout the world.[5] The U.S. is by far the largest producer with 58 million hectares of land, an area slightly smaller than Saskatchewan. Canada is fourth, after Argentina and Brazil, with 7 million hectares of land or an area about the size of New Brunswick, planted in GM crops. In all of Europe there are only 100,000 hectares of genetically modified crops while Japan refuses to allow them. It is interesting to note that of the 12 million farmers who grow these crops, 90% of them are from developing countries and are resource poor.[6] This would mean that genetically modified crops grown in the developed world are grown on large and/or corporate owned farms.

Little is known about the environmental or health effects of GM organisms. In a 2004 lecture, Canadian geneticist and environmentalist, Dr. David Suzuki stated "it is impossible to predict precisely what the effects of transgenic manipulations will be."[7] Suzuki argues that scientists have been far too quick to endorse genetic engineering and in doing so have engaged in poor science, endangering both our environment and our health. He also says that multinational corporations have become one of the main sources of funding for scientists in academic institutions and this has had an obvious impact. There are some early indications that we have opened a Pandora's Box with genetically modified organisms. In Japan, Canadian GM canola has escaped and is now growing like a weed around ports, causing Japan to consider a ban on Canadian imports of canola. One 1999 study showed a 50% increase in allergic reactions to soybeans.[8] GM soybeans have a gene from a Brazil nut that appears to be affecting people who are allergic to nuts but who are not allergic to traditional varieties of soybeans. Another study found health problems in animals that were fed GM corn. Monarch butterflies and other beneficial insects have been found to die after feeding on the pollen of GM crops.[9] To top it off, the multinational corporations that produce GM seeds have, to date, successfully prevented any food labelling that would indicate the presence of GM ingredients in our foods. Consumers are exposed to GM products in foods that contain soybeans, corn, canola, rice, potatoes, and tomatoes, as well as many other products.

GM seeds threaten the viability of organic crop production because organic plantings are contaminated through cross-pollination and windborne GM pollen or seed. A European Union report found that seed contamination rises to a level at which organic farming is not viable when even 10% of a given region is planted in GM crops. About 55% of Canadian farmland is planted in GM crops. Europe has a policy of zero tolerance for GM contamination and so Canadian organic farmers have suffered greatly through the loss of European markets. GM canola is grown all over the prairies and has contaminated seeds, crops, and fields so extensively that certified organic grain farmers no longer attempt to grow canola. The Saskatchewan Organic Directorate (www.saskorganic.com), a group of organic farmers, producers, processors, and buyers, has been fighting a long legal battle with multinationals Monsanto and Bayer, arguing that these companies have denied them their right to farm organically. If biotech companies claim to own the genes to their seeds, then with that ownership should come responsibility for contamination, including full compensation to organic farmers for damages and clean up costs. In December of 2007, the Saskatchewan Organic Directorate lost its application to the Supreme Court of Canada for a class action lawsuit, but it is still exploring other forms of legal action. This is an incredibly important legal battle that is being watched all over the world—if you wish to support this action you can do so through the Directorate's Organic Agriculture Protection Fund.

There are signs that consumer and farmer resistance is having an effect. Many feel that because of the Saskatchewan Organic Directorate's legal battle with Monsanto, the biotech giant has backed off from plans to introduce

GM wheat in North America. In 2007, a U.S. Federal judge overturned USDA approval of Monsanto's Round-Up Ready Alfalfa, arguing that it could contaminate conventional and organic alfalfa. The judge ruled that the USDA had failed to abide by federal environmental regulations when it gave initial approval and ordered a preliminary injunction to ban the sale and planting of GM alfalfa. As consumers, we can avoid GM foods by purchasing organic products, by lobbying for a far more precautionary approach as well as mandatory labelling, and also by growing our own foods.

The latest seed technology being developed by multinational seed companies has been called 'Terminator Technology.' Terminator seeds employ something called 'Genetic Use Restriction Technology,' in which an outside chemical is used to control the expression of a plant's genetic trait. In other words, the seeds that Terminator plants produce are sterile at harvest. This technology was developed to prevent farmers from re-planting harvested seed, thereby making farmers dependent and maximizing seed industry profits. To date, there is an international moratorium on the use of Terminator seeds, reflecting strong public and international opposition to the technology. However, aggressive lobbying by Canada, Australia, and New Zealand, who many feel are acting as puppets for the United States, may well bring an end to the moratorium. One can only hope that public opposition and common sense will prevail.

Sources and Further Information

www.banterminator.org

Greenpeace International, *How to Avoid Genetically Engineered Foods*, a small booklet available from Greenpeace, 250 Dundas St. W., Toronto, Ont. M5T 2Z5

Jason, Dan, The Whole Organic Food Book, Raincoast Books, Vancouver, 2001.

Lappé, F.M. & A., *Hope's Edge: The Next Diet for a Small Planet,* Tarcher/ Putnam, New York, 2002.

The National Farmers Union, 2717 Wentz Avenue, Saskatoon, Sask., S7K 4B6, *www.nfu@nfu.ca*

The Saskatchewan Organic Directorate, P.O. Box 310, Rockglen, Sask., S0H 3R0, *www.saskorganic.com*

Seeds of Diversity Canada, P.O. Box 36, Station Q, Toronto, Ont., M4T 2L7 *www.seeds.ca*

Suzuki, David, *Battling the Biotech Gene Giants,* A DVD recording of Dr. Suzuki's talk to the National Farmers Union as well as excerpts from his upcoming film about the Saskatchewan Organic Directorate's legal battle. Available for $25 from the Saskatchewan Organic Directorate or free with a donation of $100 to the Directorate.

Endnotes

1   Lappé, F.M. and A., *Hope's Edge: The Next Diet for a Small Planet*, Tarcher/Putnam, New York, 2002, p. 144.

2   Ibid, p. 144.

3   Jason, Dan, *The Whole Organic Food Book,* Raincoast Books, Vancouver, 2001, p.174

4   InterPares, *Community-Based Food Security Systems*, InterPares Occasional Paper #4, Ottawa, 2004

5   *www.isaaa.org,* 2007 report (International Service for Acquisition of Agricultural Biotechnology Applications)

6   Ibid

7   Pugh, Terry, *Precautionary principle ignored by advocates of biotech, say Suzuki,* in The Union Farmer Quarterly, Volume 10, #4, Winter 2004, National Farmer's Union, Saskatoon.

8   Jason, Dan, *The Whole Organic Food Book,* Raincoast Books, Vancouver, 2001, p. 176

9   Ibid, p. 177

MARCH

Earth's crammed with Heaven
And every common bush
Afire with God

From *Aurora Leigh*, Book vii by Elizabeth Barrett Browning (1806 – 1861), *British poet*

In the Garden
Making Transplants

In some parts of Canada March is warm enough to get out in the garden, but for most of us the landscape is still predominantly white and the days are too cold for outside work. We can, however, get out our seeds and get a jump on spring by making some early transplants.

Transplanting is the practice of starting plants in small containers in a controlled environment and then later planting them out in the garden. Not all vegetables are suited to transplanting, but for those that are, it ensures even and good germination. When you direct seed a vegetable, you are at the mercy of the climate for proper germination. If the weather is too hot, cold, wet, or dry, there is a good chance that the seeds that you plant will have either moderate or poor germination rates. This results in unproductive areas in the garden that would not occur if you had planted vegetables that had already germinated and were many weeks old.

There are many other good reasons to make transplants. You can start plants earlier than they can be seeded in the garden. This is especially true for peppers and tomatoes, which would not produce fruit in our growing season if direct-seeded. It is also valuable for vegetables such as spinach and lettuce because they can be growing inside in late March and early April when the weather outside is still erratic. In a small garden that is pressed for space, it allows vegetables to do part of their growing in small containers, reducing the time they spend in the garden, thereby making it possible to plant an area of the garden twice in one season. Because transplants are put out when they are three or four weeks old (or two months old in the case of tomatoes and peppers), they are already far ahead of any weeds that may start to grow and they are better able to cope with whatever pests may wish to feed upon them. As well, transplanted crops are set in the garden at the correct final spacing and do not need to be thinned as they grow; they quickly fill in their growing space, shading the soil and crowding out the oncoming weeds. Finally, some vegetables, such as lettuce, endive, spinach, and green onions will not germinate well in hot weather and so summer plantings of these are best started indoors in a cooler spot.

This is not to say that most vegetables cannot be direct seeded. Many people plant their whole garden from seed, buying what transplants they need from a nursery. Keep in mind that most nurseries use chemical fertilizers and that you will find a far greater selection of vegetable varieties in a seed catalogue. However, transplants do require some care before and after they go into the garden. They must be watered regularly and after they have germinated they should be kept outside under the protection of a small cold frame (see April section). Once in the cold frame you must ensure that they get adequate ventilation, do not get too hot, and do not dry out. Eventually it comes down to personal preference.

Transplanting Supplies

- Two or three 15 kg bags of composted sheep manure (I have never had good luck with cow manure—I think it is too strong for delicate seedlings).
- A large bag (35 litre) of soil-less mix containing good quality peat and vermiculite.
- Bone meal is good for root development and blood meal provides a steady supply of nitrogen—you can buy these separately or as a mix.
- A large plastic container so you can make up a large amount of starting mix at once and store it over the season.
- Transplant containers. Most gardening stores sell 'mini greenhouse' trays with 24, 36, or 48 individual cells and a plastic lid. These work well for smaller seedlings as do cut-off milk cartons, peat pots, and paper cups. Some of the vegetables, notably tomatoes, peppers, cucumbers, squash, and zucchini require bigger containers. You will need 4-6" pots for your tomatoes and 3-4" pots for the other vegetables. The pots in which nurseries sell their perennials are perfect for this.
- Several rectangular trays to hold your larger transplant pots. I buy 12" x 15" trays from a restaurant supply store and also use them to make Sunflower sprouts (*see Winter Eating later in this chapter*).
- A good south facing window or a light table.

Starting Mix

I start my first seedlings in early March and at this time I make up a large container of starting mix. For the mini green-

A mini greenhouse tray containing 48 cells with endive, basil, and green onions.

house trays I use equal amounts of soil-less mix and sheep manure. Transplants need some degree of soil sterility, so it is not a good idea to use your own compost or some local manure. I also add a small amount of blood and bone-meal—about two cups per ten gallons of mix. I make a large amount of this mix at one time so that it is handy whenever I want to start some transplants. Each time I make a set of transplants I transfer a few gallons of the mix to a small five gallon pail and moisten the mix **before** putting it in the containers. I then fill each container almost to the top and gently firm it down—it should be compact enough that the soil does not fall away from the seedling when planted in the garden, but not so dense that the plant has trouble growing.

Planting

Generally seeds should be planted at a depth proportional to their size. Lettuce, endive, basil, and green onions can be placed on top of the soil and covered with a light layer of starting mix; beets, spinach, Swiss chard, tomatoes, and peppers need a slightly thicker covering; and cucumbers, squash, and zucchini should be pressed about 1/2" into the soil. If the seeds are all brand new, two seeds per cell should ensure good germination; if both come up you keep the healthiest one. If they are a few years old—well, you decide how many seeds you want to plant! You can always thin them when they germinate (note—spinach seed should be placed in the refrigerator for one or two days before planting as this greatly improves germination).

It is a good idea to label your trans-plants; I use masking tape and a water-

These transplants of 8-10 green onions are planted as one and grow into a large bunch from which the green onions can be pulled individually or all at once.

proof marker to identify the vegetables and the different varieties of a vegetable. All pots and trays should be covered once they have been seeded to prevent them from drying out. Newspaper, some thin plastic, or the cover that comes with the mini-greenhouse trays all work well. Most vegetables will germinate well at room temperature, however tomatoes, peppers, and eggplant need more warmth (70-80°F). In a warm house the top of the refrigerator often works well. If your house is cold, consider using a small space heater in an enclosed space. I made a tiny hothouse under my desk using a blanket to keep the heat in and my tomatoes and peppers had 100% germination in a little more than one week. Check the trays often to see when the first few seedlings appear—when they do the cover should come off and the trays need to go on a windowsill or on to the light table. For vegetables that require a week or longer to germinate, you will have to watch that mould does not develop. If it looks like it might be a problem, allow the flat to germinate without a cover, watering lightly if necessary.

Multi-plant Transplants

Multi-plant transplants are a neat time-saving trick that I learned in my market garden. A multi-plant transplant is a cell that contains from two to ten seedlings of a vegetable, for which there is no inten- tion of thinning. This is especially useful for plants that are spaced close together in the garden.

Say you want to plant 400 onions, each requiring a spacing of six inches. Using a conventional single plant trans- plant, that would mean making, seeding, and handling 400 transplants. With a multi-plant transplant, you have four onion seedlings in each transplant cell, setting them in the garden at a larger

I built this wooden shelf unit for my kitchen. Most of the year, it holds my pots and pans as well as some large houseplants, but in early March I use cup hooks and small chain to attach a 4-foot, 2-bulb fluorescent light to the underside of one shelf. This serves as my light table for about two months.

spacing. This reduces the amount of transplants by 75%, thereby also reducing their care and handling by 75%. The onions in the multi-plant transplant get the same overall amount of garden space as the four single onion transplants would get and the seedlings gently grow away from each other and achieve their normal size.

This method works well for onions, leeks, and beets (four seedlings per cell), green onions (ten seedlings per cell), and for spinach and basil (two seedlings per cell). If there has been poor germination and I have transplants with, say, only four or six green onions, I will combine two sets of transplants in the garden.

Light and Light Tables

Once the seedlings have sprouted and are visible they must have adequate light. Often a south facing window is sufficient, but if the seedlings get 'leggy'—tall and skinny and reaching for more light—you will need to provide artificial light. If you have the space you can buy or build a simple light table. Fluorescent fixtures can often be found at recycled building supply places; you may need to convert the electrical connection to a cord with a three-pronged plug. A power bar at the wall makes it easier to turn the light on and off without having to unplug it. If you don't feel like buying or building anything, you can prop up the ends of a fluorescent fixture on a few short pieces of 2x4, using the blocks of wood to raise and lower the lights as necessary. The top of the seedlings should be about 2-3" below the fluorescent tubes. The gurus of transplanting recommend that you use a double fluorescent fixture and that one bulb be a regular fluorescent and the other be something called 'a gro-light' which emits a different frequency and colour of light. The two in combination are supposed to be optimum for mimicking outside light.

Soil Block Makers

As a commercial market gardener, I used something called a soil block maker to make my transplants. This is essentially a metal extrusion mold that compresses a very wet starting mix into a number of self-contained cubes. These are then ejected onto homemade wooden trays. Soil block makers produce the healthiest transplants I have ever seen and there are no plastic trays to handle, but they do require a bit of a financial investment. There are a number of different recipes for the starting mix—I use 5 gallons of soil-less mix, 5 gallons of composted sheep manure, 2 1/2 gallons of sand, and

1 cup of blood and bone meal. If you are interested in the technique, it is described in detail in **The New Organic Grower** by Eliot Coleman. As far as I know, there is no longer a Canadian supplier for soil blockers but Johnny's Selected Seeds in Maine sells a variety of sizes for both commercial and home garden use.

Soil Block Makers (from left to right): 1 ½" model that makes 20 cubes, 2" model that makes 12 cubes, 4" model that makes 1 cube (for large plants such as tomatoes), 2" model that makes 4 cubes (good for the small garden) and ¼" model for starting tiny seedlings. The ¼" cubes fit into a hole in the 2" cubes and the 2" cubes fit into a hole in the 4" cube for easy repotting.

Picture courtesy of Johnny's Selected Seeds, Winslow, Maine

Watering

I water my transplants by hand, carrying the tray over to the kitchen sink and gently pouring water from a large glass or a Mason jar. Be sure not to over water your transplants—water them as you would a houseplant, allowing them to dry out somewhat before watering.

Damping Off

Seedlings are generally easy to grow but they can be affected by a fungus disease in the starting mix and get something called 'damping off.' If the stem of a seedling appears to be eroding right where it meets the soil, then you have damping off. If this is the case, the seedling may survive with decreased vigour or it may keel over and die. Most starting mixes contain some amounts of fungus, however the fungus will grow only when the seedlings are over-watered, do not get enough air circulation, or have insufficient light. To combat the disease, some seed companies sell fungicide treated seeds and some gardening books recommend sterilizing your starting mix. It is my experience that these measures are not necessary if the growing conditions are good.

MARCH GARDEN SUMMARY

☐ Decide what vegetables you want to start as transplants.

☐ Make a transplant schedule.

☐ Assemble your transplanting supplies.

☐ Prepare a starting mix and plant some seeds.

In the Summer Gardens

• Start transplants of onions, peppers, tomatoes, green onions, lettuce, and spinach.

In the Winter Storage Garden

• Start transplants of onions, leeks, and tomatoes.

Other Possibilities

• Start transplants of celery, celery root, and eggplant.

Sample Transplant Schedules

If this is your first year of gardening you may be unsure about just how much transplanting you want to do. Some people like the sense of organization and controlled planting that comes with starting seeds as transplants. Others prefer to throw a few seeds in a small patch of garden and then water them well. There are advantages to both and ultimately it comes down to personal preference. I do recommend that you start as many transplants as possible in the heat of summer because germination can be very poor in hot weather.

Following are schedules for each of the four garden plans, assuming that you are going to make transplants for everything that you can. These schedules give:

- the approximate dates to start each vegetable;
- the number of cells to seed (I try to fill an even number of trays);
- the dates the seedlings go into the garden;
- the number of seedlings that are planted in the garden (this is always less than the number of cells initially seeded because they don't all germinate—if you have more than you need, choose the biggest and the healthiest seedlings);
- * designates multi-plant transplants.

Note—I start a large number of green onions in July, which I plant and leave in the garden over the winter. They usually survive and produce wonderfully in early April.

350-SQUARE-FOOT GARDEN

Date transplants are started	Number of cells planted in trays	Date planted in garden	Number of cells planted in garden
Early March	8 peppers	Early June	4 peppers
Late March	12 tomatoes	Early June	7 tomatoes
	48 × 2 spinach*	Mid April	32 × 2 spinach*
	12 lettuce	Mid April	8 lettuce
	12 × 10 green onions*	Mid April	6 × 10 green onions*
Mid April	48 × 2 spinach*	Early May	32 × 2 spinach*
	8 × 4 beets*	Early May	6 × 4 beets*
	8 endive	Early May	6 endive
	10 lettuce	Early May	8 lettuce
	16 × 10 green onions*	Early May	12 × 10 green onions*
	6 Swiss chard	Early May	3-4 Swiss chard
Mid May	24 × 2 basil*	Early June	18 × 2 basil*
	9 lettuce	Early June	8 lettuce
	6 × 10 green onions*	Early June	5 × 10 green onions*
	9 × 4 beets*	Early June	8 × 4 beets*
	2 zucchini	Early June	1 zucchini
	8 cucumbers	Early June	6 cucumbers
Mid June	24 × 2 basil*	Early July	20-24 × 2 basil*
Early July	10 lettuce	Early August	8 lettuce
	10 endive	Early August	8 endive
	18 × 10 green onions*	Early August	12 × 10 green onions*
	48 × 2 spinach*	Early August	32 × 2 spinach*

Even germination and an earlier harvest with transplants: the spinach on the left was direct seeded in early April. The spinach on the right was started inside in mid March and planted in the garden in early April. Both pictures were taken in mid May.

500-FOOT GARDEN

Date transplants are started	Number of cells planted in trays	Date planted in garden	Number of cells planted in garden
Early March	12 peppers	Early June	7 peppers
Late March	12 tomatoes	Early June	7 tomatoes
	48 × 2 spinach*	Mid April	32 × 2 spinach*
	10 lettuce	Mid April	8 lettuce
	14 × 10 green onions*	Mid April	12 × 10 green onions
Mid April	48 × 2 spinach*	Early May	32 × 2 spinach*
	8 × 4 beets*	Early May	8 × 4 beets*
	9 endive	Early May	8 endive
	9 lettuce	Early May	8 lettuce
	15 × 10 green onions*	Early May	12 × 10 green onions*
	6 Swiss chard	Early May	3-4 Swiss chard
Mid May	24 × 2 basil*	Early June	18 × 2 basil*
	9 lettuce	Early June	8 lettuce
	6 × 10 green onions*	Early June	5 × 10 green onions*
	9 × 4 beets*	Early June	8 × 4 beets*
	2 zucchini	Early June	1 zucchini
	8 cucumbers	Early June	6 cucumbers
Mid June	36 × 2 basil*	Early July	36 × 2 basil*
	4 lettuce	Early July	3 lettuce
	4 × 10 green onions*	Early July	4 × 10 green onions*
	4 × 4 beets*	Early July	3 × 4 beets*
Early July	10 lettuce	Early August	8 lettuce
	10 endive	Early August	8 endive
	18 × 10 green onions*	Early August	12 × 10 green onions*
	48 × 2 spinach*	Early August	32 × 2 spinach*

TWO EXTRA BEDS OF STORAGE VEGETABLES

Date transplants are started	Number of cells planted in trays	Date planted in garden	Number of cells planted in garden
Early March	48 × 4 onions*	Mid April	40 × 4 onions
Mid May	8 winter squash	Early June	5-6 winter squash

WINTER STORAGE GARDEN

Date transplants are started	Number of cells planted in trays	Date planted in garden	Number of cells planted in garden
Early March	96 × 4 onions*	Mid April	80 × 4 onions*
	30 × 4 leeks*	Mid April	24 × 4 leeks*
Late March	12 paste tomatoes	Early June	8 tomatoes
Mid May	12 rutabaga	Early June	8 rutabaga
	20 × 4 beets*	Early June	16 × 4 beets*
	16 cabbage	Early June	12 cabbage
	15 winter squash	Early June	10 winter squash

Winter Eating— Still Continued!

March is not that much different from February except that spring is starting to look really good! I often wonder if the tradition of Lent originated as people were contemplating their diet in late March. I continue making sprouts and once my light table is up I start to make sunflower seed sprouts. These sprouts need light and they must be grown on a thin layer of soil. Sunflower sprouts have a wonderful, nutty taste that my children seem to like. They are great in salads, sandwiches, and wraps or sometimes I just munch on them as they are. If you want to explore further, you can also make corn, buckwheat, and pea sprouts using this method.

If you enjoy dry beans and pulses such as lentils and split peas, it is a good time to incorporate them into your meals. As much as possible I try to be more creative in my cooking to liven up this last month of winter. One of our favourite March dishes is butter-fried onions with thyme and balsamic vinegar—many people do not think of onions when they think of vegetables but they really do have a wonderful flavour when cooked slowly over a low heat. A fancy stew or curry using carrots, onions, turnips, and potatoes is another nice meal as are vegetables roasted in the oven.

I also use some of my frozen Swiss chard and make *spanokopita* (recipe in October/November section) or a goat cheese quiche. It is a good idea to check your squash on a regular basis because they will often start to go mouldy. If this happens, it is probably wise to cut off the mouldy sections and bake all of your remaining squash at once. Place whole sections on a cookie sheet, seeds and all, bake them and then put them in freezer bags. The seeds can be removed from the individual sections when you defrost the squash and are ready to use it.

In the fruit department, I continue to use the applesauce and the berries that I have in my freezer and I make a lot of stewed fruit and fruit crisps. Sometimes I order a case of organic apples or oranges from the health food store.

Directions for Making Sunflower Sprouts

You will need –

- Sunflower seeds – not the bird seed variety. They are available from health food stores and through the companies listed in the February section.
- The same starting mix you used for starting transplants
- 4 12" x 15" restaurant trays, available second hand or from restaurant supply stores.
- A sunny window sill or a light table

Day 1 – place 1 ½ cups of seeds in a bowl of water and soak overnight.

Day 2 – drain the seeds and let them sit in the bowl until the next day

Day 3 – Rinse the sprouts with water, drain, and then let sit in the bowl until the next day.

Day 4 – Look at your seeds. You should see the small white beginning of a sprout on most of them. (If there are a lot that haven't sprouted, repeat Day 3. If you are satisfied that most of the seeds are beginning to sprout then take 2 restaurant trays and cover them with a ½" layer of starting mix. Spread half the sprouted seeds on each tray – it will be very dense. Then cover each tray with an upside down second tray. This is important because the sprouts must get established in the soil before they see the light!

Day 5 or 6 – Once the sprouts have anchored themselves in the soil remove the top tray and place the sprouts in a south facing window or under a fluorescent light.

The sprouts take four or five days to grow. Water the tray when the sprouts are beginning to droop. They can be cut when they are about three inches tall, after the first and second leaves have appeared. Use a serrated knife and cut them as close to the soil as possible. Place in a large bowl of water and wash off the dirt and any black seed shells that are still attached. If you wait until the third and fourth leaves appear you will find that they do not taste good. This takes another few days so keep an eye on the trays.

Available Foods

Fresh Eating	In My Freezer	In My Root Cellar	At the Grocery
Mung bean sprouts	Tomatoes	Carrots	Carrots
Alfalfa sprouts	Corn	Cabbage	Cabbage
Sunflower sprouts	Swiss Chard	Onions	Onions
	Pesto	Garlic	Parsnips
	Rhubarb	Potatoes	Mushrooms
	Strawberries	Turnip	Sprouts
	Blueberries	Squash (in a closet)	Apples
	Cranberries	Dried Fruit	
	Applesauce		

Menu Ideas for March

Menu ideas for March are much the same as for January and February—try to use a lot of sprouts as well as onions, garlic, and potatoes.

Cabbage, Apple, and Sprout Salad
Chickpea and Sprout Salad
Butter Fried Onions with thyme and
    balsamic vinegar

Cheese and Onion Pie
Onion Soup
Cheesy Potato Soup
Spicy Indian Potatoes
Potato Pancakes
Homemade Baked Beans
Tomato Garlic Soup
Black Bean Soup

A Few Recipes

Cabbage, Apple, and Sprout Salad

1/3 medium green cabbage
2 apples, quartered and cored
2 cups sunflower sprouts, washed
Salt and pepper

Grate the cabbage and the apples. Combine all the ingredients in a bowl and dress with oil and vinegar or a mayonnaise based dressing. You can jazz this salad up with chopped hard boiled eggs and toasted sunflower seeds. Serves 4-6. (Note: sunflower sprouts wilt if left in a dressing overnight so only dress as much salad as you plan to eat)

Chickpea and Sprout Salad

2-3 cups cooked chickpeas
1/2 red onion, finely chopped
1-2 carrots, grated
2-3 cups sunflower or buckwheat sprouts
¼ cup oil
¼ cup cider or balsamic vinegar
Salt and pepper

Combine all the ingredients except the sprouts in a bowl and let sit overnight—this takes the bite out of the onion. Add sprouts just before serving. Serves 6.

♥ Butter Fried Onions with Thyme and Balsamic Vinegar

4 large onions, thinly sliced
4 tbsp butter
2-3 tbsp balsamic vinegar
1 tsp thyme
Salt and pepper

In a cast-iron pan, melt the butter and cook the onions over very low heat for about 20 minutes, until soft and golden. Add remaining ingredients and serve. Serves 4. (Adapted from *The Greens Cookbook* by Deborah Madison)

♥ Cheese and Onion Pie

1 9" pie shell
3-4 medium onions, sliced
3 tbsp butter
1 tbsp Dijon mustard
4 eggs
1/2 cup milk
1 – 1 1/2 cups grated cheddar cheese
Salt and pepper

Preheat oven to 400°F (200°C). In a cast-iron pan, melt the butter and sauté the onions over low heat until they are soft, about 10-15 minutes. Bake the pie shell for 5 minutes. Remove pie shell from the oven and lower the temperature to 350°F (175°C). Mix together the eggs, milk, mustard, salt, and pepper. Alternate layers of onions and grated cheese in the pie shell, then pour the milk mixture over it all. Bake for 45-50 minutes or until set. Serves 4-6. (Adapted from the *Harrowsmith Cookbook*)

Onion Soup

4 medium onions, thinly sliced
3 tbsp butter
3-4 cups stock
2 tbsp lemon juice
1 cup white wine
1/2 tsp Worcestershire Sauce
1 tsp thyme
1 tbsp tamari sauce
1/2 tsp dry mustard
Salt and pepper

Melt the butter in a pan and sauté the onions over low heat until soft—about 15 minutes. Add the stock, lemon juice, Worcestershire sauce, thyme, tamari, mustard, salt, and pepper. Simmer gently for about 20 minutes. Top with Parmesan cheese. Serves 4.

♥ Cheesy Potato Soup

3-4 tbsp butter
2-3 onions, chopped
1 clove garlic, minced
4 medium potatoes, peeled and cubed
1 large carrot, peeled and chopped
3 cups stock
Salt to taste
2 cups milk
1 cup grated Cheddar cheese
Freshly ground pepper

In a large saucepan melt the butter over medium heat. Add the onion, garlic, potatoes, and carrots and sauté about five minutes. Add the stock and salt, cover and simmer until vegetables are tender. Remove from the heat and purée in a food processor or with a hand blender. You can also use a potato masher to purée the soup. Return to the pot and add the milk, grated cheese, and pepper and reheat gently. Serves 4-6.

Spicy Indian Potatoes

6 medium potatoes, cubed, cooked, and cooled
1 - 2 inch piece fresh ginger
4 cloves garlic
3 tbsp oil
1/8 tsp cayenne
1/2 tsp salt
1 tsp whole fennel seeds (optional)

Cut the potatoes into bite-sized cubes and boil until just soft. Drain them and then put the lid back on the pot. Shake the pot a little to soften the edges of the potato pieces. When the potatoes are fried, these crumbly edges will be good and crispy. Peel the ginger and the garlic and grate finely. Heat the oil in a large cast-iron pan over medium heat. Add the fennel seeds and let sizzle for a few seconds. Then add the garlic-ginger mixture, cayenne, and salt and cook for another minute or two. Add the potatoes and fry for 5-7 minutes, stirring often. The potatoes should be coated with the spices and a nice golden brown colour. Serves 4. (Adapted from *Indian Cookery* by Madhur Jaffrey)

Potato Pancakes

6 medium potatoes
3 eggs
1 onion, finely chopped
1/2 tsp salt
1/2 tsp pepper
2 tbsp flour

Peel and grate the potatoes. In a bowl, combine the grated potatoes with the remaining ingredients, blending well. Heat a greased, cast-iron frying pan over medium heat and drop spoonfuls of potato mixture onto the pan. Flatten them slightly and fry until golden brown on both sides. Serve with sour cream, salsa, and/or applesauce. Serves 4.

Homemade Baked Beans

4 cups cooked navy beans, with liquid
2 onions, chopped
1/2 tsp salt
1/3 cup blackstrap molasses
1/4 cup ketchup or salsa
1/4 cup honey
1 tbsp dry mustard
1 tsp ginger
1/2 tsp pepper
4-6 slices bacon (optional)
Preheat oven to 325˚F (160ºC). Place navy beans, without liquid in a 9 x 13" baking pan or deep casserole. Add the remaining ingredients and mix together. If you use bacon, cut in 1/2" pieces. Add enough bean liquid to cover and mix again. Cover and cook about 1 hour. Check occasionally and add more bean liquid or water if necessary. Serves 6.

Tomato Garlic Soup

1 whole bulb garlic
1 onion, finely chopped
3 tbsp oil
2-3 cups stewed or frozen tomatoes
1/2 tsp tarragon
1 tsp basil
3 cups stock
Salt and pepper

Peel and finely chop the garlic. In a large pot, sauté the garlic and onion in oil over low heat. Peel and chop the tomatoes, then add the remaining ingredients and simmer for 15-20 minutes. Some leftover red wine adds a nice flavour. Serves 4.

♥ Black Bean Soup

8 cloves garlic, finely chopped
4 large onions, chopped
1/8 -1/4 tsp chili flakes
3 tbsp oil
4 cups cooked black beans, with liquid
2 cups stock
2 tbsp ground coriander
2 tbsp ground cumin
1 tsp pepper
1 tsp oregano
1 tsp thyme
1/2 tsp salt

In a large pot, sauté onions, garlic, and chili flakes in oil over low heat. When soft, add the black beans, the stock, and the spices. Simmer for 20-30 minutes. Serve topped with finely chopped sweet onion and sour cream or grated cheddar cheese. Serves 6-8.

Food for Thought

The Genuine Progress Indicator

When one stops and thinks about the parameters that surround modern food production, one cannot help but wonder why polluting our environment with agricultural chemicals and transporting food many thousands of kilometres is economically feasible. Knowing my interest in the subject, a neighbour showed me some *Canadian (??)* fish she had purchased—it was caught in Manitoba, processed and packaged in China, and then sold in Ontario. How can this fish possibly be affordable? The reasons lie within the foundations and principals of Western economic accounting, a system whereby only the movement of money and the generation of profit are considered. In this system, less tangible variables, such as the cost to society of pollution, environmental degradation, and poverty do not enter the economic equation and are therefore not part of the cost of the food that you buy in the grocery store. Increasingly, there are many who believe that we must measure economic costs in a far more comprehensive and holistic manner. To this end, the Genuine Progress Indicator has emerged as one of the most viable alternatives to present day economic accounting.

My first introduction to the whole idea that economic thought might be flawed came from an excellent Canadian National Film Board documentary entitled **Who's Counting? Marilyn Waring on Sex, Lies, and Global Economics**. A cellist by training, Marilyn Waring was elected to New Zealand's Parliament in 1975 and soon after was appointed chair of her country's national accounts committee. Having very little economic training, Waring perfected what she termed "the art of the dumb question" and embarked upon an education in the world of political economics. Inquiring about the workings of her government's financial decisions, Waring often found that the explanations given to her made absolutely no sense, to which her aides would reply—"we know, but that is the way it is done."

As she progressed through three terms of office, Waring became increasingly concerned about the implications of a system of national accounting that relied on limited definitions of value and ignored large segments of society. One of the most troubling economic indicators was the Gross Domestic Product or GDP, considered by many to be the broadest measure of the health of a nation's economy. The United Nations System of National Accounts defines the GDP as the "output of goods and services produced by labour and property located within a country." The GDP was developed in 1932 by Simon Kuznets as a series of uniform accounts for the U.S. government. It became official policy in 1946 when it was introduced to provide a measure of wartime production capacity and is now used by virtually every country in the world. The most obvious problem with the GDP is that it assumes that every monetary transaction that passes through an economy adds to the welfare of the community, i.e. it does not discriminate between constructive activities such as education or food production and destructive activities such as pollution control, war, or crime. As Ms. Waring very aptly points out—"the Exxon Valdez was the best thing that ever happened to the GDP of Alaska," By ignoring any activity that does not directly pass through the market, the GDP does not account for the unpaid work done primarily by women in their homes and community and in subsistence agriculture. The health of a country's social and natural resource capital are also ignored as the GDP is only interested in the final market value of a product.

Waring's research led her to examine the concept of *time use* as a far more accurate account of how a society functions. She has argued convincingly that international business systems do not adequately meet the environmental and social needs of both local and global economies. By exposing the truth of economic accounting, she and others were able to question the power dynamics behind economic policies and priorities and the value systems upon which those decisions are based. Marilyn Waring is currently a professor at the University of Auckland where she employs *time use* concepts in her work with indigenous populations in the South Pacific. Her work has been instrumental in the development of the Genuine Progress Indicator and Waring continues to be involved with the issue in both Canada and Europe.

Finding a better way to assess the wealth of a nation is certainly problematic. Economists generally recognize four categories of capital:

- human knowledge and skills;
- human made technology and infrastructure;
- natural resources and ecosystems.
- social and cultural abilities.[1]

Many of these categories provide non monetary contributions to society. Finding ways to quantify these categories is not simple. One can try to assign some sort of dollar value but this could present the mistaken idea that the categories are interchangeable, which is far from true. As we are beginning to realize, there are no substitutions for clean water, a vibrant fishery, or for peace.

A San Francisco group, Redefining Progress, was one of the first organizations to formally develop a Genuine Progress Indicator (GPI) that accounts for non monetary aspects of society and that discriminates between constructive and destructive expenditures. Its GPI looks at such issues as:

- crime and family breakdown;
- household and volunteer work;
- income distribution;
- resource depletion, pollution, and long term environmental damage;
- leisure activities and time use;
- defence spending;
- public infrastructure;
- dependence upon foreign capital.

According to Redefining Progress, the 2004 U.S. figures for GDP overestimated the health of the U.S. economy by about 7 trillion dollars; much of this is a result of money that passed through the U.S. economy in the form of expenditures resulting from the accounting scandals of Enron,

WorldCom, and others!

In Canada, there has been much interest in the GPI. The Canada Well-Being Measurement Act was introduced to Parliament in 2000, by then-Liberal MP Joe Jordan in association with Peter Bevan-Baker of the Green Party and received official motion status in June of 2003. The Act calls for "the development and periodic publication of a set of indicators of the economic, social, and environmental well being of people, communities, and eco-systems in Canada."

Unfortunately, the bill seems to be on a back burner at this time.

Alberta's Pembina Institute developed its own Genuine Progress Indicator in 2001. According to its research, the GDP of Alberta increased by 483% from 1961 to 2003. During this same time, the Genuine Progress Indicator fell by 19%. This reflects a decline in quality of life and a deterioration in the environment and considers factors such as the level of household debt, the gap between rich and poor, greenhouse gas emissions, forest depletion, and issues of obesity and problem gambling.[2]

GPI Atlantic is a non-profit research group dedicated to constructing an index of sustainable development for the province of Nova Scotia. GPI Atlantic has identified and researched 22 social, economic, and environmental indicators and is currently publishing reports on each of them. To date, nine reports have been completed and abstracts for these reports can be found on the GPI Atlantic website (*www.gpiatlantic.org*).

GPI Atlantic's report on *The Economic Value of Unpaid Housework and Child Care* stresses the essential contribution that work performed in the household brings to our society. It gives this work a positive value of about $275 billion in the Canadian economy and looks at the consequences of women's double work burden in terms of increased stress and loss of free time. The report argues that our economy and our workplace have not considered the emerging reality of women's labour force participation and that valuing unpaid work brings attention to the need to balance family and workplace (and I would add environmental) responsibilities.

The Costs of Crime report, written in 1999, estimates that 'crime costs Nova Scotians $1.2 billion a year, or $3,500 per household, a number that is equal to 6.3% of provincial GDP. Interestingly, imprisonment is one of the fastest growing sectors of the so-called booming U.S. economy. By using the GPI, the costs of crime are seen as having a negative impact on our economy.

The report on *Farm Economic Viability in Nova Scotia* paints a depressing picture of an industry in deep trouble. While indicators such as gross farm output and total cash receipts look healthy, others such as net farm income, expense to income ratio, percent return on investment, and debt to net income ratio are all far below figures for a viable industry. These figures show that while many farms generate a great deal of income, far too much of this income goes to pay off expenses and to finance debt. Farm income has declined an average of 60% since 1971 with farm subsidies also declining, although marketing boards have helped Nova Scotia's dairy and poultry industries to remain viable. One of the few areas that has proven to be profitable is the direct marketing of organic produce to consumers. On the environmental side, soil is eroding at a rate six times faster that it can be replenished and the decrease in soil quality is estimated to cost Nova Scotians $11.5 million per year. As one examines these issues, it becomes apparent that many of the agricultural innovations that we have seen in the past century would not have been considered financially viable if the myriad of hidden costs had been considered.

By putting real number values on the many complex parts of our economy, Genuine Progress Indicators can bring new insight into the real cost of the foods that we eat. These numbers clearly show that cheap food is not always a bargain and that committing ourselves to paying a fair price for food enables farmers to properly care for their land and the environment. They also demonstrate that not all things that generate a profit are beneficial to society and by the same token, many things with no apparent monetary value have very real worth. Genuine Progress Indicators also demonstrate that respect for the environmental health of an ecosystem is fundamental to the well being of a nation. Implementing such an indicator would end the domination of the GDP in government policy and it would force politicians to acknowledge the economy that ordinary people actually experience in their day to day lives. It would also seriously change the price of that fish.

Sources and Further Information

Measuring Progress, in Alternatives Magazine, University of Waterloo Department of Environmental Studies, Waterloo, Ontario, volume 33, #2/3, June 2007.

GPI Atlantic, 535 Indian Point Rd., Glen Haven, N.S., B0J 3J0 *www.gpiatlantic.org*

Nickerson, Mike, *Measuring Well-Being,* The Seventh Generation Initiative, P.O. Box 374, Merrickville, Ont., K0G 1N0.

Redefining Progress *www.rprogress.org*

Waring, Marilyn, *If Women Counted: A New Feminist Economics,* Fitzhenry and Whiteside Ltd., Toronto, 1988.

Who's Counting? Marilyn Waring on Sex, Lies, and Global Economics. National Film Board of Canada, 1996. (available from most public libraries)

Endnotes

1 Spangenberg, J.H., *Precisely Incorrect,* in Alternatives Magazine, University of Waterloo Department of Environmental Sciences, Waterloo, Ontario, June 2007, page 33.

2 Taylor, Ann, *Alberta's Boom Not Without Bust,* in Alternatives Magazine, University of Waterloo Department of Environmental Studies, Waterloo, Ontario, June, 2007, page 42.

APRIL

Man must feel the earth to know himself
And recognize his values
— Charles A. Lindbergh (1902 – 1974), *American aviator, author, and inventor*

In the Garden

April is a month of energy and enthusiasm. The weather is perfect for working outside and many people do not realize that a great deal of planting and growing can happen in April. Lettuce, spinach, green onions, green garlic, salad greens, radishes, and peas prefer the cooler temperatures and they will all tolerate frost and even a late snowfall.

Soil Health

If this is your first year of gardening, it is probably a good idea to learn a little bit about your soil. Soil is classified in three broad types—sandy, loamy, or clay. Loamy soil is the ideal—it is relatively light and easy to dig and contains a nice mix of sand, clay, silt, and organic matter. As its name implies, sandy soil contains more than its fair share of sand. To its advantage, it is light and easy to dig, however it is often quite infertile and it needs to be watered frequently as it dries out quickly. Clay soil is heavy and, when squeezed will form—to varying degrees— a solid mass in your hand. It is much harder to dig and tends to have poor drainage in wet weather. It is sticky when wet and hard and crusty when dry. To its advantage, a clay soil is usually quite fertile and its water retaining capabilities are a bonus when the weather is really dry.

If we look at the nature of soils we can begin to understand how to look after them. Soil is comprised of air, water, minerals, and organic matter. Organic matter is defined as decayed plant and animal matter. Virgin soils contain between 8% and 20% organic matter and this organic matter is an essential component of a healthy soil. It is food for earthworms and micro-organisms such as bacteria and fungi. These, in turn, make organic matter and mineral particles, and nutrients available to the plants that you grow. In addition to organic matter, agricultural science has identified seventeen elements that are essential for plant growth—these are described in detail in the chart at the end of this section.

Your soil will come with its own initial supply of nutrients and organic matter. Some soils are more fertile than others and you will have to make some conclusions about your own garden. You can have your soil tested by a soil testing company or you can buy a kit for home gardeners. You can also use what I would call an intuitive method of testing—look at your soil and work your hands through it. Does it feel nice or is it full of gravel, sand, or clay? Before you turned it, what kind of vegetation did it support? Did you remove the sod from a dense and healthy lawn or from something that was sparse and weedy? How does it fare in dry weather? All of this information should give you a feel for the quality and nutrient content of your soil. Once you have assessed your soil, you will have to decide if it needs to be improved or maintained through the regular application of organic matter.

In good soils, a yearly application of 2-3" of organic matter is usually sufficient. Sandy or clay soils will benefit from much more organic matter: as much as 25-50% of your soil depth can be new material every year. In sandy soils, this organic matter provides much needed nutrients and works to hold moisture. Sand itself does not retain water so up to 80% of the moisture in sandy soils is held by the organic matter. In clay soils, organic matter works to separate the clay particles, thereby loosening up the soil and allowing air and water to move more freely. One must be careful not to confuse organic matter with black earth or peat, both of which will lighten the soil, but may not provide much in the way of nutrients, bacteria, and living organisms. ***Work to improve your soil, not to replace it with purchased ingredients.***

For the purpose of the small home garden, organic matter usually comes in the form of composted garden and kitchen wastes as well as composted animal manures. I make my own compost but I also supplement this with composted manure. I prefer to get manure from animals that are primarily grass fed. Sheep and horse manures fit this bill. These manures tend to be relatively free of the chemical pesticide, herbicide, and fertilizer residues found in manures from animals fed commercial grains. Manure from large meat producing operations may contain hormone and antibiotic residues

Usually manure is mixed with some sort of bedding, something that the animal stands on when it is in its pen. This bedding is generally straw, wood shavings, or sawdust. If possible, try to get aged manure in which the poop and the bedding have started to break down into a homogenous substance. I incorporate whatever manure I bring home into my compost pile (see October/November section) and spread it on my garden after it has sat for a year. ***It is not a good idea to add raw manure directly onto your garden as it may contain pathogens that can contaminate drinking water. It also contains high levels of nitrates, a water soluble form of nitrogen that can accumulate in certain crops.***

Straw is the ideal bedding in terms of suitability for a vegetable garden, but most commonly shavings are used for bedding—this is fine but they do make your soil more acidic over time. Your soil's acidity or alkalinity is called its pH—with 0 being the most acidic, 7 neutral, and 14 the most alkaline. Vegetables grow best in soil that has a pH of between 6.0 and 6.8. Acidic soils will have a pH that is below 6.0. If you suspect a pH problem, you can add something called agricultural lime every three to four years at the rate of one quart per 100 square feet of garden. Wood ashes also work; add them at the rate of one quart per 100 square feet of garden every one to two years. If you are unsure you can also buy a kit to test your soil's pH at most gardening stores.

If you feel that your soil is seriously lacking in nutrients, there are a number of organic amendments that you can add. Blood meal, kelp, and fish emulsions are good sources of nitrogen; bone meal and rock phosphate contain phosphorus; and greensand, a fine rock powder, contains potassium as well as many other micro nutrients. A good gardening store or farm co-op should be able to help you

NUTRIENTS	FUNCTION	SOURCES
PRIMARY NUTRIENTS		
Carbon, hydrogen, and oxygen	Building blocks of all organic matter	Water and Air
Nitrogen	Increases and improves leaf growth	Air, compost, manure, fish emulsion, seaweed, blood meal
Phosphorus	Stimulates root growth Important for seed development	Compost, manure, bone meal, rock phosphate
Potassium	Increases plant vigour Protects plants from diseases	Compost, manure, green sand
SECONDARY NUTRIENTS		
Calcium	Important to the cell wall	Compost, manure, bone meal
Magnesium	Aids in photosynthesis	Compost, manure, Epsom salts
Sulfur	Builds proteins	Compost, manure
MICRO NUTRIENTS		
Boron, chlorine, copper, iron, manganese, molybdenum, nickel, and zinc	Necessary for enzyme production, the absorption of other elements, and the utilization of nitrogen	Compost, manure, green sand

Transplanting

If you have made transplants, they will do much better if they are handled with a certain amount of care. If your transplants are still indoors it is a good idea to get them used to the outside light before planting them—this is called *hardening off*. As long as the weather isn't really miserable, bring them outside for six to ten hours a day for three or four days. When you are ready to plant, thoroughly soak each transplant. Then gently push on the bottom of each cell to remove the transplants and lay them all out on top of the soil, using the measuring stick to get an even spacing. Plant the seedlings and water them by hand, using a small plastic container. Try to give each transplant about half a litre of water, taking care to pour the water slowly so as not to swamp the seedling. *If the weather is very hot, it is a good idea to do your transplanting in the evening; this allows the seedlings to become established overnight before being hit by the hot sun.* These little bits of extra care take very little time and produce far healthier plants.

Cutworms are small, brown or grayish 1-2" worms that eat the roots of the transplant below the soil. You know you have a cutworm problem if a healthy looking seedling suddenly wilts and dies. The worm will then move through the soil and attack the next set of roots that it finds. There can be several cutworms in an area and they can do a lot of damage over a period of several days. I must admit that they leave me with a rather sick feeling in my stomach, especially if the problem occurs in my tomato patch where I have nurtured my transplants for many months. If you notice a dying transplant, the best thing to do is to dig the ground around it and try to find the worm. If this isn't successful you can place protective collars around your plants; these can be made out of light cardboard or newspaper and should encircle the plant, 1-2" below the soil and 1" above the soil. My final solution is to talk to the cutworm and ask him (her?) to please move on and stop destroying my beautiful seedlings!

A wide bed with lettuce, endive, green onion, beet, and basil transplants in the June garden

Watering

Plants need sufficient water to germinate, grow, and withstand pests and diseases. When Mother Nature does not co-operate, your garden should have a good watering every five to seven days depending upon the air temperature, the amount of cloud cover, and your soil type.

WATERING TIPS
- ☐ Water thoroughly, usually for about one hour.
- ☐ Use a gentle sprinkler and a water timer.
- ☐ Soak the soil to a depth of four or five inches.
- ☐ Water in the evening—this allows the water to really soak in.
- ☐ Watering on a hot sunny day can burn your plants.
- ☐ Plants can look wilted in the evening—they will pick up overnight—if they look wilted in the morning they need water.
- ☐ Place rain barrels underneath your eaves trough and use for watering individual transplants or for spot watering.

Shelter for Your Transplants

As the weather warms up, you should move your seedlings to some sort of outdoor shelter. With the exception of tomatoes and peppers, all of your plants will do better outside once the weather warms up. Many garden centres have small greenhouses for sale or you can easily make your own. Keep in mind that your structure will have to accommodate tomato plants that will be almost two feet high by the end of May. I make a *mini* (keyword – mini) greenhouse with four secondhand windows and secondhand lumber; both are easy to find at places that sell recycled building materials. Two of the windows sit horizontally on the frame and the other two are almost vertical. I provide rudimentary ventilation by moving the top windows, either up or back, and when the tomatoes get really tall I remove them altogether. The vertical windows are held in place with some bent nails on the long 2x4. The back and sides are closed in with plastic stapled to the wood. If possible place the structure in a protected spot that is warmer in the spring—perhaps a patio or the south side of your house. Below is a diagram to illustrate my design.

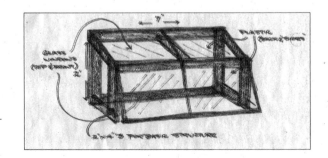

Cold Frames

Growth rates in plants are dependent upon the temperature of the soil: they are much slower in cold soil. One way to plant early and bring additional warmth to the soil is by planting an early spring crop in a cold frame. This is basically a low wooden frame with a glass cover that is placed directly over the soil and your plants grow within this frame. Cold frames are a common feature in many small gardens but personally I find them awkward to work in—mainly because of the wooden sides. I prefer to use the floating row cover to bring extra warmth to my April plantings. In my experience it is just as effective, less confining to work in, and you do not have to manipulate the glass either to let the rain in or the heat out.

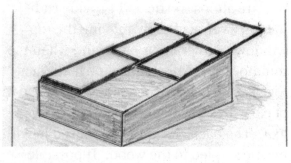

Straw

Finally, in the June section I recommend covering your walkways and the bare soil around your plants with a layer of straw. This is called mulching. Bales of straw can be hard to find in June so it is a good idea to pick up two or three now from your local gardening centre or farm co-op.

Marking Out Your First Beds

As soon as the ground can be worked, you should begin digging and planting. To mark out your bed for planting:

- Have a look at your garden plans and mark out an area for your April beds.
- Dig this area thoroughly, if possible to the depth of the tines on your garden fork.
- Remove any weeds that are present and break up any clumps of soil with your hands.
- Smooth the area over with your fork or a rake.
- Starting at one edge of the garden, use your four-foot measuring stick to mark the four corners of the bed. Place a rock or small stick at each corner.
- To make your walkways, stand beside one of the markers, perpendicular to the bed, and sidestep your way down the length of the bed, aiming for the marker at the other end and packing down the walkway as you go.
- Repeat this process to make a walkway on the other side of the bed.
- Plant the bed you have marked out according to your garden plan and then make your next bed in the same way.

Planting Techniques
Green Garlic

Green garlic is the green shoot of a garlic clove, harvested long before it becomes a garlic bulb, and eaten much like a green onion. It has a delicious, garlicky flavour and is good both cooked and fresh. I plant 50-60 cloves of garlic in the fall and the green shoots are ready to eat in early April. In the spring, I plant green garlic in early April and in May. To plant, separate the individual cloves of garlic (do not peel them) and lay them out on the soil, 3-4" apart. Then use your thumb to push the cloves about 2" into the ground so that the pointy tip is facing up and the flat end is facing down. Harvest when the shoots are 8-12" tall; I prefer to use a garden fork or shovel to loosen the plant from the soil.

A bed of salad greens should look like an even, dense carpet of plants. When the greens are about 2" high, take a peek under the row cover. If the seeds are too close together, the plants will look crowded and they will be smaller than their neighbours. Thin by gently removing small sections of greens where necessary—this will allow the remaining plants to grow.

Salad Greens

To plant salad greens make rough lines in your four-foot bed, marking out a small section for each variety of green you want to plant. In a 7 x 4 foot section of greens, I divide the area down the middle (i.e. two 2x7 foot sections) and then divide each of these into three or four smaller sections.

Salad green seeds are planted by broadcasting them directly onto the soil. To do this, place some seed in the palm of one hand and then pick it up with the thumb and forefinger of your other hand, rubbing the fingers together in a gentle back and forth motion and letting the seeds drop evenly onto the soil. Use about one teaspoon of seed for every four to six square feet of garden—the exception to this is red kale, which has a much larger seed and needs about two teaspoons of seed per 4-6 square feet of garden. The idea is to distribute the seeds evenly over the soil—it takes a bit of practice and some concentration, but it isn't hard. When you have seeded all your varieties of greens, lightly cover the seeds by passing your hand over the soil once.

My typical planting of greens

Kale	Tatsoi	Red Mustard	Kyona
Arugula		Lettuce	

Flea Beetles are tiny black beetles that love to eat any plants that are members of the mustard or cabbage families. This includes radishes, turnip, and rutabaga, cabbage, broccoli, Brussels sprouts, cauliflower, and salad greens such as tatsoi, kyona, kale, and red and green mustard. I protect my greens by covering them with a section of floating row cover immediately after planting—I don't believe you can grow nice salad greens without doing this. The greens grow underneath the cover and I leave it on until harvest. Rotenone is an organic pesticide made from the roots of two bean family plants that is effective against flea beetles. However, it is moderately toxic and takes a week to decompose. It comes in a fine powder and must be dusted on the plants as necessary.

Spinach, Lettuce, and Green Onions

Spinach, lettuce, and green onions can all survive some cold weather and do well if planted in April. If you started these vegetables indoors in March, they should be ready to go in the ground by the middle of the month. Have a look at the plant spacing diagrams in the February section. Lettuce seedlings need a 1' spacing so mark out your bed using a measuring stick or a ruler, then plant the seedlings. Spinach transplants can have 1-2 seedlings per transplant cell. They should be placed about 6-8" apart, both across and parallel to the bed. Green onions should have 8-10 seedlings in each transplant cell and need a spacing of 6-8".

Lettuce and spinach can also be seeded directly at this time. Plant lettuce in rows that are 1' apart, the seeds within the rows should be placed at 2-3" intervals and later thinned to 1' intervals. Plant spinach in rows that are 6-8" apart; the seeds should be 1-2" apart within the rows and later thinned to 3-4" apart. The thinnings can be added to your salads. Green onions can be direct seeded but as the plants are small, I recommend that you broadcast the seed over the area you wish to plant, aiming for a spacing of about 1".

Radishes

Radishes are another spring crop that should be sown directly into the garden; make sure that the soil is well broken up so the radishes can develop properly. Radishes should be planted in rows that are 6" apart, and the seeds within the row should be placed at 1-2" intervals and later thinned to 2-3" intervals.

Peas

Peas are a cool weather crop and should be planted as soon as you can work in the garden. Varieties tend to be either tall or dwarf: both have a place in my summer garden. *Soaking your pea seeds in water the day before planting helps them to germinate faster, providing they don't dry out for a long time after they are planted.*

Traditional varieties of peas grow to be 4-6' tall and must be staked when they are about 8" tall—we will do this in June. The traditional method of planting involves digging a 2-4" deep trench and placing the seeds in the trench at 2-3" intervals. Once you have done this, dig a second trench parallel to the first one and 6-8" from it and plant it in the same way. Don't worry if the soil from the second trench spills over into the first one, both trenches need

Snow Peas that have been broadcast and then mulched with straw. The planting is somewhat irregular but it is very quick to do and the plants produce as well as those planted in formal rows.

to be covered when you have finished planting. An easier method involves broadcasting the seeds in an 8" wide band, aiming for a spacing of 4-6", and digging them in with your fork. (If you are confused, read the next paragraph!)

The quickest and easiest way to plant dwarf varieties of shell, sugar snap, or snow peas is to broadcast the seed. Count out approximately ten pea seeds for every square foot of garden to be planted. Then sprinkle the seeds over the soil, aiming for an even distribution and a spacing of about 3-4". To bury the seeds, simply turn the soil with your garden fork—the planting depth will not be exact but that is fine. Any seeds left on top can be pushed an inch or two into the ground with your finger.

Onions and Leeks

When I first started gardening, I would plant my onions in May and was always disappointed because they never seemed to grow very big. This is because the size of the mature onion depends upon the amount of green growth that the plant achieves before the summer solstice. For this reason, onions should be planted in April so they can take maximum advantage of the increasing light levels. If you are planting onion sets they need a spacing of 6". Lay the bulbs out on the soil and gently push them into the soil with your thumb, pointed side up, so that the top of the bulb is about 1" below the soil.

If you grew multi-plant transplants of either onions or leeks you should have three or four seedlings in each of your transplant cells and these should be spaced 1' apart. Mark out your wide bed and using your measuring stick, place four transplants across the bed, then move down 1' and repeat the process. I prefer to lay out all of my transplants, then put them all into the soil, and then finally water them all—I think it is faster and there is less switching between tasks.

The Floating Row Cover

The floating row cover is great in the April garden because it captures the sun's warmth and adds about 4°F of heat to the soil underneath it. It acts much like a cold frame and the plants mature faster and are healthier. The cover allows 80% of the light through and all of the rain and is light enough that the plants grow up underneath it. I like to cover most or all of my April planting. To do this lay the cover over the bed—if it is too long you can cut it or roll the extra up at one end. Then find something to hold the edges in place—I use 3-6" rocks placed at 18" intervals around the whole perimeter. Pieces of wood also work well. I leave the cover on until sometime in May when the weather has warmed up.

Planting a Perennial Garden

As much as possible, perennials should be planted sometime in April or in early May. This allows them to become established before the hot, dry weather sets in. I incorporate my smaller perennials into my flower gardens and the larger ones are planted on the edge of my vegetable garden, but they too can be worked in anywhere you would like. Once a perennial garden has been established, it needs some routine weeding as well as an annual application of compost or composted manure. This can be added to the top of the soil around the plants sometime in the fall or in the spring before they start to grow.

Herbs

Perennial herbs such as thyme, oregano, and tarragon all do well in flower beds or in a formal perennial bed—they also need some light compost and a spacing of about 1'. Mint is very invasive and should be planted where it can be dug back annually. Chives, garlic chives, and perennial onions do best in partial shade—I keep mine in a shady section of a flower bed that is close to my front door. Before planting, dig in a bit of compost and then plant them at a 1' spacing. Perennial onions grow much like a large bunch of green onions, dividing continuously over the summer and eventually forming a large clump from which you can pull individual sections the next spring.

Rhubarb

Rhubarb needs a lot of compost to do well – several shovels full are a good idea. Space the roots about 3' apart, adding compost or well rotted manure to the hole before you plant the root. Again, two or three plants are ample for most families.

Sorrel

Sorrel is a tangy, large leafed plant that is more common in Europe than it is in North America. It has a wonderful lemony flavour and is a good source of vitamins A, B, and C as well as iron. Sorrel is easily grown from seed. Broadcast some seed in a small area and thin to two or three plants spaced about 12-18" apart. In June, the plants will send up flower stalks—you can cut the stalks or let the plants to go to seed. Sorrel is a perennial but as the plant gets older the leaves do become tougher so every few years it is a good idea let this reseeding happen.

Jerusalem Artichokes

Jerusalem artichokes, also call sun-chokes, are the tuberous roots of a type of sunflower plant. Each small tuber will spread under the ground into many pounds of tubers and above ground you will see one tall sunflower-like plant. To plant, lay about a dozen tubers on the ground so that they are 1' apart. Then dig down with your fork and bury the tubers 8-10" in the ground. Jerusalem artichokes can be harvested in the fall or the following spring. They survive the winter without any loss of quality and do not need to be mulched. I prefer to wait until spring to harvest because they provide something fresh at a time when there isn't that much in the garden. When the harvest is finished, usually sometime in May, you should dig up all the remaining tubers—it is hard to get all of them and the ones you miss will send up new shoots so you may have to do some thinning. Then add some compost, and replant 12-16 individual tubers at a 1' spacing.

Asparagus

Asparagus should be planted in fertile soil that drains well. Individual crowns must be planted 2' apart. To plant, dig a 12-18" deep hole at each planting site. Add 6-8" of compost or aged manure to the hole so that there is a bit of a mound in the center of the hole. Spread the roots of the asparagus crown over this mound. Cover the crown completely so that it has several inches of soil on top of it. When the first shoots appear, fill in the rest of the hole with soil. You must not harvest your asparagus for at least one and preferably two years after you have planted it. Keep it free of weeds and allow the shoots to grow into ferns. When the ferns die back in the fall, the energy that is stored in them will be transferred into the roots below.

APRIL GARDEN SUMMARY

☐ Dig the area to be planted in April.

☐ Spread 2-6" of compost and/or aged manure and dig it in.

☐ Mark out your April beds.

In the Summer Gardens

- In mid-April, plant green garlic and direct seed salad greens, radishes, and peas

- In mid- to late April, direct seed or transplant spinach, lettuce, and green onions.

- Cover the whole bed with a length of floating row cover to speed up growth and to protect the salad greens and radishes from flea beetles.

- In mid-April transplant onions or plant onions sets—these do not need to be covered.

Transplants

- In mid-April, make transplants of spinach, beets, endive, lettuce, green onions, and Swiss chard. These will be planted in the garden in May.

In the Winter Storage Garden

- In mid-April, plant the onion transplants or onion sets as well as the leek transplants.

In the Perennial Garden

- Plant herbs, chives, garlic chives, perennial onions, rhubarb, sorrel, Jerusalem artichokes, and asparagus.

Other Possibilities

- Direct seed spring turnip, kohlrabi, dill, and coriander.

Harvesting and Eating

April is a difficult month in the kitchen and requires some creativity and patience. The winter vegetables are just about finished and there is very little to be harvested from the garden. I try to manage with what I have, knowing that very soon there will be an abundance of wonderful vegetables coming my way. I continue to make sprouts on a regular basis and there are still potatoes, onions, garlic, carrots, and cabbage in the root cellar. I bring up about two dozen carrots at a time, clean them all, and then place them in a bowl of water; about half of them are still delicious for fresh eating and the other half are suitable for cooking.

There are a few vegetables available in the garden—perennials such as chives, garlic chives, perennial onions, and Jerusalem artichokes as well as green garlic that was planted the previous fall. Parsnips that have spent the winter in the garden under a thick layer of straw should be dug in April. Often there are volunteer plants from last year's garden—green onions, kale, spinach, and arugula that have survived the winter—I harvest everything I can find and use it as much as possible throughout April.

In the fruit department, I continue to use the apples, rhubarb, and berries that I have in my fridge and freezer and again, I usually share a case of organic oranges with a friend.

If this is your first year of growing your own food you probably won't have anything to harvest from your garden. Don't worry, it doesn't take long to establish a few perennials and in the meantime, you can try to buy some local vegetables from your grocery store. If you have access to a Farmers Market, you can sometimes supplement your diet with a few wild plants, notably fiddleheads and wild leeks.

On the Wild Side: April is a great time to harvest wild foods to supplement your fairly minimal garden pickings. Apart from fiddleheads and wild leeks, there is also wild asparagus, stinging nettles, cattail roots, and, easiest of all, dandelion greens. Stinging nettle must be harvested with gloves on. It loses its sting once cooked and tastes much like cooked spinach; it is good with eggs or in soups and is high in iron, calcium, and vitamins A and C. Young cattail shoots taste something like baby corn. Dandelion greens are great in a salad with crumbled bacon and egg and a hot vinegar dressing. The Peterson Field Guide Series publishes A Field Guide to Edible Wild Plants, which is very comprehensive and has excellent illustrations.

Harvesting Techniques
Green Garlic

Pick green garlic as you would a green onion—pull it from the soil, cut off the root, peel away the outer skin and clean the bulb, and then use the both the bulb and the green in soups, bean salads, fried rice, and pasta dishes.

Chives, Garlic Chives, and Perennial Onions

Simply cut chives and garlic chives with scissors as needed. As the weather warms up the plants will begin to flower—avoid harvesting the flower stalks as they are tough. Perennial onions grow like a continuously dividing bunch of green onions—harvest about half of each clump and leave the rest to divide over the summer.

Parsnips

Parsnip is traditionally an early spring vegetable, having been grown the previous summer and left in the garden, covered with a thick layer of straw to prevent it from freezing. It is an underrated food and is delicious in soups and stews as well as roasted in the oven. Each time you want to harvest some parsnips, remove a small section of straw and allow the frost to leave the ground. Then take your garden fork and gently dig up the roots. As much as possible, remove only as much straw as you need because parsnips will start to sprout if they are not kept cool.

Jerusalem Artichokes

Jerusalem artichokes should be harvested as soon as the frost is out of the ground. Begin by cleaning up the area, removing the dead flower stalks and taking them to the compost. Then take your garden fork and carefully dig a section, harvesting the larger tubers and composting the smaller ones. The inside of the tuber looks much like a potato; as the weather warms up the tuber gets ready to send up a flower stalk and the inside takes on a deep red colour—when this happens it is no longer good to eat. You will have to scrub and slice the tubers to find the ones that are suitable. Jerusalem artichokes are delicious raw (grated or thinly sliced) as well as lightly steamed, roasted, or sautéed in butter. I like to grate them, add an egg, salt, and pepper, and fry them like I would a potato pancake. They are an excellent source of Vitamin B, calcium, magnesium, and iron.

Available Foods

In My Garden	In My Freezer	In My Root Cellar	At the Grocery
Green Garlic	Squash	Potatoes	Turnips
Chives	Tomatoes	Onions	Onions
Perennial Onions	Pesto	Garlic	Garlic
Parsnips	Rhubarb	Cabbage	Cabbage
Jerusalem Artichoke	Strawberries	Carrots	Carrots
Sunflower sprouts	Blueberries		Parsnips
Mung bean sprouts	Applesauce		Some squash
Alfalfa sprouts			Sprouts
			Mushrooms
			Apples

From a market—wild leeks and fiddleheads
In the wild—wild leeks, fiddleheads, stinging nettle, and cattails

Menu Ideas for April include:

Coleslaw made with cabbage, carrots, and sunflower sprouts (still a staple)

Stir-fry with onions, garlic, cabbage, carrots, and mung bean sprouts

Fried Rice with onions, cabbage, green garlic, and chives

Fish baked with green garlic, chives, and lemon

Spaghetti with onions, garlic, and mushrooms

A spring soup made with green garlic, onions, and chives (and stinging nettle)

Any kind of bean or lentil salad with onions, chives, and green garlic

Rice Salad with dried cranberries, hazelnuts, green garlic, onions, and chives

Pasta with olive oil, green garlic, and wild leeks

Steamed or Fresh Carrots

Butter-fried Onions with thyme and balsamic vinegar

Sautéed Onions and Mushrooms

Roasted Onions, Carrots, and Parsnip

Jerusalem Artichokes Sautéed with Kale and Onions

Parsnip or Jerusalem Artichoke Fritters (my kids love them)

Gingered Parsnip and Carrot Soup

Pan-fried or Steamed Jerusalem Artichokes

Cream of Jerusalem Artichoke Soup

Steamed Fiddleheads served with lemon and butter

Scrambled Eggs with steamed stinging nettles and butter

Strawberry-Rhubarb or Apple-Rhubarb Crisp

Apple, Strawberry, and Rhubarb Compote

Strawberry or Blueberry Smoothies

Gingered Parsnip and Carrot Soup, Mixed Bean Salad, and a Strawberry-Rhubarb Crisp using frozen fruit

A Few Recipes

Spring Coleslaw

3-4 carrots, grated
1/3 medium green cabbage, shredded
2 cups sunflower sprouts
1/4 cup oil
juice of 1/2 lemon
2 tbsp maple syrup

In a bowl combine the carrots, cabbage, and the sprouts. Add the remaining ingredients and season with salt and pepper. This is a very lightly dressed salad; sometimes I add mayonnaise or a creamy dressing to give it some variety. Sunflower sprouts do not survive sitting in salad dressing for any length of time it is best to add the sprouts just before each meal. Serves 4-6.

Spring Soup

3-4 cups stock
1/2 to 3/4 cup finely chopped chives, green garlic, and/or green onions
4-5 Jerusalem Artichokes and/or carrots, peeled and cubed
1/2 pound cubed tofu or chicken
Juice of 1 lime
Large handful of rice noodles

Combine all the ingredients in a pot and bring to a boil. You can also add protein by stirring in one or two well beaten eggs into the boiling soup. Serves 3-4.

❤ Garlic Noodles (our favourite April meal)

4-6 cups pasta such as penne or fusilli
6-8 green garlic
2 bunches wild leeks (optional)
3 tbsp butter
3 tbsp olive oil
1/2 tsp salt

Cook the noodles in boiling water until done, then drain. While they are cooking, clean the green garlic and wild leeks and chop finely, using the whole plant. In a large pan, melt the butter and olive oil over low heat. Add the green garlic, wild leeks, and salt and sauté very lightly. Toss the mixture with the cooked pasta and top with grated cheese and/or dried chili flakes. Serves 4.

Black Bean and Barley Salad

1 cup dry black beans, soaked and cooked
     (or 1 can black beans)
1/2 cup cooked barley
6-8 shoots green garlic
1 large bunch chives
1 medium onion

Clean and chop the green garlic and chives. Finely chop the onion. Rinse both the black beans and the barley with cold water. Drain well. Combine all the ingredients and season with salt and pepper. Dress with oil and red wine or cider vinegar. You can also add sunflower seed sprouts to this salad as well as dried herbs such as parsley, oregano, and basil. Serves 4-6.

❤ Spring Fried Rice

1 – 1 1/2 cups rice, cooked and cooled
6-8 shoots green garlic
1 onion
2-3 carrots
Large bunch chives
2 tbsp oil
1 1/2 cups mung bean sprouts (optional)
2 tbsp tamari or soy sauce
Juice of 1 lime

Clean and chop the green garlic, onion, and chives. Peel the carrots and cut them into 1/2" pieces. In a large pan, sauté the chopped vegetables in oil. Add the cooked rice and cook over medium heat for 5-10 minutes. Add the bean sprouts and cook a few minutes longer. Flavour with tamari, salt and pepper, and lime juice. If you like your food spicy, add 1/4 - 1/2 tsp dried chili flakes to the pan when you are sautéeing the green vegetables. Serves 4.

❤ Mixed Bean Salad

3 cups cooked beans, such as kidney
     beans, chickpeas, navy beans
6 shoots green garlic
1/2 onion, chopped
1/2 cup chopped chives
1 tsp each dried oregano, basil, and parsley
1 tbsp Dijon mustard
4 tbsp oil
3 tbsp lemon juice
1/2 tsp salt
2 cups cooked pasta, such as macaroni

Clean and chop the green garlic. Combine the first five ingredients in a large bowl. Mix well. Add the remaining ingredients, one at a time, mixing well after each addition. Serves 4-6.

♥ Parsnip or Jerusalem Artichoke Fritters

4 large parsnips or 2-3 cups Jerusalem
   artichokes
3 tbsp oil
6-10 dashes hot sauce
1/2 tsp salt

Preheat oven to 375°F (190°C). Peel the parsnips or artichokes and cut them into thin (about 1/4") rounds. Place slices in a bowl and toss with oil, hot sauce, and salt. Place slices on a large cookie sheet and bake for about 20-25 minutes, turning once or twice, they should be slightly brown and soft enough to eat. Serves 3-4.

Jerusalem Artichokes Sautéed with Kale and Onions

2-3 cups Jerusalem Artichokes, sliced thinly
3-4 cups kale (that has survived the winter
   in the garden)
2 tbsp oil
1 onion, chopped
3 green garlic, finely chopped
1 cup diced cooked sausage such as
   Kielbasa or Chorizo (optional)
Salt and pepper

Parboil the Jerusalem Artichokes in an inch of water until just tender. Drain. Chop the kale into bite size pieces. In a large pan, sauté the onions and green garlic in oil for 3-4 minutes. Add the Jerusalem Artichokes and kale and continue cooking 5-10 minutes, until all the vegetables are tender. Add the sausage (optional), heat through, and season with salt and pepper. Serves 4.

Roasted Onions, Carrots, and Parsnip

4 medium onions
4 medium carrots
4 medium parsnip
3 tbsp oil
1/2 tsp each thyme and parsley
Salt and pepper

Preheat oven to 350°F (175°C). Clean the onions, carrots, and parsnips. Cut the onion into 1/2" wedges. Cut the carrots and parsnip into 1" slices. Place in a 9 x 13" glass baking dish. Add the oil, herbs, salt and pepper and mix well. Bake for about 45 minutes or until vegetables are tender. Serves 4-6.

Cream of Jerusalem Artichoke Soup

2 tbsp oil
2 medium onions, chopped
6-8 Jerusalem artichokes, peeled and
   chopped
4 large potatoes, peeled and chopped
2 tbsp flour
4 cups stock
1 cup light cream
Salt and pepper

In a large sauce pan, sauté the onions, Jerusalem artichokes, and potatoes in oil for about 5 minutes. Add the flour and stir to mix. Add the stock and simmer until the vegetables are cooked. Remove from heat and purée until smooth. You can also use a potato masher to purée the soup. Add the cream and season with salt and pepper, reheat before serving. Serves 4.

Gingered Parsnip and Carrot Soup

2 cups sliced carrots
2 cups sliced parsnip
2 medium potatoes, peeled and diced
1 onion, chopped
1 inch fresh ginger
2 tbsp butter
Small bunch chives
4 cups stock
1 cup light cream
1 tsp lemon juice
Salt and pepper
1 tsp paprika
1/8 tsp cayenne

Peel and finely grate the ginger. In a large saucepan, melt the butter over medium heat. Add the carrots, parsnip, potatoes, onion, and ginger and sauté for about 5 minutes. Add the stock and simmer until the vegetables are tender. Using a potato masher, a hand blender or food processor purée the vegetables. Return soup to the stove and add the cream, lemon juice, spices, salt, and pepper. Simmer for another few minutes. Garnish with finely chopped chives. Serves 4.

Food for Thought
The Many Faces of Organic Agriculture

Over the past thirty years, organic agriculture has gone from what was essentially an alternative system of farming to an accepted and viable industry. In a landmark statement in 2007, the United Nations declared that organic agriculture has the greatest potential for feeding the developing world. Similarly, after nine years of research, a study done by Iowa State University found that organic systems of farming showed greater yields, increased profitability, and improved soil quality over conventional farming practices. The biggest differences were evident in soil and water quality. Organic soils cycled nutrients more efficiently, were more structurally stable, and had superior water retention abilities, thereby reducing surface run-off and preserving groundwater supplies. In this article we will look at organic agriculture as a means of farming, a grassroots movement, and as a billion dollar industry.

Sir Albert Howard is generally considered the western founder of organic agriculture. He began his work in Britain in the 1920s by postulating that the newly emerging synthetic fertilizers would destroy the soil and this unhealthy soil would inevitably result in unhealthy people. Howard developed models of agriculture that were based upon natural systems, arguing that one did not have to understand how something worked in order for it to work. In 1943 he published *An Agricultural Testament*, in which he advocated for a closed nutrient cycle, based upon mixed cropping, the use of animals, and the recycling of nutrients. Howard's ideas made their way to North America in the 1950s and found considerable support within the 'back to the land' and 'hippie' movements of the 1960s.

Another important name in the organic movement is Wendell Berry, an American farmer and philosopher, whose numerous books have inspired millions of readers. According to Berry, organic agriculture should encompass three key components:
- the food is grown in a gentle way, without chemical inputs;
- the farm to table route is both personal and small scale, thereby benefiting the rural community;
- the food itself is relatively simple and unprocessed.

Berry saw small-scale agriculture as essential to the health of rural communities, and people in general. He argued that rural communities, though often poor in terms of monetary assets, had all their basic needs met within the community. There was a sense of caring, fellowship, and fun, a passing on of knowledge through the generations, a feeling of self-reliance and independence, and work schedules that followed both the rhythms of the day and of the seasons. Berry argued that the industrial economy fails to care for the long-term welfare of people or land and is dishonest in that it does not account for the costs of depleted land, bankrupt farmers, or displaced workers.[1]

As a method of farming, organic

agriculture is regulated by individual governments. The Organic Agriculture Centre of Canada (OACC) defines a broad set of principles and standards that farmers must abide by in order to be certified as organic producers. These standards include:

- the use of all genetically modified products, synthetic fertilizers, pesticides, and herbicides are forbidden;
- farmers cannot use sewage sludge (humanure) as a fertilizer;
- animals must be raised in humane conditions, 'appropriate to their behavioural needs' and without the use of hormones, antibiotics, or parainsecticides;
- organic foods cannot be irradiated, nor can they contain synthetic ingredients such as preservatives or fungicides in either their processed form or in their packaging;
- organic farmers must seek to protect the environment, decrease pollution, and work towards long-term soil fertility and biodiversity;
- the use of organic seeds and manure from organic farms is encouraged but not required;
- organic certification makes no claims about the health, safety, or nutrition of the food produced, nor does it guarantee against contamination from nearby soils, water, and/or air.

Central to the idea of organic agriculture is the creation and maintenance of a healthy soil, rich in a wide variety of nutrients, bacteria, and living organisms whose activities release food for plants gradually and in a balanced, bioavailable form.[2] A fertile soil contains appropriate plant foods in the correct proportions for optimal plant growth. It has a compositional structure that provides living conditions that are suitable to both soil organisms and plant roots. The principal ways of maintaining soil fertility include:

- the planting of cover crops or green manures. (Plants such as alfalfa, clover, or rye grass are seeded in an area, allowed to grow, and then tilled back into the soil. These green manures enrich soil fertility by bringing up nutrients from deep in the soil or by trapping atmospheric nitrogen on their root nodules. They also add organic matter to the soil when tilled under, though one must be careful as one can destroy the structure of the soil through over tilling.)
- the spreading of composted organic matter and animal manures;
- the use of organic products such as seaweed, bone meal, and rock phosphate that are designed to provide nutrients.

Organic farmers tend to plant a wide range of crops in order to reduce the effects of insect damage or disease to one crop. It is hoped that healthy soils produce plants that are vigorous enough to deter pests and diseases. When problems do arise they are generally dealt with manually, i.e. by hand picking, or on a larger scale, by vacuuming off insects, through the use of organic pesticides, and/or with insect barriers such as the floating row cover. There are also beneficial insects, handmade sprays, and biological controls that work to control pests without harming the environment.

As we begin to understand the nature

of soils, we can see why organic matter is so important to soil health. Organic matter is rich in bacteria, which allow for the absorption of minerals into the plants that we eat. These minerals provide our bodies with nutrition and allow us to digest and utilize the vitamins and minerals in our foods. They also support a number of functions in the growing plant, including root and cell growth, the formation of proteins, the extraction of energy from starches and sugars, and the absorption and metabolism of nitrogen.[3] Industrial farming practices have replaced green manures and animal manures with chemical fertilizers. These fertilizers generally provide only three elements—nitrogen, potassium, and phosphorus. While these three elements will allow plants to grow, they do not replenish the soil with important trace elements or with organic matter. As a result, most soils now contain less than 5% organic matter. Our soils have become very much like sieves, no longer retaining the wide range of minerals, organisms, and bacteria that are essential for healthy plant growth. The result is soils that are seriously lacking, and in many cases, virtually deficient in trace minerals. These deficiencies carry over into the foods that we eat and into our bodies.

For a long time, the effects of agricultural chemicals and industrial farming methods were seen primarily in the land itself and in the immediate watersheds. The use of heavy machinery has resulted in soil compaction, which has destroyed the oxygen carrying capabilities of the soil as well as its ability to support important

bacteria and living organisms. Runoff of manure from large feedlot operations (farms where large numbers of animals are fed grain in a small space) and residues of chemical fertilizers, herbicides, and pesticides have polluted nearby rivers and streams. Increasingly, agricultural pollution has become an issue of global proportions, affecting areas thousands of miles from the source of the pollution. As soils become depleted in organic matter they lose their ability to retain nutrients. A large percentage of the agricultural fertilizers that are applied to conventional farmlands are never absorbed by the soil. This has resulted in huge amounts of fertilizers finding their way into the watersheds of many of the world's major rivers.

The existence of an enormous 'dead zone' in the Gulf of Mexico is perhaps one of the most worrying water pollution problems facing us today. Researchers first documented an oxygen-poor zone at the mouth of the Mississippi River in the early 1970s. The zone begins early each year when melting snow and spring rains wash nutrients, including agricultural nitrogen and phosphorus from the vast Mississippi watershed, into the river. When these waters hit the ocean, they sit on top of the heavier, saltier water. Fuelled by sunlight and dissolved nitrogen, massive algae blooms thrive near the surface and the water becomes starved of oxygen, causing fish and shrimp to flee the area and killing less mobile aquatic life. In 1993, this dead zone became a national issue as heavy floods in the central U.S. caused it to double in size, to roughly 18,000 square kilometres. It is currently about 16,000 square kilometres and it may well result in the collapse of Louisiana's coastal fishery. There are currently about forty-five oxygen-starved, coastal dead zones around the world, triple the number of thirty years ago.

Organic agriculture seeks to address many of the problems associated with conventional agriculture and today we see it both as a grassroots social movement and as a billion dollar industry. At the grassroots level, the back to the land movement embraced organic agriculture as part of a radically different way of growing food. For many, it was part of a spiritual philosophy that sought to change our whole food system, advocating local and co-operative distribution systems and small, owner-managed farms. Organic agriculture offered an alternative to an impersonal, corporate food system that many perceived to be sacrificing food quality, nutrition, and the health of the environment in its pursuit of profit. There was a belief that food should not be part of a capitalist economy and the ethics of agricultural labour practices, both in North America and in the developing world, came into serious question. In many ways, grassroots organic agriculture was as much a movement to change our whole social consciousness as a way to grow food.

Today we find this type of organic agriculture alive and well in many different forms. There are small organic growers who sell directly from their farm, through farmer's markets, or through community supported buying plans (often called CSAs), in which customers agree to regular purchases of produce from a specific farmer. One can also buy organically grown meat from animals that are raised in a humane and low stress environment, with access to sunlight, pasture, and organic feeds and without the use of chemical feeds, antibiotics, or growth enhancing hormones. Increasingly, there is awareness that the broad range of issues that grassroots organics sought to address are all very much interconnected and vital to the environmental, social, and economic health of our communities.

Organic agriculture remained very much small potatoes until the late 1980s when a series of environmental scares generated a great deal of media attention. "Mad Cow Disease" or BSE (bovine spongiform encephalopathy) entering the food chain and the use of the carcinogenic pesticide Alar on apples resulted in an increased mistrust among consumers of conventional farming methods. The demand for organic foods skyrocketed and today organic agriculture is a $14 billion a year industry in North America. Organic products are now carried in most grocery stores, with 66% of consumers saying they buy some organic foods. Whole Foods in the U.S. is one of the largest organic retailers, with 184 stores and $5 billion in annual sales. Consumers can purchase organic dairy products, meats, and vegetables as well as processed foods such as pastas, potato chips, soft drinks, and cookies. This shift to major retail outlets has resulted in more and larger scale organic producers with some farms in the thousands of acres. There are organic factory farms and huge organic feedlot operations. Organic foods travel long distances and have become increasingly processed and packaged, relying heavily on fossil fuels for cultivation, harvesting, and distribution. Market share and price issues have resulted in a series of large organic corporations buying out smaller producers. Canadian producers have difficulty competing with farms in California and Mexico, where a twelve-month growing season, migrant labour, government subsidies, and huge markets shape a vastly different economic playing field.

With these changes comes controversy over the meaning of organic agriculture. Some say industry is simply substituting animal manures for chemical fertilizers, which often do not come from within the farm but are shipped in from large meat producing operations. The food may be grown organically, but increasingly it has a huge environmental footprint and the goals of environmental sustainability and socially responsible labour practices are being lost. Others argue that organic agriculture should not be seen as a movement of social consciousness but rather as a system of farming whereby there are no chemical fertilizers, pesticides, or herbicides and where animals have access to the outdoors. There is little doubt that the replacement of chemical inputs with animal manures is of great benefit to the environment and perhaps by not trying to tackle all of the issues at once, organic agriculture has avoided becoming either lost or marginalized.

It is hard to find simple answers in this debate but as awareness of the issues increases, there is a growing belief that we must substitute the word 'ecological' for the word 'organic.' Ecologically produced food must be sustainable, benefit both the environment and the community, and should not consume large amounts of fossil fuels in its production and distribution. Both consumers and governments must push for ecologically produced foods. The Canadian government does not have a good track record, either through its choices for subsidies and or through its investments in research. Europe is far more progressive; in Denmark, the government imposes a 25% tax on pesticides; other governments recognize the cost of water and soil pollution associated with conventional farming and pay farmers to convert to organic farming. This year Britain's main organic certification body, the Soil Association, announced a one-year consultation period, during which it would consider excluding foods imported by air from organic certification. The potential impact of this is enormous. As with anything, organic farmers have struggled to create viable operations within the constraints of consumer demand and market realities. It is only through an ongoing commitment to examine all of the issues that we will gain a greater understanding of what we are doing and a greater ability to make informed choices.

Sources and Further Information

Berry, Wendell, *Home Economics*, North Point Press, San Francisco, 1987.

Berry, Wendell, *The Unsettling of America: Culture and Agriculture*, Sierra Club Books, San Francisco, 1977

Eisen, Jill, *Organics Goes Mainstream*, CBC Ideas, Fall, 2006. *www.cbc.ca/ideas/features/ organics/index.html*

Jason, Dan, *Greening the Garden: A Guide to Sustainable Growing*, New Society Publishers, Gabriola Island, B.C., 1991.

Organic Agriculture Centre of Canada, *Canadian Organic Standards*, *www.organicagcentre.ca/std_ canadian.html*

Endnotes

1   Berry, Wendell, *Does Community Have a Value?,* in Home Economics, North Point Press, San Francisco, 1987, page 185.

2   Jason, Dan, *Greening the Garden: A Guide to Sustainable Growing*, New Society Publishers, Gabriola Island, B.C., 1991, page 9.

3   Karr, Michael, *Mineral Nutrient Depletion in US Farms and Range Soils,* www.canadianlongevity.net, 2006, page 4.

MAY

There is so much to be thankful for,
The drops of rain that take on new meaning,
Bear the promise of new life
And renewed energy to the rootlets and buds

— Helen Keller (1880 – 1968), *deaf-blind American author and activist*

In the Garden

May is a busy month in the garden. The first salad greens are ready to eat and everything is starting to grow. Although the gardens that I have designed do not take a lot of work it is time to get serious about your planting. Your tomatoes should be about a foot tall and too high for most light tables. Once the weather has warmed up, you should move them, along with your peppers and any other seedlings that are still indoors, outside under the protection of a small greenhouse or cold frame. Your seedlings should thrive in this protected spot, however, **you must bring your tomato and pepper plants in at night if the temperature is going to drop below freezing.**

In the summer gardens, May is the time to make a second planting of spinach, lettuce, green onions, green garlic, and salad greens. It is also time to plant dill, coriander, parsley, Swiss chard, beets, endive, beans, and carrots. In the winter garden, carrots, parsnip, and early potatoes should be planted. Every year I let some dill and coriander go to seed in my garden and in early May there is usually a good scattering of plants that are already several inches high. As much as possible, I allow these volunteers to grow until I need the section of garden they are occupying and then I harvest them. Towards the end of May, I remove the row covering from the April section of garden except for the area where the salad greens are planted—they still need the bug protection.

Planting Techniques

Swiss chard

Three or four plants of Swiss chard are sufficient in a small garden. They grow throughout the summer and into the late fall, providing an abundant harvest of greens for cooking and soups. Transplants and seeds should be spaced about 1' apart in the garden and the seeds should be planted about 1/2" deep. Other than some weeding and watering, Swiss chard needs very little attention.

Beets

Beets can be planted several times throughout the summer. If they are to be direct seeded, mark out six rows within your wide bed, about 1/2" deep. Plant the seeds 2-3" apart and cover with soil. When the seedlings are about 2" high thin them so that they are 6" apart. The thinnings are delicious in salads, and beets are sometimes planted as part of a salad green mix. If you started transplants, there should be three or four beet seedlings in every transplant cell. These need a spacing of 1' within the garden. They do not need to be thinned; the beets will grow apart from each other and reach full size within this clump.

Parsley

I buy two or three parsley plants from a local nursery rather than start them from seed because they take a very long time to germinate. They require a spacing of 1' per plant.

Endive

Endive is not commonly grown in North America. It is a member of the dandelion family, as is lettuce, and it forms rosettes of slightly bitter tasting leaves. I grow the

'frisee' variety because the centre becomes a wonderful creamy white with milder tasting leaves when mature. Plant endive as you do lettuce, either from transplants at a 1' spacing or direct seeded in rows that are 1' apart. Seeds should be planted 1-2" apart within the rows, and later thinned to 1'. Again, the thinnings are great in salads.

Beans

Bush beans and pole beans can be planted in late May, once the soil has really warmed up. If it is a cool and/or wet spring it is best to wait until early June as the seeds will not germinate if the soil temperature is below 65°F/18°C. Plant bush beans in the same way you planted snow peas or sugar snap peas. Count out approximately ten bean seeds for every square foot of garden to be planted. Broadcast the seeds, aiming for an even spacing of 2-4" and bury them by digging the area with a garden fork. In my garden plans, the first planting of beans is located where the salad greens grew in April. These greens must be pulled and composted and the area quickly dug over, after which the beans can be planted. *Tip— You can soak bean seeds in water for a few hours prior to planting to help with germination.*

Pole beans require more work than bush beans do but they taste delicious and produce over a much longer period of time. Pole beans grow to be 6' - 7' high and need to be staked. Probably the easiest way is to make a teepee with three of four poles that are 6' - 8' long and about 2" thick. Arrange the poles on your lawn and tie the tops of them together with some rope or wire. Then stand the poles up so they form a teepee and carry them to your wide bed—you may need someone to help you. Arrange the poles so that they form a stable teepee and push them into the soil as far as they will go.

Plant five or six seeds in a circle around the base of each pole; the seeds should be about 1" deep and 6" out from the pole. Thin to two or three plants per pole. The bean plants should wind their way up the poles and produce throughout the summer. Because the plants grow to be so tall, it is a good idea to plant pole beans at the edge of your garden where they do not bring too much shade to your other plants.

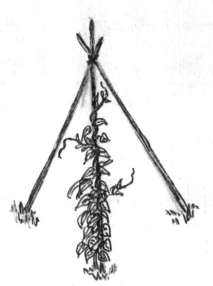

Beans growing on a teepee.

Dill and Coriander

Dill and coriander can be broadcast in much the same way that you plant salad greens. Mark out a section of garden to be planted—I usually find that about four square feet for each herb is plenty. Lightly broadcast the seed, aiming for a spacing of about 1-2" between seeds. Using a small hand fork, gently dig the seed into the ground so that it is just lightly covered with soil. You should have a nice carpet of herbs which can be thinned and harvested as needed.

Carrots and Parsnips

Since both of these vegetables form long roots, I dig my four-foot-wide bed twice before planting, loosening the soil and breaking up any hard clumps that may be present. This makes it much easier for the roots to grow straight and deep. I then make six rows in the wide bed, each row about 6-8" apart. Carrot seeds are very fine and they are hard to plant evenly but try to aim for a spacing of about 1/2" between the seeds. The same spacing is suitable for parsnips. Both carrots and parsnips take about three weeks to germinate and they should be kept moist during this time. Ideally they should be watered every three or four days. To keep the moisture in for the first two weeks you can cover the damp rows with some straw or a board. This method usually works unless the weather is unseasonably cold; in this case the covering stops the soil from warming up and hinders germination.

Maximizing Your Peas: Take a look at your plantings of peas. If there are any areas where the seed hasn't germinated, replant those sections by gently loosening the soil with a small hand fork and pushing the seeds into the ground with your thumb. Take care not to disturb the peas that have already sprouted. In this way you get a small second planting and harvest without taking up extra space in your garden.

Potatoes

Potatoes can be planted in May and in June; later plantings tend to have fewer problems with pests. In the winter storage garden, I do a small planting in May for early eating and a larger planting in June for storage. You can buy seed potatoes from a gardening center or order them from a seed catalogue. You will need one potato eye for every square foot of garden. An eye is the spot where there is new growth emerging from the potato and there are several eyes on one potato. As a general rule, I leave small potatoes whole and cut the larger ones into two or three pieces—these pieces are called slips. Each slip should contain at least one and preferably two good eyes.

The slips need to be planted deep in the ground because the potatoes form above the seed piece. Many people dig a deep trench and lay the slips in the trench; this works well but it is a lot of work. I find it easier to lay all the slips on the soil so that they are 1' apart in rows that are 1' apart. Pick up one slip at a time and in its spot dig your garden fork down into the soil, as deep as it can go. By prying the fork forward a few inches you can usually open up a space in the soil that is about 10" deep. Still holding the fork, bend down and push the potato eye down into the gap in the soil and bury it as deep as you can. Repeat this procedure until all of the slips are planted.

Colorado Potato Beetles and Badminton: These small brown and yellow striped beetles appear in the spring and lay clusters of yellow egg masses on the underside of the potato leaves. They hatch into brown, slug-like larvae in June and can eat an amazing amount of the plant if they are not stopped. If you are diligent you can destroy the yellow egg clusters. Once the eggs have hatched, the larvae can be hand picked or controlled by dusting with Rotenone. I prefer something I call "potato bug badminton." This method involves a badminton racket, a bucket of soapy water, and a person who lightly bats the potato plants over the bucket, thus causing the beetles to fall into the bucket. Some larvae escape the bucket and fall to the ground where they begin their crawl back up the plant, but a round of potato badminton every week or so always wins the battle for me. Keep all the equipment at the edge of the garden where it is handy for the whole summer.

Transplants

In May, your tomato and pepper seedlings must be moved into bigger containers. Tomatoes do best in pots that are about 6" in size, while peppers need a 3-4" pot. The pots in which nurseries sell perennials are perfect for this. Use the same starting mix that you used to start your transplants. Put about 1" of soil in the bottom of the pot and then carefully place the seedling in the pot, filling the sides and top with more starting mix. Make sure that everything is well watered so that there is a minimum of stress to the roots.

Cucumbers, zucchini, and winter squash can be direct seeded in the garden in late May but I prefer to start them indoors in early May. The resulting seedlings are better able to deal with pests and the harvest is a few weeks earlier. To make transplants, fill a 3-4" pot with your starting mixture and put two or three seeds in each pot. Cover with plastic or newspaper and thin to one plant per pot when the seeds have germinated.

For the summer gardens, I also start some early basil as well as another set of lettuce, beet, and green onion transplants. For the winter garden, it is time to start transplants of cabbage, beets, and rutabaga. All of these transplants will be planted out in early June.

Four-Legged Friends

As your plants start to emerge, you will soon get a sense of whether or not there are other creatures who are interested in your garden. Perhaps because I live in a small village I have not had any significant problems, but I have talked to gardeners in Kingston who lose a great deal of produce to squirrels and rabbits. I have both a cat and a dog and they spend much of their time outside and I think this is the real reason that I do not have animal problems. Pets, however, are not for everyone and gardens do need protection.

If your pest problem is of the small variety I would start with covering up the more attractive parts of your garden with a securely rocked down floating row cover. It is not the prettiest way to grow a garden but often the culprit will get discouraged and move on and you can remove the cover. Other solutions include using the live traps (also called Have a Heart traps) that can be purchased at most gardening centers. We once had a groundhog problem in our market garden. The male part of our team suggested sitting in the garden with a shotgun. I could not imagine spending the night sitting beside a groundhog hole, and, I guess when it came down to it, my partner couldn't

either. Eventually we bought a live trap, put some lettuce in it, and set it directly over the groundhog hole. The next day we struck gold and whisked the cute little guy a long way down the road. Another option is a short fence, which works well for animals that do not burrow as well as for wandering dogs and cats (your own or the neighbours').

Deer, unfortunately, are another kettle of fish. Their eating habits are truly amazing as they will take just one bite out of everything that you have in the garden. In my market garden I could lose one-hundred lettuces in a night—one bite at a time. The area was far too big to fence and I didn't like the idea of leaving a dog outside overnight because the garden was far from the house. My solution was to set up my tent and spend about a week camping out. I found that the deer soon moved on. Some people suggested that I mark my territory (i.e. pee!) and spread blood meal (hopefully not my own!) around the perimeter of the garden. These methods might have helped, but I still camped out! If camping does not appeal to you then I would suggest fencing, especially if this is a long term project.

The fence must be at least 7' tall and it must be attached to secure posts. The T-posts sold for agricultural fencing work well but they can be expensive. I used 5/8" reinforcing bar (re-bar) cut into 12' lengths for stakes in my market garden. This might be a cheaper solution. You will also need a fencing tool and staples to attach the fence to the ground and to the posts.

A fence post pounder is a simple and

effective tool that saves tempers and hands. It costs about $50 and is essentially a heavy metal sleeve that is open at the bottom and closed at the top. Place it over your post, stand the post and the pounder vertically, then raise and lower the pounder onto the post.

Most deer fencing is made from UV-resistant polyethylene and comes in various weights and mesh sizes. I found 7' x 100' lengths on the Internet for between $25 and for $250; they are long-lasting and effective. Lee Valley Tools carried the cheaper one.

MAY GARDEN SUMMARY

☐ Mark out, dig, and spread compost or manure on the area to be planted in May.

In the Summer Gardens

- In mid-May, direct seed or transplant spinach, lettuce, endive, Swiss chard, beets, and green onions.
- In mid-May, direct seed carrots, salad greens, dill, and coriander. Plant green garlic and transplant parsley.
- In late May, direct seed bush beans or pole beans.

Transplants

- In mid-May, start transplants of basil, lettuce, green onions, beets, zucchini, cucumbers, and winter squash to be planted in the garden in June. Transfer tomato and pepper transplants to larger pots.

In the Winter Storage Garden

- In mid-May, direct seed carrots and parsnips and plant some early potatoes.

Transplants

- In mid-May, start transplants of rutabaga, storage beets, storage cabbage, and winter squash to be planted in the garden in June. Transfer tomato transplants to larger pots.

Other Possibilities

- In May, direct seed fennel, kohlrabi, bush peas, radishes, dry beans, corn, and spring turnip.
- In mid-May, direct seed or start transplants of broccoli, Brussels sprouts, cabbage, cauliflower, and melons.
- In late May, plant sweet potatoes.
- If you do not wish to start transplants you can direct seed cucumbers, zucchini, and winter squash in late May.

Harvesting and Eating

May is an amazing month. It begins with a feeling that there still isn't a lot to eat and that patience is running out. In the garden, I continue to harvest chives, green garlic, parsnip, and Jerusalem artichokes. Believe it or not, there are still some very respectable carrots in the root cellar as well as one last head of cabbage that is good after the outer leaves have been peeled away. I make my last batches of sunflower seed, mung bean, and alfalfa sprouts and there are still a few more meals with coleslaw and sprouts on the menu in early May. Early May is the peak of fiddlehead season; it only lasts for two or three weeks before the plants grow into beautiful ferns. Wild leeks are also at their best and we use a lot of them in soups, stir-fries, and fried rice. I am lucky to be able to find both fiddleheads and wild leeks in my area but they are also available at the Kingston Farmer's Market along with local asparagus.

By mid-May, there are salad greens, spinach, and sorrel as well as radishes, green onions, and green garlic in the garden. I plant a lot of green onions in the early spring because I like to harvest about half of them when they are still quite small. I also usually have a good supply of volunteer dill and coriander that has seeded itself from last year's plants and by the middle of the month they are large enough to harvest. I find another 'volunteer vegetable' in my fridge because about a third of the remaining onions from last fall have a long sprout of green growing from their center. In the spirit of using what I have, I cut up these green shoots and use them like green onions in cooking. Rhubarb is also ready to harvest in late May.

Harvesting Techniques
Asparagus
Once you decide you are ready to harvest your asparagus, cut back the old ferns, weed the area, and add some compost. Harvest only spears that are the size of your finger or larger. Allow the smaller spears to grow into ferns. As your plants mature, the harvest will get bigger and will last for five to eight weeks. Towards the end of each year's harvest you must let the remaining shoots grow into ferns so they can return energy to the plant roots.

Sorrel
By the first week of May, the first small leaves of sorrel are ready to harvest. Sorrel has a lemony flavour that is great with eggs and fish, either on its own or in a white sauce. Pick individual leaves as you need them—the plant will keep on producing all year. By June, it will start to go to seed, sending up a large seed head, and the leaves will become quite tough. Cut the plant back to the ground on a regular basis if you don't want it to go to seed. In the fall the texture of the leaves becomes tender again and sorrel can be harvested into November.

Coriander and Dill
Coriander and dill that self-seeded the year before can be harvested as soon as the plants are 4-6" high. They grow randomly all over the garden—I try to harvest ones that are in areas I am planning to dig soon, leaving the others to grow bigger. Just break off the stems as necessary— they are both nice in salads and in most bean dishes.

Salad Greens
Check your bed of salad greens in early May. It should look like a dense carpet of growth without any bare patches of soil. If some areas are too crowded, the plants will seem a bit tight and they will be smaller. Give these areas a quick thinning by pulling out small clumps to make more room for the remaining plants. Depending on the weather, your salad greens should be 4-6" tall by the first week of May and ready to eat. To harvest, remove the row covering and pull any weeds that

you see, taking care not to get too much soil on the greens. Then use a sharp, serrated knife and simply give your greens a haircut by gathering up a handful at a time and cutting them off at the base—if the greens are long try to cut them slightly above the ground so you do not have so much stem. The first few salads are small and precious but by the third week of May we have a big bowl of greens at almost every meal. To save time, I cut enough for several meals and wash it all at once. The first cutting is by far the tenderest but the plants do grow back and can be cut a second and third time, especially if they have had sufficient water. Sometimes I like to let the arugula grow to about 8 or 10" in height and then use it in an arugula pesto. After the last cutting, salad greens should be dug under or pulled and composted otherwise they will grow quite tall and take nutrients from the soil. Huge amounts of rainfall, i.e. more than 1-2" in a short period of time, will cause salad greens to grow too fast and their quality will suffer considerably so cut them and use them right away.

Harvesting tip: Salad vegetables such as greens and lettuce must be harvested early in the day as they lose moisture and about 70% of their sweetness by mid morning, rejuvenating themselves overnight. I discovered this by chance when I had my market–garden—I once tasted a beautiful red lettuce in the evening. It was bitter and I was quite upset since it was part of a bed of about 100 equally bitter lettuces that were due to be sold the next week. Just to be sure, I checked them again the next morning and to my surprise they all tasted beautiful and sweet. Later I saw an article in a gardening magazine that explained why this happens.

Radishes and Spinach

Take a look at the radishes and spinach that were planted in April and, if necessary, thin them so that they are 2-3" apart. Both should be ready around the middle of May. Harvest spinach by pinching off individual leaves. As the plant matures it will start to go to seed, especially in hot weather. You can delay the process by breaking off the seed head. We eat radishes raw, placing them in a bowl on the table. They are also good sliced and added to salads. Radish tops are wonderful cooked and used in soups. They seem a bit prickly when you wash them but this texture disappears once they are cooked.

Rhubarb

Rhubarb can be harvested throughout May and June. All of the larger stalks can be picked without damaging the plant—gently pull the base of each stalk, then cut away the bottom of the stalk and the leaf. Rhubarb is one of the easiest and quickest vegetables (rhubarb is a vegetable) to store. To freeze, simply wash the stalks and cut into 1" pieces, then put directly into plastic bags. I try to freeze about a dozen one-quart bags a year. I also cook a large pot of rhubarb and can half a dozen or so one-quart Mason jars.

A note on canning foods: Many foods such as rhubarb, strawberries, raspberries, and tomatoes are easily cooked and stored in sealed glass jars—this is called canning. Canning can be more convenient than freezing because the food does not have to be defrosted and therefore does not require you to be organized! I have no idea which method uses the least energy. It is beyond the scope of this book to give directions on canning foods—there are many good books out there and there are many different ideas about just how much sterilization is necessary as well as how much sugar one must add. Bernardin, a company that makes the lids used in canning publishes a great booklet that is advertised on the lid box or visit *www.homecanning.ca..*

Available Foods

In My Garden	In My Freezer	In My Root Cellar	At the Grocery
Chives	Tomatoes	Carrots	Carrots
Green Garlic	Rhubarb	Cabbage	Cabbage
Jerusalem Artichoke	Strawberries	Onions	Onions
Parsnips	Blueberries	Garlic	Garlic
Garlic Chives			Potatoes
Sorrel			Parsnips
Spinach			Mushrooms
Salad Greens			Sprouts
Radishes			Asparagus
Green Onions			Apples
Dill			
Coriander			
Sprouts			

At the market—wild leeks and fiddleheads In the wild—wild leeks, fiddleheads, cattails, and asparagus

A May harvest of baby greens, spinach, lettuce, radishes, and coriander.

Menu Ideas for May Include:

Spring Coleslaw
Steamed Parsnips
Parsnip Fritters
Carrot and Parsnip Soup
Sorrel and Chive Omelette
Sorrel and Potato Soup
Sorrel Sauce with Fish or Eggs
Quinoa Salad with chives, green onions, and green garlic
Bean Salad with chives, green onions, and green garlic
Garden Salad with spinach and baby greens (the staple)
Spinach and Mushroom Salad
Eggs Florantine (or Fish)
Tomato Spinach Soup
Steamed Fiddleheads with butter and lemon
Stir-Fry with onions, green garlic, wild leeks, and mung bean sprouts

Fried Rice with onions, carrots, green garlic, and wild leeks
Pasta with olive oil, green garlic, green onions, and/or wild leeks
Pasta with Arugula Pesto
Spring Soup made with green onions, green garlic, radish greens, and/or wild leeks
Wild Leek and Potato Soup
Black Bean Quesadillas with green garlic and fresh coriander
Steamed Asparagus
Roasted or Barbequed Asparagus
Asparagus, Mushroom, and Goat Cheese Quiche
Rhubarb Pie
Rhubarb Torte
Rhubarb and Apple Crisp
Rhubarb Juice
Stewed Rhubarb with maple syrup and milk, yogurt, or cream

A Few Recipes

Sorrel and Potato Soup

2 tbsp butter
2 onions, chopped
3 cups sorrel leaves
4 cups stock
6 medium potatoes, peeled and cubed
Small bunch chives

Wash the sorrel leaves, remove the thicker stems and chop. In a soup pot, melt the butter over medium heat. Sauté the onions for about 5 minutes, then add the chopped sorrel and potatoes and sauté for another minute or two. Add the stock and simmer for about 30 minutes. Remove from heat and gently purée the soup with a potato masher, a hand-held blender or in a food processor. Season with salt and pepper and garnish with chopped chives. Serves 4.

♥ Sorrel Sauce for Fish or Eggs

3 cups fresh sorrel
2 tbsp butter
2 tbsp flour
2-3 cups milk
1 large bunch chives
Salt and pepper
4-6 filets of white fish or
4-6 fried eggs

Wash the sorrel and remove the tough stems. Chop it finely. Wash and chop the chives. In a cast-iron pan, melt the butter over medium heat. Add the sorrel and sauté for 3-5 minutes. Add the flour and blend well—the sorrel begins to disinte-grate as it cooks and is easy to blend with the butter and the flour. Cook for 2-3 minutes. Gradually add the milk, using a whisk to make a smooth sauce. Add the chives, then season with salt and pepper and simmer for a few minutes, stirring often. You can serve this sauce with any kind of eggs or you can layer a casserole dish with fish filets and sauce and bake for 15 to 20 minutes at 400° F/200°C. Serves 4-6.

Sorrel Omelet

2 cups sorrel leaves
1 large bunch chives or wild leeks
6 eggs
1 tbsp butter

Wash sorrel leaves and remove the thicker stems. Wash the chives or wild leeks. Finely chop the vegetables. In a bowl, beat the eggs together. Heat a large pan and add butter. Gently sauté the sorrel and chives for about 3 minutes. Add the beaten eggs and mix with the sautéed vegetables. Cook over low heat. To cook the top of the omelet you can either cover the pan with a lid or place the pan under the broiler for a few minutes. Serves 4.

♥ Eggs Florentine (or Fish)

6-8 cups spinach leaves, tightly packed
4 green onions, chopped
1 onion, chopped
6-8 eggs
4 tbsp butter
1/2 cup flour
2 cups milk, heated
Salt and pepper

Wash spinach and steam until cooked. Drain and chop and place in a bowl; there should be about 2 cups of cooked spinach. In a wide, heavy saucepan melt butter over medium heat. Sauté the onions until lightly cooked, about 3 minutes. Stir in flour and cook for about 2 minutes. Gradually add hot milk, stirring constantly. Simmer until thick, still stirring constantly. Season with salt and pepper. Add spinach and incorporate it into the sauce. Reduce heat to low and cook for 3 or 4 minutes. Using a spoon, make six small depressions in the sauce and put an egg into each depression. Cover pan with a lid and simmer until eggs are cooked. This recipe is also good with any white fish such as haddock or sole. Simply place fish fillets in a buttered casserole dish and top with sauce, then bake at 425°F (218°C) for 15 to 20 minutes. Serves 3 or 4.

Quinoa Salad with Chives, Green Onions, and Green Garlic

1 cup quinoa
2 cups water
3 green onions, chopped
3 green garlic, chopped
1 large handful chives, chopped
1 large carrot, grated
1 small bunch fresh parsley, finely
    chopped
3 tbsp sesame oil
4 tbsp rice vinegar and/or lime juice
Salt and pepper

Place the quinoa in a fine sieve and rinse thoroughly with water (important!). Bring the water to a boil and add the quinoa. Cover and simmer for about 15 minutes. Turn off the heat and let sit until cool. In a bowl, combine quinoa with the remaining ingredients. Serves 4-6.

♥ Spinach and Mushroom Salad

6 cups fresh spinach
1 1/2 cup sliced mushrooms
1/2 cup toasted sunflower seeds
3-4 hardboiled eggs
1/2 cup grated feta cheese

Wash and drain spinach. Peel and crumble hardboiled eggs. Toast sunflower seeds by lightly cooking them in a dry pan until they just begin to turn light brown. Tear spinach into bite sized pieces and place in a salad bowl. Add mushrooms and sunflower seeds. Top with crumbled feta cheese. Dress with olive oil and wine vinegar or any kind of creamy dressing such as blue cheese or creamy Italian. Serves 4 or 2 as a nice summer meal

♥ Tomato Spinach Soup

1/3 lb bacon or 2 tbsp butter
1 cup diced tomatoes (from the freezer)
4 cups vegetable stock
4-5 green garlic shoots
3-4 cups fresh spinach
1/2 cup uncooked pasta such as spirals,
    shells or macaroni

Cut bacon into 1/2" pieces. Clean and chop green garlic. Wash and chop spinach. In a medium pot, sauté bacon or melt the butter over medium heat. Add green garlic and sauté for 1 or 2 minutes. Add tomatoes, chopped spinach, and broth and cook for about 15 minutes. Add pasta and cook for another 10 or 15 minutes until noodles are tender. Serves 4.

Black Bean Quesadillas

3 cups cooked black beans
3 tbsp oil
1 medium onion, chopped
4-6 green onions
1/8 tsp dried chili flakes
1 tsp dried oregano
1 tsp cumin
1 cup fresh coriander leaves
1 package 8" tortillas
6 green garlic shoots
1 1/2 cups grated cheese
Salsa
Sour cream

Clean and chop the green garlic. In a large pan, sauté the onion, green garlic, and chili flakes in oil until soft, about 5 minutes. Add the black beans along with some of the bean liquid as well as the oregano and cumin. Simmer for about 10 minutes, then using a potato masher, gently mash the beans and continue to cook until thick. Season with salt and pepper. Clean and chop the green onions and the coriander. To assemble, spread about 1/3 cup of bean mixture on half of each tortilla. Top with green onions, coriander, and grated cheese. Fold the tortilla over. Cook each tortilla on a lightly buttered pan over low heat for 6-7 minutes, turning once. Serve with sour cream and salsa.

Asparagus, Mushroom, and Goat Cheese Quiche

3/4 pound fresh asparagus
2 cups sliced mushrooms
1 bunch green onions
2 tbsp butter
1 9" deep dish pie shell
3 eggs
1 cup milk
1 tsp salt
1/2 tsp pepper
1 tsp thyme
2 tbsp flour
1 cup crumbled goat cheese

Preheat oven to 350°F (175°C). Lightly steam the asparagus, remove from the pot, and cut into 1-2" pieces. Clean and chop the green onions. In a large pan, melt the butter over medium heat. Sauté the green onions and mushrooms until soft, then add the chopped asparagus and sauté for another few minutes. Remove from the heat. In a bowl combine the eggs, milk, salt, pepper, thyme, and flour and mix well. To assemble the quiche, place the vegetable mixture in the bottom of pie shell. Add the crumbled goat cheese. Carefully pour over the milk mixture. Bake for 35-40 minutes or until set. Serves 4. This recipe is also good with any combination of cooked spinach, wild leeks, and mushrooms.

Roasted or Barbequed Asparagus

1 pound asparagus
2 tbsp olive oil
Lemon juice or balsamic vinegar

Preheat oven to 450°F (230°C) or fire up the barbeque. Wash the asparagus and remove the tough ends. Drizzle asparagus with olive oil, coating evenly. Place directly on barbeque or place on a lightly greased cookie sheet and bake for 15 minutes. Serve as is or drizzled with a bit of lemon juice or balsamic vinegar. Serves 4.

Pasta with Arugula Pesto

1 pound pasta
4 cups of arugula
3 cloves garlic
1/2 cup sunflower seeds
1/2 tsp salt
1/2 cup olive oil
1/2 cup Parmesan cheese
Freshly ground pepper

Wash arugula and remove any tough stems. Place in a food processor with garlic, sunflower seeds, salt, and olive oil and process thoroughly. Add the Parmesan cheese and pepper and blend for a few more seconds. Cook and drain the pasta and then toss with the pesto. This dish is great when your greens are too big to be used in salads. Serves 4.

♥ Wild Leek and Potato Soup

2 dozen wild leeks
4 medium potatoes
3 tbsp butter
6 cups chicken or vegetable stock
Salt and pepper

Clean and wash the wild leeks. Coarsely chop the whole plant, bulb and green. Peel and dice the potatoes. In a large saucepan, melt the butter over medium heat and sauté the leeks and potatoes for about 5 minutes. Add stock and simmer for about 20 minutes. Purée the soup with a potato masher, or a hand blender and season with salt and pepper. Serves 4.

Fresh Rhubarb Pie

2 9" pie crusts
6-8 cups chopped fresh rhubarb
1 1/2 cups sugar
1/2 cup flour
1 tsp grated orange rind
2 eggs

Preheat oven to 425°F (220°C). In a bowl, mix together rhubarb, flour, sugar, orange rind, and eggs. Place in one pie shell and cover with the other. Seal the edges and brush with butter if you wish. Bake for 10 minutes and then reduce heat to 350°F (175°C) and bake for another 20-25 minutes or until pastry is golden. The moisture content of rhubarb depends upon the amount of rain it has had, sometimes this pie can be quite runny but the juices are delicious so I never worry about it. Serves 6-8.

Rhubarb Torte

1/2 cup butter
2 tbsp sugar or honey
1 cup flour
3 1/2 cups chopped rhubarb
2 tbsp flour
1 cup sugar
3 egg yolks
1/2 cup milk
3 egg whites
1/4 cup sugar

Preheat oven to 325°F (160°C). Combine butter, sugar, and flour until mixture is crumbly. Press into an 8" x 8" pan and bake for 20 minutes. In a medium pot, cook rhubarb, sugar, flour, egg yolks, and milk until mixture is thickened—the rhubarb will be soft but not mushy. Cool and then pour over crumb crust. Beat egg whites and sugar until stiff. Spread meringue over rhubarb, brown in 400°F (200°C) oven for about 5 minutes. Cool before serving. Serves 6.

Rhubarb Muffins

3 cups flour
3 tsp baking powder
3/4 cup sugar or honey
2 cups chopped rhubarb
2 eggs
1/4 cup oil
1 cup orange juice
3/4 cup nuts or sunflower seeds

Preheat oven to 350°F (175°C). In a bowl, combine flour, baking powder, and sugar. In a 2-cup measure, combine orange juice, eggs, and oil. Pour wet ingredients into flour mixture and stir until just blended. If mixture is too dry, add a bit of water. Stir in rhubarb and nuts or sunflower seeds. Drop into greased muffin tins and bake for 20 or 25 minutes or until a knife comes out clean. Makes 12 muffins.

Rhubarb Juice

8 cups chopped rhubarb
20 cups water
8 whole cloves and/or 1" grated ginger
Honey and/or lemon juice to taste

Place the rhubarb, water, cloves, and ginger in a large pot and bring to a boil. Simmer for 10 minutes. Let cool, then pass through a fine sieve. Add honey and/or lemon juice to taste.

Eggs Florentine with a Salad of Baby Greens, Spring Soup, Steamed Asparagus, and fresh radishes

Food for Thought
Greenhouse Gas Emissions

As the research is beginning to show, modern food production makes a significant contribution to greenhouse gas emissions, and some numbers suggest that agriculture is responsible for fully one-third of global emissions. So it would follow that growing one's own food and purchasing local and seasonal products can be an important way of reducing these emissions. But exactly what are greenhouse gas emissions and how do we begin to understand our own contributions?

Greenhouse gases are comprised of three main gases: carbon dioxide, methane, and nitrous oxide.[1] Carbon dioxide accounts for about 60% of greenhouse gases but methane and nitrous oxide have a far greater greenhouse effect. Figures for greenhouse gas emissions are presented in metric tonnes (1000 kg) or Imperial tons (2000 pounds) of carbon dioxide and they account for the relative greenhouse effects of methane and nitrous oxide.[2]

- Carbon dioxide is released through the burning of organic matter, primarily fossil fuels, but also trees. It is also released through the deterioration of soil due to poor farming practices.
- Methane is released through the anaerobic (i.e. without oxygen) decomposition of organic matter. This occurs in factory farming when manure is left to rot in huge piles, in hydro-electric projects when vegetation is submerged and rots, and in the decomposition of organic material in submerged rice paddies. Methane gas is also released in oil wells, mines, and landfill sites.
- Nitrous oxide is released primarily through transportation that uses an internal combustion engine and through the use of nitrogen-based chemical fertilizers.

The Kyoto Protocol, which became legally binding in 2005, calls for countries to reduce their greenhouse gas emissions by about 6% by the year 2010: this is below 1990 levels. There are many who believe this is completely inadequate and that we must actually reduce our fossil fuel consumption by about 70% in order for life to continue on this planet. At the 2007 United Nations Conference on Climate Change in Bali, Indonesia most experts were beginning to talk about 25-40% reductions. In the past century, our atmosphere has warmed by about 2° Celsius, resulting in warmer oceans, chaotic weather, and a loss of permafrost and arctic ice.[3] Some scientists believe that our earth will warm four to ten degrees by the year 2100 if we do not make drastic changes quickly. Many European countries are taking these predictions seriously and are aiming for much higher reductions than the Kyoto objectives. France plans to produce 20% of its electricity from renewable sources by 2010, Britain is committed to a 20% reduction of greenhouse gases by 2010, and The Netherlands is considering an 80% reduction by 2040.[4]

Another way of understanding the issues is to look at some comparative statistics:

In North America, the bulk of our emissions come from industry, followed by the transportation of goods, and then residential and commercial activities. Personal use, including cars, home heating, and food consumption account for approximately 35% of total emissions. If we include the emissions generated through producing the goods that we consume, personal use rises to about 50%.[5]

According to one source, Canada produces about 726 million tonnes of CO_2 annually. This amounts to a total of 22 tonnes per capita. The average figure for direct personal consumption is 7.7 tonnes of CO_2 per Canadian per year.[6]

The Dutch average 3 tons CO_2 for personal use, the Japanese about 2.1 tons CO_2, and Bangladesh produces about 0.03 tons CO_2 per person per year.[7]

Before the Industrial Revolution, the concentration of CO_2 in the atmosphere was about 280 parts per millions (ppm). Today it is 360 ppm and rising. To stabilize at this level would require a 70% reduction of emissions by the year 2100. The International Panel on Climate Change does not consider this kind of reduction even a remote possibility. To stabilize atmospheric CO_2 at 450 ppm would require immediate action and a 50% reduction in emissions by 2100. To stabilize at 550 ppm would require less immediate action and a 50% reduction in emissions by 2150. A concentration of atmospheric CO_2 above 650 ppm raises serious questions as to the ability of humans to adapt to such conditions without serious social and economic disruption.[8]

In order to get a sense of one's personal share of greenhouse gas emissions one must use some sort of ecological footprint or emissions calculations model. The models are all based on some gross oversimplifications but they do help assess your relative position on the environmental scale. In ***Stormy Weather: 101 Solutions to Global Climate Change***, author Guy Dauncey presents emission figures for three imaginary couples which give an idea of both the parameters and the possibilities:

Couple #1 owns a 2600-square-foot home that is heated with oil, drives 27,000 km per year in inefficient vehicles, and each take one long distance flight per year. This couple is responsible for 28 tons of CO_2 emissions per year.

Couple #2 contributes about 8 tons of CO_2 emissions to the atmosphere each year. They live in a small condominium heated by natural gas, drive a fuel efficient car a total of about 7000 km per year, and each take one short flight per year.

Couple #3 lives in a passive solar energy home, drives 4500 km a year in a fuel-efficient car, eats local, organic food, and does not fly. This couple's lifestyle results in less than 1 ton of CO_2 emissions per year.

When it comes to figuring out your own personal share of greenhouse gas emissions, Guy Dauncey's book has a great deal of thought-provoking information, including the following figures:

3.8 tons CO_2 per person are emitted by flying from New York to Paris;

- 11.2 tons CO_2 are emitted per 1000 gallons of heating oil;
- 1 ton CO_2 is emitted per 100 gallons of gasoline used;
- 8 tons of CO_2 are emitted to produce 10,000 kilowatt hours of electricity;
- One tree absorbs 1 ton of carbon over forty years.

In his book **Heat: How To Stop The Planet From Burning**, George Monbiot provides further insightful figures. Without a doubt, air travel is an extremely polluting form of transportation that has the potential to make an individual's single largest emissions impact. For example, on a trip from London to Manchester in Britain, the emissions figures per kilogram of passengers are as follows:

- Going by plane results in 63.9 kg of CO_2 emissions.
- Driving by car results in 36.6 kg of CO_2 emissions.
- Taking the train creates 5.2kg of CO_2 emissions.
- Hopping on the bus results in 4.3 kg of CO_2 emissions.[9]

Unfortunately, avoiding air travel alone will not significantly reduce greenhouse gas emissions. According to a British government report, 85% of personal domestic travel kilometres are done by car, 1.2% by plane, and the remainder by trains, buses, motorcycles, and bicycles.[10] The rise in international air travel is of growing concern—some estimates project that it if current trends continue, it will be one of the biggest contributors of CO_2 emissions by 2030.[11]

If you want to get a sense of your own personal emissions search the Internet for *greenhouse gas emissions home calculation* yields many sites. Ecological footprints are another way of assessing one's environmental impact. An ecological footprint is a measure of the amount of ecologically productive land required to support the resource demands and absorb the wastes of a person or community. Search the Internet under 'ecological footprint' and you will find several sites offering calculation models. I took the Mountain Equipment Co-op questionnaire and ended up with an ecological footprint that was about one-third of the average North American. According to the web site, if everyone on Earth lived like me, we would need 2.2 Earths. This is somewhat depressing as I live fairly simply and drive an energy efficient car. However, I do have an older, oil-heated house and living in the country requires me to do more driving than I would like.

Reducing one's impact on the environment seems to involve two basic strategies: increasing the efficiency of your energy users and reducing the amount of time that these energy users are in operation. Both involve varying degrees of time and/or money. Those that involve a reasonable to significant monetary investment include:

- switching to energy efficient appliances;
- investing in solar or wind power;
- insulating and weatherproofing your house;
- investing in new windows;
- buying a more efficient vehicle.

To assess the financial viability of these options, people often look for a payback period of three to four years. Another approach, perhaps more realistic, would be to look at the monthly interest paid on a loan to make these changes and compare it to the monthly savings generated by these changes. If you can realize energy savings equal to the interest that you pay, then you break even. If you look at this investment in terms of the environmental benefits, then it may be a very worthwhile investment. If you save more than the interest incurred, it starts to look even better. On the vehicle front, often the gas savings alone pay for the financing of a new, fuel efficient car. One must be somewhat careful when embracing this course of action because the situation is not as simple as it might appear to be. Before throwing something away it is important to consider the energy that went into producing that item as an integral part of its energy consumption. For example, more than half of the energy consumption attributable to each vehicle on the road occurs in the manufacturing process.[12] So switching to a more energy efficient car may save fuel but a very significant amount of energy is consumed in the production and manufacturing of that vehicle.

On the cheaper side of things, there are a number of things a person can do. These include:

- increasing one's use of public transportation, car pooling, walking, or cycling;
- taking local holidays;
- consuming less and living simply;
- repairing things that are broken;
- developing leisure interests that are relatively environmentally benign such as art or music;
- buying local and organic food, and of course, growing your own.

Most of these ideas involve changing one's way of doing things. For me, this type of change is an interesting issue. Having made many changes over the past twenty-some years, I would say that there are obstacles to this process. Inevitably, there seems to be an inherent human resistance to changing familiar behaviour, but once one gets beyond this, there seems to be a fundamental lack of time in our society. It takes time to recycle, to take the bus, or to repair household items. It also takes time to educate oneself about an issue and to incorporate changes into one's day-to-day life. This is often very difficult in a society where, for many, every waking hour is filled with work, driving, raising children, and managing a household. It is also an unfortunate reality in our society that the ability to make changes that involve time can be very dependent upon income.

In less affluent countries, environmental change often goes hand in hand with issues of equality and democracy as citizens struggle to improve their working and living conditions. Certainly these are issues in North America, but I also believe that environmental change must be accompanied by a different kind of social change, one in which we re-examine our values and our priorities. Our society seems gripped by a belief that we must forever work harder and longer in order to become more competitive, abandoning social and environmental concerns in order for our economy to survive. Northern European countries such as Denmark, Sweden, and Finland (which is currently rated as one of the most productive and efficient countries in the world) have proven that they can have steady and prosperous economies without abandoning their environment or quality of life. Flexible work schedules, six to seven weeks of holiday per year, free post-secondary education, and a fair minimum standard of living all contribute to a society where citizens are able to take care of both their own needs and those of the environment.

How we define our society is very much dependent upon our priorities as well as conscious decisions as to where we spend our energy and our dollars. As people struggling to live in a more environmentally sustainable fashion, I believe it is vital that we question some of the social and moral parameters that govern our society and take the kinds of steps that encourage and support responsible environmental stewardship.

Sources and Further Information

Dauncey, G. and Mazza, P., *Stormy Weather: 101 Solutions to Global Climate Change*, New Society Publishers, Gabriola Island, B.C., 2001

Heinberg, Richard, *The Party's Over*, New Society Publishers, Gabriola Island, B.C., 2004

Lapp, Steven, *Personal CO2 Calculator*, Sydenham, Ontario, 2002.

Monbiot, George, *Heat: How to Stop The Planet From Burning*, Doubleday Canada, 2006.

Torrie, R.D. and Parfett, R., *Mind the Gap*, in Alternatives Magazine, University of Waterloo Department of Environmental Studies, Waterloo, Ontario, Volume 26, #2, Spring 2000.

Endnotes

1   Dauncey, G. and Mazza, P., *Stormy Weather: 101 Solutions to Global Climate* Change, New Society Publishers, Gabriola Island, B.C., p. 10.
2   Ibid, p.10
3   Ibid, p. 16
4   Ibid, p. 22
5   Ibid, p.56
6   Lapp, Steve, *Personal CO2 Calculator*, compiled for a workshop given in 2002, Sydenham, Ontario.
7   Ibid, p.56
8   Torrie, R.D. and Parfett, R., *Mind the Gap,* in Alternatives Magazine, University of Waterloo Department of Environmental Studies, Waterloo, Ontario, Volume 26, #2, page 23.
9   Monbiot, George, *Heat: How to Stop the Planet From Burning*, Doubleday Canada, page. 180.
10 Ibid., page 146.
11 Ibid, page 171.
12 Heinberg, Richard, "The Party's Over," New Society Publishers, Gabriola Island, B.C., page 161.

JUNE

One cannot help but be in awe when
contemplating the mysteries of eternity,
of life, of the marvelous structure of reality.
It is enough if one tries to comprehend
a little of this mystery every day.
— Albert Einstein (1879 – 1955),
German physicist and Nobel Prize winner

In the Garden

June usually signals the start of genuinely warm days in Southern Ontario. While many
people traditionally plant their gardens on the long weekend in May, I try to space my
planting out over the whole summer. This is because some plants do much better in either cooler or warmer weather and also because I want to have a steady and manageable
supply of food throughout the season. I wait until early June to transplant tomatoes,
peppers, cucumbers, winter squash, and zucchini because I find these seedlings do
much better in my small greenhouse/cold frame until the weather has really warmed up.
Potatoes also benefit from a later planting because the potato beetles that attack them
have slowed down somewhat.

In the summer gardens, it is time to make another planting of lettuce, beets, green onions, bush beans, dill, and coriander as well as a first planting of basil. By now, all of the vegetables that were planted in April should have been harvested—if your garden is small and pressed for space, this bed can be replanted with many of your June vegetables. The bed should be cleaned up, lightly dug, and, if possible, a small amount of compost or well rotted manure added. In the winter storage garden, potatoes, beets, cabbage, and turnip should be planted. Planting in June means that the plants will mature in the fall (rather than late summer) when they can go directly into cold storage and again, pest problems decrease as the summer progresses.

Planting Techniques
Tomatoes

Lightly dig the area you are going to plant. You can add some compost but if your soil is reasonably healthy it is better not to do this. If there is too much the plants will grow beautiful and bushy but there will not be much in the way of fruit. To plant:

- Water your transplants and pinch off the bottom two or three branches.
- Mark out your bed so that the tomatoes are spaced 3' apart on both edges of the bed, staggered diagonally across the bed (see February for spacings).
- For each transplant dig a hole about 9" deep and fill it with water.
- Place the transplant in the hole so that the bottom 4-6" of the stalk will also be buried when you fill in the hole. When you do this, roots will form along the buried section of stalk and the plant will be stronger.
- Fill the hole with soil; this is somewhat messy as everything is quite wet.
- Water again from the top.

Tomatoes can be left to sprawl on the ground, they can be staked, or they can be grown inside of wire cages. I don't have a lot of space so I prefer to use wire cages for my more compact determinate varieties. The larger indeterminate varieties will sprawl and topple the cages so they are better staked or left on the ground. Staking and pruning are covered in detail in the July section.

Tomatoes are relatively easy to grow but they do need a consistent supply of water. Blossom end rot occurs when there isn't enough moisture in the ground and results in black ends on some of the fruit. In cool, wet summers tomatoes can get a blight that starts as a small brown spot on the leaves and eventually spreads to the whole leaf. This comes from a fungus in the soil and the best way to prevent it is to try to make sure that soil does not splash onto the plants during watering—mulching can help.

Tomato hornworms: These three- to four- inch-long worms are an amazing sight to behold. They are the larvae of a large white moth and will eat both your tomatoes and the foliage at an alarming rate. They are not always easy to spot but if you see large bites in your fruit or whole sections of stalk that have been chewed, it is time to do some serious looking. The best way to control them is by hand-picking – Sorry!

Many larger transplants benefit from some extra care when they are set out in the garden. Digging a hole and filling it with water before transplanting helps to minimize root stress.

Peppers

Peppers need a spacing of about 1 1/2'. As with tomatoes, too much compost will result in bushy plants but few actual peppers. Before you start:

- ❧ Make sure your transplants are well watered.
- ❧ Lightly dig your wide bed and mark your transplant locations.
- ❧ At each transplant site dig a hole that is slightly deeper than the transplant and fill the hole with water.
- ❧ Place a pepper plant in each hole, fill the hole with soil, and water again from the top.

Pepper plants are relatively pest and disease free; the biggest challenge is that they get enough heat to set and mature fruit. If possible, try to plant them in a protected area or against a south facing wall. You can trap heat by covering the plant with some sort of translucent container such as a cut-off milk jug or one of any number of products available at gardening stores. Another method involves planting the peppers in large 10-12" pots that have had the bottoms cut out of them. The bottom 4-6" of the pot is submerged in the soil and the remainder is left above the ground.

Basil

Basil is a trouble free summer herb that is easy to grow. It can be direct seeded in rows that are 6-8" apart; the seeds within the row should be 2-3" apart and later thinned to 6-8" apart. Transplants should be planted in rows that are 6-8" apart with seedlings spaced 6-8" apart. Basil transplants can contain either one or two seedlings per cell.

Cucumbers, Winter Squash, and Zucchini

Cucumbers should be planted in two rows within the wide bed, with plants spaced about 18" apart. Cucumber plants will sprawl over your lawn and garden. If you are really pressed for space, you can grow them on some sort of vertical trellis. Winter squash is planted in one row down the centre of the wide bed with plants about 2' apart. Zucchini can be planted in two rows within the wide beds, with plants spaced 3' apart and staggered across the bed

If you are direct seeding any of these vegetables, use the same spacing and plant two or three seeds at every interval, and later thin this to just one plant per interval. If you started transplants, dig a hole that is slightly bigger than the transplant. Because all of these vegetables have fairly sensitive root systems which suffer when exposed to air or dry soil, it is a good idea to water the transplant well and then fill the hole with water before putting the seedling in.

Pest Problems: These vegetables are all members of the squash family and are susceptible to two fairly common pests.

- Squash bugs are flat, grayish brown bugs about 1/2" long. They are slow and can easily be hand-picked but you must keep an eye out for them throughout the season. If your plants look chewed up or the leaves are wilting, look closely at the stalks and underneath the leaves for the bugs.
- The cucumber beetle is a yellow and black striped beetle that chews on the leaves and can destroy small seedlings. You can watch out for these beetles and pick them off by hand (though they are quick and hard to catch) or you can dust the leaves with Rotenone. You can also cover your plants with a floating row cover until they are well established. I prefer the last option, as I don't have to remember to check on my plants and the cover has the added benefit of trapping heat so the plants grow faster. Once the plants start to flower you must remove the row cover so that pollination can occur.
- Try to remember that healthy plants are less likely to suffer serious insect damage so work to maintain a fertile and healthy soil and water often in dry weather.

Cabbage

Cabbage needs a fairly fertile soil so if you have some extra compost you can add it to your wide bed. I do not direct seed cabbage because I find that when I do this, the tiny plants really struggle to get ahead of the pests. Transplants need a spacing of about 2'. Plant seedlings two across in the wide bed and stagger them diagonally to make better use of the space. After planting, cover your wide bed with a section of floating row cover to protect against flea beetles and cabbage moths.

Cabbage Pests: Unfortunately all members of the cabbage family have more than their fair share of pest problems.

- Flea beetles like to eat the small leaves. The floating row cover provides an effective barrier or you can dust with Rotenone.
- The cabbage butterfly is a white butterfly which lays clusters of light green eggs on the underside of the leaves. These eggs hatch into well camouflaged green worms that make some nasty holes in your plants and leave an unpleasant trail of digested cabbage. The floating row cover will prevent the moths from laying their eggs in the first place. Bacillus Thuringiensis is a naturally occurring bacterium that is fatal to cabbage worms when ingested. It can be purchased at gardening stores under the name of Dipel or Bt. This product must be mixed with water and put in a spray bottle—it will control cabbage worms if sprayed weekly throughout the summer.

Rutabaga

I prefer to plant rutabaga from transplants because flea beetles like the small turnip leaves. Transplants require a 1' spacing and again, it is a good idea to cover your wide bed with a section of floating row cover, at least until the plants are well established. Direct seed rutabaga in rows that are 1' apart, with seeds 2-3" apart. Thin to 1' apart within the rows when the seedlings are several inches high.

Transplants

I really encourage you to make transplants in June because summer rainfall can be very erratic and the temperatures hot. Lettuce in particular will not germinate at temperatures above 70°F. Sometime in June, it is a good idea to start more basil as well as lettuce, beets, and green onions, all of which will be planted in the garden in July. Once the plants are up and established, move them outside to your mini greenhouse or cold frame. If the weather is hot, the seedlings will do best in a protected spot outside of the greenhouse or with all of the greenhouse glass removed. They need to be protected from heavy rains which can damage them or wash the soil out of the trays so make sure they are covered at night or if you will be away.

Carrots and Parsnips

It is a good idea to look at your bed of carrots and parsnips to see how well it has germinated. If there are blank areas, loosen the soil with a small hand fork and reseed. If possible, keep this bed well watered for several weeks.

Weeding

Around the beginning of June, I usually find it is time to do some weeding. Weeds can be put in plastic pails and carried to your compost. They can also be left in the walkways to decompose but many people believe that this can cause disease problems. Weeding is always easier when the ground is wet, so try to weed after a rain or after you have watered your garden. I do my weeding with a small hand fork because it is more successful at getting out the roots than simply hand pulling.

Staking Shell Peas

The shell peas that were planted in April will need to be staked before they get too tall. If you have access to sticks or tree branches that have been trimmed, then 3' - 4' long sections of these provide good support for your peas. Choose sections with a few side branches and simply push them into the ground between the double rows of peas at about 12-18" intervals. Another easy method is simply to put a line of tomato cages over your double row of peas.

You can also use eight to twelve stakes that are about 5' long. Hammer stakes at each end of each row of peas and put additional support stakes throughout the rows. Near the base of the peas run string along the outside of the stakes, wrapping it once around each stake, and working it up about 6" with each completed round.

'Tying Up' Your Endive

Once your endive plants have reached full size they must be 'tied up' to deprive the leaves of the plant of light for four to six days. This results in milder tasting and creamy white leaves in the centre. To do this, bring the leaves of the plant together and tie a small string or fit a rubber band around the outside of the plant. The tie should keep the plant upright but not be overly tight; if it is too tight the endive will rot in the center. Let the plant grow for five to six days before harvesting. To harvest, cut the head off at the base and remove the outer leaves. The centre should be creamy white. Endive plants tend to mature at different rates, so I begin by tying up the biggest three or four plants, and then when I harvest these I move the ties to another three of four plants, and so on.

Mulching

Mulching is a process whereby you cover the bare soil in walkways and around plants with a layer of material that conserves moisture and blocks sunlight so that weeds don't grow. I like to mulch most of my garden in early June because this is usually when things start to dry out. I use straw to mulch my garden: it looks and smells nice and in the fall it will decompose and add organic matter and nutrients to the soil. Straw comes in bales that are made up of 2-3" sections called flakes.

To mulch with straw:

- Take a flake of straw, fluff it up, and spread it out over the bare sections of your garden.

- Spread a good layer of mulch in the walkways. Between plants it takes more time as you have to line up the straw fibres and curve them around the vegetables.

- Do not mulch areas where you have broadcast seeds or where there are six rows of a vegetable within the bed (e.g. carrots, spinach, basil) as these plants are close enough together that, once established, there is very little bare soil.

- Wait until late June to mulch your tomatoes, peppers, cucumbers, squash and zucchini. *If you mulch too early and the ground is still somewhat cool, the mulch will act as insulation and slow down the growth of these vegetables.*

I prefer to use straw as mulch for the reasons mentioned above but you can also use:

- 🌱 grass clippings, as long as they are not from a gas-powered mower;
- 🌱 old hay, but beware—it may be full of weed seeds;
- 🌱 shavings and sawdust (these will decompose but over time they will make your soil more acidic).
- 🌱 Some people say they use newspaper, burlap bags, and old carpet but I prefer not to put anything that may contain industrial chemicals on my garden.

JUNE GARDEN SUMMARY
- ☐ Dig, compost, and mark out your June beds.
- ☐ Weed and mulch your garden.
- ☐ Stake rows of shell peas.
- ☐ Tie up your endive.

In the Summer Gardens
- In early June, transplant tomatoes and peppers. Transplant or direct seed cucumbers, zucchini, and winter squash.
- In mid-June, transplant or direct seed lettuce, green onions, beets, and basil. Direct seed dill and coriander and plant potatoes.
- In late June, make a second planting of bush beans.

Transplants
- In mid-June, make transplants of basil, lettuce, green onions, and beets to be planted in the garden in July

In the Winter Storage Garden
- In early June, transplant tomatoes. Transplant or direct seed winter squash, rutabaga, beets, and cabbage.
- In mid- to late June, plant a main crop of storage potatoes.

Other Possibilities
- Direct seed salad greens, fennel, kale, and corn.
- Direct seed or make transplants of broccoli and Chinese cabbage.

Common Organic Pest Remedies

As the summer progresses, you may have to deal with a variety of insects that want to feed on your garden. When it comes to pest control, you must decide how much damage is acceptable and when it is time to take action. Organic methods of pest control include barriers such as the floating row cover, hand picking, trapping, and the use of a number of organically acceptable products. Hand picking is definitely the most benign method and works for larger bugs such as squash bugs and Colorado potato beetles. I find it takes daily picking for about seven to ten days to win the battle, and be sure to look on the undersides of your plant leaves when you are doing it. As I describe each vegetable, I try to include information on pest control but I also thought it would be useful to summarize some of the products on the market, their makeup, and their uses.

Product	Active Ingredients	Uses	Precautions
Dipel: comes as a liquid or in granulated form and must be mixed with water and sprayed on plants.	Bacillus thuringiensis: a bacterium that is fatal when ingested by pests.	Fatal when ingested by caterpillars, worms, and larvae, particularly cabbage worms and cabbage loopers.	Will also kill beneficial insects that feed on the plants, generally not a problem in a small garden.
Rotenone: comes as a powder which must be dusted on plants.	Extract from the roots of two bean family plants.	Kills most chewing insects including squash bugs, cabbage worms, tomato horn worms, flea beetles, and Colorado potato beetles.	Toxic to beneficial insects, birds, and fish. Moderately toxic to humans and animals. Residues remain on plants for about one week.
Pyrethrin: comes as a powder which must be dusted on plants.	Derived from the blossoms of the Dalmatian daisy. It acts as a nerve poison.	Kills cabbage worms, Colorado potato beetles, flea beetles, tomato hornworms, and squash bugs.	Moderately toxic to animals and other small insects.
Diatomaceous Earth: comes as a powder which must be dusted on plants, preferably when they are wet so it adheres better.	Made from the crushed skeletons of single celled freshwater plants.	Kills soft bodied pests such as slugs, larvae, caterpillars, and aphids by abrading and drying their outer body.	Non toxic but it is abrasive so it may irritate mucous membranes. Avoid inhaling it.
Insecticidal Soap	Made from fatty acid salts	Kills aphids, whiteflies, and spider mites.	
Floating Row Cover	Made of spun-bonded polypropelene	Acts as a barrier so insects cannot chew on plants or lay their eggs on them.	Eventually it must be disposed of.
Yellow Sticky Traps	Yellow colour attracts insects	Effective on aphids and whiteflies	
Slug and Earwig Traps	Homemade traps made from a coffee can with a hole cut in one side. Bury can is buried so the hole is even with the soil and then fill with 1-2" of beer. The lid keeps rain out.	Traps slugs and earwigs	

Harvesting and Eating

For me, June is one of the most wonderful times in my garden. The really hot weather hasn't hit yet, everything is so green and lush, and there is such a feeling of abundance. In the early morning, when the world is still quiet and peaceful, I go outside and pick something for supper, enjoying this time of gentle simplicity.

In early June, our salads consist of baby greens and the last of the spinach. Spinach leaves become thinner after the first few pickings and are not as good in salads—I try to use them in a soup or curry. Later there are heads of lettuce and endive. ***Remember that salad vegetables must be harvested in the morning because they lose 70% of their moisture and sugar content by mid-morning, replenishing it during the night.*** After each section of salad vegetable is fully harvested, I take my fork and quickly turn the soil so that the area is ready to be replanted later in the summer. I still make a lot of bean, rice, and pasta salads, using green onions, green garlic, radishes, and fresh herbs. My root cellar is empty in June and I do rely on the grocery store for staples such as onions, carrots, and potatoes. For a treat, we continue to buy some local asparagus.

Keep it simple: When I first started growing my own food I often felt overwhelmed by the idea of having to cook everything I grew. One day I visited another gardening friend and saw a big bowl of fresh vegetables on her kitchen table, her kids grazing from it as they went in and out of the house. I soon realized that this was a far easier, and probably more nutritious, way of doing things.

Harvesting Techniques

Endive
Endive is harvested in much the same way as lettuce: cut the plant off at the base, remove the string or rubber band, and then peel off the darker outer leaves. The creamy white centre leaves have the mildest taste; however I also use the paler green leaves found outside of the centre. We use endive in a wonderful Spanish salad called *Xató* that I first tasted when I was selling vegetables to Chez Piggy Restaurant in Kingston. The salad is made with garlic and finely chopped almonds. I use far less olive oil than the Chez Piggy recipe because one can easily go through a whole bottle in just a few meals.

Peas
Generally the dwarf varieties of peas are ready in early June; the taller varieties mature in late June and early July.
- Snow Peas are traditionally picked when they are quite flat and are good fresh, steamed, or in stir-fries.
- Sugar Snap peas are eaten when they are round and full—you can eat both the pod and the peas but you must first peel the stringy spine from the back of the pea. Sugar Snap peas are good steamed with butter or lightly cooked

in a stir-fry but I prefer to eat them fresh. After harvesting I wash them and place them in a bowl on the table, and we eat them as snacks and during our meals.

∽ Shell peas often don't make it past the garden in our family—we tend to eat them right off the vine while we are outside. Occasionally I harvest enough to shell and lightly steam for supper.

Beets

If you have grown your beets in clumps of four, you will probably find that some of them are bigger than their neighbours. You don't have to harvest a whole clump of beets at once but can pull the larger ones first. One of our favourite ways to eat beets is in a beet sandwich. This idea comes from England where beets were called "poor man's steak." The beets are cooked and then sliced and served in a sandwich with mayonnaise and, if you like, horseradish. I recommend an open-faced sandwich using a toasted dark rye bread. Beet greens are not everyone's favourite vegetable but they are highly nutritious and this is incentive for us to eat them. We usually steam them and serve them with butter and a bit of fresh lemon juice. They are also nice mixed with sautéed onion, garlic, and bacon and a small amount of cider vinegar.

Swiss Chard

Swiss chard will continue to grow from the same plant throughout the summer and well into the fall. The outer leaves can grow to be quite big and are not as nice as the inner leaves. I try to harvest Swiss chard when the leaves are less than

a foot tall, pulling the stalks gently away from the center of the plant. In the summer, I sauté Swiss chard with garlic and onions; later in the fall I use it in casseroles and stews.

Strawberries

Of course, one of the best things about June is that strawberries are in season. Sometimes we forgo a proper supper and enjoy a light meal of a green salad and/or a bean salad, followed by strawberry shortcake for dessert. I try to pick a lot of strawberries, both for fresh eating and to freeze or can for the winter. They are a local food and our area has one or two organic pick-your-own farms, so for me, strawberries make a lot of sense

---

Storage Tip: I freeze strawberries in 1-quart bags, aiming for between 20 and 24 bags a year. You can put the cleaned and hulled berries straight into the bags or freeze them on cookie sheets and then bag them. This allows you to take out a few strawberries at a time later in the winter. Strawberries are also easy to can— they can be made into jam or gently cooked and canned with only a little bit of sugar.

Available Foods

In My Garden	In My Freezer	At the Grocery
Green garlic	Tomatoes	Asparagus
Green onions	Rhubarb	Onions
Parsley	Strawberries	Carrots
Coriander		Parsnips
Dill		Lettuce
Radishes		Cucumbers
Spinach		Mushrooms
Salad Greens		Tomatoes
Lettuce		Strawberries
Endive		Apples
Sugar Snap or Snow Peas		
Swiss Chard		
Beets		
Beet Greens		

Menu Ideas for June Include:

Green Salad with baby greens, spinach, and lettuce

Spinach and Coriander Curry

Steamed, Roasted, or Barbequed Asparagus

Asparagus, Mushroom, and Goat Cheese Quiche

Asparagus and Pasta Salad

Caesar Salad

Spanish Endive Salad

Cobb Salad (endive, lettuce, chicken, eggs, and more)

Pasta Salad with green onions, green garlic, and asparagus

Black Bean Salad with green garlic, green onions, and coriander

Navy Bean Salad with green onions, radishes, parsley, and dill

Rice Salad with green onions, dill, parsley, hazelnuts, and dried cranberries

Stir-Fry with green onions, garlic, and snow peas

Pasta with garlic and asparagus

Chicken with dill sauce

Curry with red lentils, onions, mushrooms, and spinach

Fresh or Steamed Sugar Snap or Snow Peas

Sugar Snap or Snow Pea and Mushroom Salad

Steamed Beet Greens with butter and lemon

Steamed Beets

Beet Sandwiches

Thai Noodle Salad with fresh greens and coriander

Strawberries and cream, yogurt, or milk

Strawberry Shortcake

Strawberry Nut Torte

A Few Recipes

Asparagus and Pasta Salad

3 cups macaroni or other small noodle
3 cups cooked asparagus
4 green garlic, finely chopped
4 green onions, finely chopped
¼ cup mayonnaise
2-3 tbsp lemon juice
1 bunch dill, stemmed & chopped
Salt and pepper

Cook the pasta until tender, drain and rinse with cold water. Lightly steam the asparagus until just tender. Drain and cut into 1" pieces. Combine all the ingredients in a bowl and mix well. This salad is also nice with 1-2 cups of cubed leftover meat, such as chicken or lamb. Serves 6.

♥ Spinach and Coriander Curry

2 onions, chopped
4-6 cups spinach
3-4 cloves garlic, minced
1-2 tbsp mild curry paste
2 chicken breasts or ½ lb firm tofu
1 1/2 cups stock
1/2 cup red lentils
2 large bunches coriander
2 tbsp oil
1 1/2 cups coconut milk, or light cream, or yogurt
1-2 tbsp honey
1 tsp cumin
1 tbsp lemon juice
Salt and pepper

Cut the chicken or tofu into bite-sized pieces. Wash, stem, and coarsely chop the spinach. Wash, stem, and finely chop the coriander—there should be about 1 cup when chopped. In a medium pot, add the oil and sauté onions and garlic over medium heat for about 3 minutes. Add the curry paste and the chicken or tofu and cook another few minutes. Add the stock and the red lentils and bring to a boil, cooking for about 10 minutes—be careful that the lentils do not stick to the bottom of the pot. Add the spinach, coriander, and remaining ingredients and simmer another 5 minutes, seasoning to taste. Serves 4.

Navy Bean Salad

4 cups cooked navy beans
1-2 bunches green onions
12-16 radishes
Large handful fresh dill
Large handful fresh parsley
4 tbsp lemon juice
4 tbsp oil
Salt and pepper

Clean the green onions and the radishes. Finely chop the green onions. Thinly slice the radishes. Wash and drain the dill and the parsley, remove the thicker stems, and finely chop the leaves. Combine all the ingredients in a large bowl, mixing well. Season with salt and pepper. Serves 6.

❤ Black Bean Salad

3 cups cooked black beans
4-6 green garlic
1 bunch green onions
Large handful fresh coriander
3 tbsp oil
Juice of 1-2 limes – about 3 tbsp
Salt and pepper

Clean the green garlic and green onions and chop them finely. Wash and drain the coriander, then remove the thicker stems. Finely chop the leaves and the thin stems; you should have about 1/2 cup of chopped coriander. Put all the ingredients in a bowl and mix well. This salad is one of our summer favorites. You can spice it up with a few dashes of hot sauce. Later in the summer, we add finely chopped hot peppers and fresh corn to this salad. Serves 6.

Herbed Rice Salad

1 cup rice, cooked and cooled
1 bunch green onions
Large handful fresh dill
Large handful fresh parsley
1/2 cup hazelnuts
1/4 cup dried cranberries
3 tbsp oil
3-4 tbsp lemon juice

Clean the green onions and chop finely. Wash and dry the dill and parsley. Remove the larger stems and chop finely. Coarsely chop the hazelnuts. Combine all the ingredients in a large bowl, mixing well. Season with salt and pepper. Serves 4.

❤ Thai Noodle Salad (our version)

1 lb cubed chicken, tofu, or pork
3 cloves chopped garlic
3 tbsp Vietnamese fish sauce
Juice of 1 lime
3 tbsp tamari
6 cups mixed salad greens
1 bunch green onions, chopped
1 large bunch coriander, chopped
2/3 cup chopped peanuts (optional)
1 pkg thin rice noodles

Marinate the meat or tofu in fish sauce, lime juice, tamari, and garlic for 2-6 hours. Sauté in oil until cooked. Remove from the pan and place in a bowl. Place green onions, coriander, and peanuts in bowls. Soak the rice noodles in boiling water until soft, drain and place in a bowl. Wash the greens and place them in a bowl. Put all the bowls on the table and let each person make their own individual salad by placing a large handful of greens on their plate, topping with rice noodles, meat or tofu, green onions, coriander, and peanuts. Make a dressing with 3 tbsp tamari, 2 tbsp fish sauce, 2 tbsp lime juice, 2 cloves crushed garlic, 1 cup water, and 1/4 tsp dried chilies and spoon some over each salad. Serves 4.

❤ Spanish Endive Salad

2-3 heads curly endive
1/2 cup olive oil
3 tbsp red wine or balsamic vinegar
2-3 cloves garlic, finely chopped
1/2 cup almonds, finely chopped

Peel off and discard the outer leaves of the endive, stopping when you start to see leaves that are creamy coloured at their base. Wash these leaves thoroughly; 2 or 3 soakings in water are usually necessary to get rid of all the dirt. Spin the endive dry. Make a dressing with the olive oil, wine vinegar, and garlic. Tear the endive into bite-sized pieces, place the pieces into a salad bowl and toss with the dressing. Allow the endive to marinate for 30 minutes to 1 hour before serving, and then toss with the chopped almonds. This is a delicious salad that even my fussiest eater loves. Serves 4-6. (adapted from the *Chez Piggy Cookbook* by V. Newbury and P. DeGreen)

Cobb Salad

1 head lettuce
1 head endive
3 green onions
1 chicken breast, cooked
3 hardboiled eggs
6 slices cooked bacon (optional)
1/2 lb blue cheese
French or Italian dressing

Wash the lettuce, endive, and green onions. Tear the lettuce and endive into bite-sized pieces and place in a large bowl. Chop the green onions and add to the bowl. Dice the chicken breast and eggs and crumble the bacon. Arrange on top of the greens. Crumble the blue cheese over everything. Serve with your favourite French or Italian dressing. Serves 6. Later in the summer you can add diced tomatoes to this salad.

♥ Beet Sandwiches

2 beets, cooked and cooled
Mayonnaise
Horseradish (optional)
Light or dark rye bread

Remove the skins from the beets and cut into 1/4" slices. I like to make open-faced beet sandwiches with a really dark pumpernickel or whole grain rye bread that has been toasted. My kids prefer a more conventional sandwich with two layers of light rye bread.
Serves 1-2.

Sugar Snap or Snow Pea and Mushroom Salad

2 cups sugar snap or snow peas
1 cup mushrooms, sliced
1-2 tbsp sesame seeds
1/4 cup oil
1/4 cup rice vinegar
1-2 cloves garlic, finely chopped
1/4 tsp dried chilies (optional)
1 tbsp tamari sauce
Lettuce leaves

Rinse the peas and blanch them by cooking in boiling water for 1 or 2 minutes, then draining and rinsing under cold water. Toast the sesame seeds by frying them in a dry pan over medium heat until light brown. Remove from the pan immediately. Combine the snow peas, mushrooms, and sesame seeds. Toss with the remaining ingredients. Serve over lettuce leaves. Serves 4.

Spanish Endive Salad, Herbed Rice Salad, Sugar Snap Pea and Mushroom Salad, and a bowl of fresh strawberries.

Chicken with Dill Sauce

1 lb cooked chicken, either pieces or cubed
    leftovers from another meal
1/4 cup butter
1 onion, chopped
2 green garlic, chopped
1/3 cup flour
4 cups stock
2 egg yolks
2 tbsp lemon juice
1 large bunch dill
Salt and pepper

Wash, stem, and finely chop the dill. In a large pan, melt the butter and sauté the onion and green garlic over medium heat for 3-5 minutes. Add the flour and mix with onion and garlic. Slowly add the stock, stirring constantly. Cook over low heat, until thickened. Remove 1/2 cup of the sauce and stir it into the egg yolks. Return this to the pan and add the lemon juice and fresh dill. Simmer a few minutes and season with salt and pepper. Add the chicken to the sauce and serve over rice. If you have an abundance of fresh shell peas, they are wonderful added to the sauce and cooked for a few minutes. Serves 4.

Strawberry Shortcake

3 cups flour
1 tbsp baking powder
2 tbsp sugar
3/4 cup butter
1 egg
3/4 cup milk
1-2 quarts strawberries
2 cups whipped cream

Preheat oven to 350°F (175°C). In a bowl, mix the dry ingredients. Cut in butter with a pastry cutter until well blended. Beat the egg and combine with the milk, add to the flour mixture, mixing only until just blended. Spoon dough into a greased, 9" baking pan, then bake for 30 minutes. Allow to cool. Wash and hull the strawberries, cutting the larger ones if desired. Whip the cream, adding a few teaspoons of sugar if you wish. Place strawberries on top of shortcake, cover with whipped cream, and serve. Serves 6-8.

Strawberry Nut Torte

4 egg yolks
3/4 cup sugar
3 tbsp hot water
1 cup ground almonds or hazelnuts
1 tsp baking powder
2 tbsp flour
4 egg whites
1 1/2 cups whipping cream
3-4 cups strawberries

Preheat oven to 325°F (160°C). In a large bowl, beat the egg yolks, sugar, and water until foamy. Combine the ground nuts, baking powder, and flour and add to the egg yolk mixture. In a smaller metal bowl, beat the egg whites until stiff. Gently fold the egg whites into the cake batter. Grease two round cake pans and divide the batter between them. Bake for 40 minutes, allow to cool, and then remove from pans. Whip the cream and wash, hull, and slice the strawberries. To assemble the cake, place one layer on a plate and top with half the whipped cream and strawberries. Add the second layer of cake, followed by the second half of the whipped cream and strawberries. Serves 6-8.

Food for Thought
Waste Reduction

If we are going to seriously take stock of our impact on our environment, then waste reduction is another place where individual personal action can make a huge difference. A great deal of garbage is associated with food—both in terms of packaging and organic waste. Growing one's own food, buying local and seasonal produce, and eating simply all considerably reduce one's use of packaged foods while composting of kitchen and garden waste can significantly reduce the amount of garbage you send to the landfill.

Canada really seems to struggle when it comes to garbage issues, throwing away **more garbage than any other country in the world**. We discard a whopping 2.7 kg of waste per person per day, or 985 kg per person per year; the equivalent of 20 refrigerators full per household per year. The cost of disposing of this waste is estimated at $1.5 billion per year or about $50 per citizen annually. Most residential waste consists of 33% paper, 33% organic waste, 20% metal and plastic, and the remaining 14% is wood, rubber, leather, textiles, and building materials.[1] This waste takes anywhere from a few weeks to thousands of years to decompose and much of it contains a host of toxic and environmentally damaging chemicals that seep into our soils and our ground water.

Canada first began to sense that it might have a garbage problem in the 1970s and this awareness led to a scatter-ing of recycling projects with varying degrees of success. These initiatives seemed to fade until the early 1990s when people began complaining about ever expanding landfills and all the associated issues of land and groundwater pollution, smell, and toxic contamination. Since then most provinces have legislated mandatory municipal recycling services. This has resulted in a provincial average of 30% waste diversion. Nova Scotia is the Canadian leader in this field. In 1998 it banned the landfilling or incineration of all organics, including food waste, yard waste, and paper, and a year later achieved 44% waste diversion. This kind of public policy makes a huge difference: Nova Scotia's annual per capita garbage figures are 460 kg per person, just under half the national average.

There are many who feel that today's garbage issues are a direct result of municipal waste removal programs because they involve a public policy in which producers take no responsibility—physical or financial—for the waste that they generate. There are few incentives for producers to curb their use of excessive and wasteful packaging and/or toxic materials or to incorporate systems for reuse and recycling into the design of their products.[2] Many people also feel recycling is nothing more than "welfare for waste," costing taxpayers a great deal of money and once again diverting responsibility away from producers.[3] The 30% reduction in waste that we have achieved through recycling is far less than what is possible and not enough to keep pace with the increases in total waste that our society continues to experience.

Nevertheless, recycling does have a significant impact especially when one considers the conservation of materials. Using recycled materials eliminates the process of primary resource extraction and avoids the use of a host of other materials necessary for production and manufacturing.[4] The Recycling Council of Ontario *(www.rco.on.ca)* publishes a fact sheet entitled ***Recycling and Waste Reduction Statistics*** that gives one a good understanding of the issue. For example:

- It takes 95% less energy to make sheet metal from recycled cans than it does to make it from raw materials.
- About 3.5 billion aluminum cans are recycled in Canada each year, representing enough energy to heat 36,000 homes for one year.
- A steel mill using recycled scrap reduces water and air pollution and mining waste by about 70%.
- Recycling one tonne of newspaper saves 19 trees, 3 cubic metres of landfill, 4000 kilowatt-hours of energy, 29,000 litres of water, and 30 kilograms of air pollution effluent.
- Recycling glass avoids the mining of limestone, glass sand, soda ash, and feldspar. In 2005, an estimated 3.4 billion refillable glass bottles were produced in Canada. These have a life-span of fifteen uses and represent savings of $46 million in crude oil or the equivalent of the electricity used by 90,000 Canadian homes in one year.[5]

Perhaps one of the most important changes to waste management problems now being considered is called 'extended producer responsibility' or EPR. This is legislation that makes producers responsible for the whole life cycle of their products, including take back, recycling, and final disposal. EPR would reduce the incidence of poor product design and excessive packaging and ensure that such waste disasters as Canada's shift from refundable glass beverage containers to aluminum cans and plastic bottles would no longer make economic sense.

Europe has already instituted many EPR laws; perhaps most notable is legislation introduced in 2003 that governs the manufacturing and disposal of electronic waste.[6] European consumers must be able to take their e-waste to municipal collection points or to the retailer. Producers are responsible for picking up the waste and transferring it to a certified recycling facility and they cannot charge for this service. They must also guarantee future disposal responsibility should they go bankrupt or merge with another company. For e-waste that is older than 2003, the cost of disposal is shared by all existing companies, proportionate to their share of the market. E-waste legislation is currently being looked at in Ontario, Alberta, and British Columbia.

Giles Slade, author of ***Made to Break: Technology and Obsolescence in America***, argues that electronic waste is already out of control and that we are heading for an environmental nightmare. Electronic waste contains a host of toxic metals, including mercury, lead, arsenic, cadmium, beryllium, antimony, nickel, and zinc. An estimated five to seven million tons of electronic waste ended up in U.S. landfills in 2001.[7] The U.S. is one of the few countries not to ratify an international agreement making it illegal to ship toxic waste. As a result, Third World countries with lax environmental regulations allow citizens to dismantle American electronic waste, selling what is reusable, and often smashing the remainder with hammers.

Slade also takes direct aim at the practice of obsolescence in the electronics industry. There are currently three billion cellphones and 68 million iPods worldwide. Deliberate marketing strategies encourage consumers to replace these items every year to eighteen months. Unfortunately, their small size leads many to see them as disposable when, in fact, their huge numbers result in a very significant total volume of toxic metals entering landfills.[8] Cathode ray tubes contain the highest concentrations of toxic waste—**there are 5-10 pounds of lead in the average TV**. This is something to consider because in 2009 the U.S. government will switch to a high-resolution digital television signal rendering about 300 million analogue televisions obsolete.

Up until recently it has been extremely difficult to dispose of electronic waste in Canada but with changing municipal regulations and increasing prices for metal and oil, electronic waste disposal and recycling in Canada is quickly becoming a viable industry. In order to learn more about what is currently available in my area, I looked up Recycling Services in the Yellow Pages and had a fascinating conversation with a representative of a

Kingston company called Kimco. He indicated that his company would take most things that have an electronic component, from computers to appliances. There is a fee but apparently people are willing to pay rather than have their waste going into landfills. Kimco acts as a collection and sorting facility and then ships items on to the appropriate recycling corporation. There is a market for almost anything, from keyboards to Christmas tree lights, but the biggest problem is that this market is by the ton and therefore items must be collected and stored until there is sufficient quantity to ship. Apparently companies all over the world are investing in new and innovative technologies to recycle and reuse electronic waste. In Barrie, Ontario a company called GEEP recycles electronics and turns the reclaimed plastics into diesel fuel, which they use to power their facility. Another company called Vermont Gold has a whole line of jewellery made from gold that has been reclaimed from electronic products.

There are a number of communities in Canada that have very successful waste reduction strategies. The Regional District of Kootenay Boundary in the southern interior of British Columbia consists of eight municipalities with a total population of 32,000. Through a multi-faceted series of initiatives, the district has achieved a 72% reduction in overall garbage while saving money and providing a source of community pride and spirit.[9] Beginning in 1995, the district instituted a ban on the disposal of cardboard, expanding this ban over the next six years to include all recyclables and yard wastes. During this period they also phased in a user pay system for household garbage as well as almost universal access to curbside recycling. Partnerships with retail and community groups and educational campaigns lent further support to the philosophy of zero waste, as has a committed lobbying effort aimed at bringing in Extended Producer Responsibility legislation in the province. Future initiatives include centralized composting facilities and curbside green waste collection; this is projected to eliminate about 45% of Kootenay Boundary's remaining garbage—pretty impressive for a small municipality.

One of Canada's most committed municipalities is the village of Annapolis Royal in Nova Scotia. Provincial legislation in the late 1990s forced the closure of the county's waste incinerator and also banned the disposal of organic and recyclable materials. Plans to create a regional waste authority that would truck waste to Halifax did not make sense to the town's 600 residents so they decided to work with their council to find a different solution. In 1997, Zero Waste 2005 was formed with the goal of eliminating as much waste as possible in a manner that was as easy as possible for residents and businesses.[10] Inherent in the philosophy of the project was a desire to keep the project small and local so as to create a model that other small communities could easily replicate.

A major focus of Zero Waste 2005 was the elimination of organic food and yard wastes. To do this, the project distributed approximately 125 Green Cones for backyard composting and built three centrally located, low-tech composting bins to accommodate any backyard overflows. It also purchased two Earth Tubs designed to compost large quantities of organics for the town's public works yard. These serve residents, local restaurants, and grocery stores. In addition, local businesses were asked to reduce their packaging and to move away from foam and plastic packaging. Several four-stream garbage collection stations were installed in the downtown area to collect paper, beverage containers, organic waste, and residual materials. Much of the success of the project has come from yearly mailings to residents as well as a strong commitment from volunteers and public works staff, all of whom received extensive training in the proper use of both the Earth Tubs and the Green Cones.[11]

Annapolis Royal's waste management system costs about $30,000 per year— right on par with the Canadian average of $50 per person. This represents an increase of 25% over its pre-1997 budgets but is an impressive $15,000 less than the cost of joining the regional waste authority.[12] In 1998, the United Nations placed Annapolis Royal on its very prestigious list for "Global Best Practices for Human Settlement."

When I think about all of this information a few things strike me. I am really surprised by how little we spend on waste management in Canada; about $50 per citizen does not seem to be a huge expense. It would follow that with a little bit more money a great deal more could be accomplished. Through diligent recycling, it is within the grasp of most households to reduce their garbage by about 50%, given that household waste is approximately 33% paper and 20% metal or plastic. If one has enough of a backyard to have a compost pile, this waste can be reduced by another third. *If you do the math, this would mean it is possible to generate less than 15% of the Canadian average or about 150 kg of garbage per year per person.* This is less than 3 kg of garbage each week and I know from my own experience that this is not unreasonable. Our family of three manages to fit all of our garbage into one plastic grocery bag each week without much extra effort—well, it is my daughter's job to do the recycling so she may disagree with this! It is our experience that the easiest way to recycle is to separate the recycling from the garbage before it goes into the garbage can—rummaging through a garbage can and trying to separate the paper from the chewing gum is no fun. We have a waste basket for paper and under the kitchen sink there are three pails, one for other recyclables, one for compost, and one for garbage.

Waste reduction is another area where making a difference is something that is very "doable"—both on a personal and on a municipal level. As several communities in Canada have found, tackling this issue can allow us to feel so much more positive about ourselves and our communities.

Sources and Further Information

The Spring, 2006 issue of **Alternatives Magazine,** published by the University of Waterloo Department of Environmental Studies. The issue is dedicated to examining Waste Reduction and includes the following articles:

Zero Waste Wins by Paul Connett

Practical Tools for Zero Waste by Raymond Gaudart

Embodied Energy by Clarissa Morawski

Hope in Wasteland by Helen Speigelmann

Unplugged by Beverley Thorpe

Slade, Giles, *Made to Break: Technology and Obsolescence in America,* Harvard University Press, Cambridge, Massachussetts, 2006.

The Recycling Council of Ontario, *Recycling and Waste Reduction Fact Sheet, www.rco.on.ca*

www.citizenswasteinfo.org

www.annapolisroyal.com

District of Kootenay Boundary website – *www.rdkb.com*

Endnotes

1   Recycling Council of Ontario, *Recycling and Waste Reduction Statistics,* www.rco.on.ca/factsheet, page 3.

2   Speigelmann, Helen, *Hope in Wasteland'* in Alternatives Magazine, University of Waterloo Department of Environmental Studies, Waterloo, Ontario, Spring 2006, page 11.

3   Ibid, page 10.

4   Morawski, Clarissa, *Embodied Energy,* in Alternatives Magazine, University of Waterloo Department of Environmental Studies, Waterloo, Ontario, Spring, 2006, page 19.

5   Ibid, page 19.

6   Thorpe, Beverley, *Unplugged,* in Alternatives Magazine, University of Waterloo Department of Environmental Studies, Waterloo, Ontario, Spring 2006, page 25.

7   Slade, Giles, *Made to Break: Technology and Obsolescence in America,* Harvard University Press, Cambridge, Massachusetts, 2006, page 262.

8   Ibid, page 264.

9   Gaudart, Raymond, *Practical Tools for Zero Waste,* in Alternatives Magazine, University of Waterloo Department of Environmental Studies, Waterloo, Ontario, Spring 2006, page 13.

10 www.gtacleanaironline.ca, *Annapolis Royal, Nova Scotia, Eliminating Waste by 2005,*

11 Ibid

12 Ibid

JULY

The Earth is mother,
Of all that is natural,
Of all that is human.

— Hildegard of Bingen (1098 – 1179), *German abbess, poet, mystic, and composer*

In the Garden

As the summer progresses you will probably find that there is far less work to do in your garden. Almost everything has been planted, the garden has been mulched and weeded, and it is time to enjoy summer. My summer garden plans allow for a small amount of planting in July to ensure a continuous harvest of salad vegetables. To make room for this planting, you will have to dig under areas of the garden that were planted in April and/or May. Any weeds or plants that are too big to turn under should be pulled and put on the compost. I like to let a *few* (Keyword – few!!) dill and coriander plants go to seed as next spring these will germinate all over your garden, maturing long before your first plantings do.

It is important to keep your garden well watered during the summer months. If your area has watering restrictions this can be difficult, but one can water a garden without a sprinkler by filling large buckets and regularly watering at the base of each plant. You can also keep several large containers under sections of eavestrough to collect and store what rain water there is. ***Remember that watering in the evening is far more beneficial for your garden.*** There is also some ongoing weeding as well as regular rounds of insect control, especially in the winter storage garden

The flats of basil, lettuce, beets, and green onions that were started in mid-June should be planted in early July. ***If the weather is really hot, it is a good idea to do your transplanting in the late afternoon or evening.*** You should then give your garden a good watering and mulch the newly planted bed. If you are planting these seeds directly in the garden and the weather is dry you must make sure that they are watered every three or four days to ensure good germination.

I also like to plant some coriander and dill, as well as a section of salad greens. I don't include lettuce in my summer greens mix as it germinates poorly in the July heat but I make sure that I plant some tatsoi, arugula, and kale. After harvesting these greens for salads, I thin the plants and allow them to grow to full size for harvest in the fall. These plantings germinate well in midsummer as long as they are watered once or twice after they have been seeded.

Weeding

Weeding is an ongoing job, but it is really up to you how neat and tidy you want your garden to look. Weeds are definitely not beneficial to young plants; they compete for water, nutrients, and space, and interfere with your seedling's ability to develop. However, once plants have grown to approximately two thirds of their maturity, I find that a few weeds have little effect; this is especially true for vegetables such as beets, lettuce, or green onions that do not stay in the garden all summer. It is a good idea to keep your cucumber, pepper, and tomato plants and any winter storage vegetables fairly clear of weeds and do what you can in the rest of the garden. ***It is important, however, not to allow any weeds to go to seed in the garden.*** The number of seeds that one weed can produce and the length of time (about seven years) that some of these seeds can survive in your garden is truly one of the many wonders of nature.

Thinning Carrots and Parsnips

I wait until July to thin carrots and parsnips because the tiny seedlings are very delicate and it is easy to disturb the roots of those you want to keep. For this reason it is also not a good idea to do all of your thinning at once. Thin the whole bed several times over the month, aiming for a final spacing of 3-4" apart. As the carrots get larger, you can eat the thinnings. The best way to thin a dense clump of plants is to put your finger on the carrot or parsnip that you want to keep and hold it in place while you gently pull the others out. Again, this should be done in several stages if necessary. If there are large gaps where no seed has come up, these sections can be replanted by gently loosening the soil with a small garden fork and dropping in a few seeds. As long as the area is kept well watered, the seed should germinate.

Tomatoes

Staking — As your tomato plants get bigger, you will have to decide how you want them to grow. As I mentioned earlier, determinate varieties of tomatoes grow to a finite size that I find quite manageable. These tomatoes can be left to sprawl on the ground. This method requires little work but there is a greater chance of rot or insect damage in wet weather. Alternatively you can gently tie your plants to wooden stakes or allow them to grow within wire cages. All of these methods work well. Indeterminate tomatoes should be staked as some varieties grow to be 9' - 10' tall. Wooden stakes work well, as do the metal T-posts used in agricultural fencing.

Pruning — When staking indeterminate varieties of tomatoes it is a good idea to also do some pruning. Pruning involves restricting the plant's growth to one or two main stems. This makes the plant easier to tie up, reduces sprawl, and results in fewer fruit that are larger in size. To understand pruning you must be able to tell the difference between a branch and a sucker.

- Look at your tomato plant and find the main stem—it will have branches growing from it and these branches will have leaves and flowers on them.
- Then look at where a branch meets the main stem—here you will often see a tiny shoot, which in gardening terms is called a "sucker." If left to grow, these suckers will become secondary stems and have branches growing from them.
- Another way to think about it is that stems have branches on them while branches have leaves and flowers on them.

Once you are confident that you have this figured out you can begin pruning. It is a good idea to do this once a week to keep on top of the process.

- Look at your tomato plants and pinch off all the suckers that you find. Usually you are simply pinching the small shoots that form at the intersection of the main stem and its branches, but sometimes these shoots will go unnoticed and you will have to break off a fairly significant secondary stem with many of its own branches.
- As you work on pruning your tomato vine gently tie the main stem up and around your stake.

Peas

Your peas should have finished producing by late July. Remove the stakes from the shell peas and then remove and compost all of the plants.

Cucumbers, Zucchini, and Winter Squash

If you covered your plants with a floating row cover, this should be removed once the plants begin to flower. This is necessary for the flowers to be pollinated. As much as possible, try to train your plants to stay within their beds. Continue to keep an eye out for striped cucumber beetles and squash bugs and use Rotenone if necessary. I find that watering once or twice a week in dry weather helps these plants withstand insect damage.

Potatoes

You really have to be diligent about controlling potato bugs or you could lose most or all of your plants. Try to go after them at least once per week or ten days.

Cabbage

If your cabbage plants are not growing under a floating row cover you should incorporate a weekly cabbage worm inspection into your garden routine. The worms are pale green and hard to see but their dark green castings (the remains of your chewed up cabbage leaves) can't be missed. If you don't trust your ability to find the worms, you should spray your plants with Bt every week or so. Since this is a liquid it will wash off so try to spray after a heavy rain or after you have watered your garden.

Transplants

Again because of the hot weather and often dry conditions I encourage you to start seeds indoors in July. These will go into the summer garden in early August and should provide you with vegetables well into the fall. The timing of this planting is fairly critical because after the sum-mer solstice the light levels are decreasing steadily, causing a parallel decrease in growth rates. I have found that my transplants must go in the garden between about August 3 and 10 in order for them to mature. If they are planted before this time, they mature too soon and do not remain in good condition throughout the fall. If they are planted after this time there is a surprising difference in the growth rates and the plants will not reach full maturity. I start my transplants between July 7 and 13 for this schedule to work. I start a large number of lettuce, endive, spinach, and green onions; they should mature near the end of September and hold their quality well into October and November

JULY GARDEN SUMMARY

- ☐ Dig, compost, and mark out your July beds.
- ☐ Continue watering and weeding as needed.
- ☐ Begin to thin your carrots and parsnips.
- ☐ Stake and prune your tomato plants.
- ☐ Remove pea plants and put them on the compost.
- ☐ Check squash, zucchini, and cucumbers for cucumber beetles on a regular basis.
- ☐ Check potatoes for Colorado potato beetles on a weekly basis.
- ☐ Check cabbage plants for cabbage worms on a weekly basis.

In The Summer Gardens

- In mid-July, transplant or direct seed basil, lettuce, endive, green onions, and beets. Broadcast dill, coriander, and salad greens.

Transplants

- Before mid July make transplants of lettuce, endive, green onions, and spinach to be planted in the garden in August.

Harvesting and Eating

As you can see from the **Available Foods** table, things start to explode in July. Even with small plantings of all your vegetables, you will probably find that you have more produce than you can eat. I hope you have a few hungry neighbours! The table is a bit misleading because not all the vegetables are ready to harvest at the same time. Vegetables such as peas are harvested in early July but are finished by the middle of the month. The first tomatoes, cucumbers, and hot peppers will be ready from the middle to the end of July, depending on how hot the summer has been; green peppers take longer to ripen. Tiny new potatoes are often ready for harvest by the end of July; they also can be found at roadside markets, along with broccoli and cauliflower. Local fruit is still hard to find but there are usually raspberries for sale. We are lucky to have a few good stands of wild blackberries in our village and I pick as much as I can. I also try to make one trip to a local Pick Your Own operation and get some raspberries for the winter.

I am a very lazy cook in the summer; there are many days when it is just too hot to want to do much of anything. Once we have eaten the last of the peas and green salads we move on to our standard July vegetable: the cucumber. At first we eat them sliced, then in salads with yogurt or sour cream, and then in our favorite summer salad of tomatoes, cucumbers, and basil and sometimes feta cheese. We also eat cooked beets, zucchini, and green and yellow beans and I try to finish the rest of the tomatoes that are in my freezer.

Storage Tips: To freeze raspberries, simply lay the berries on cookie sheets and place in the freezer, and then transfer to plastic bags. I don't wash raspberries because I feel they are clean and because they lose a lot of juice when you wash them.

Harvesting Techniques

Beans
Beans should be picked before they get too big. If you can see the seeds bulging under the skin they are getting tough. You should not harvest beans when the plants are wet as this can encourage the spread of disease.

Cucumbers
Often homegrown cucumbers have a slightly bitter taste just under the skin, especially when they get bigger. To get rid of this bitterness, slice off the first half inch or so from one end of the cucumber. Take this end and rub it in a circular motion against the open end of the cucumber for about ten seconds. You should notice a white foamy substance starting to form; this is the bitterness that is being drawn out of the cucumber. Cut off a second slice to get rid of the foam. Repeat the process at the other end of the cucumber.

Garlic Basil Pesto freezes easily and I make several large batches that I freeze in small plastic containers.

To make pesto, wash and stem enough basil to fill a 2-cup measure. Place this in a food processor and add 3 cloves of garlic, 1/2 cup olive oil and 1/4 tsp of salt. Purée until smooth. Sometimes I add 1/2 cup of sunflower seeds to the mix. I don't add cheese to my pesto—we prefer to add it when we serve it.

Basil

Do not cut your basil plants but instead pick off a few stems at a time; the plants will keep growing and can be harvested several times over. Eventually the plant will produce flowers and seed clusters. To delay this and prolong the harvest, pinch off the flowers on a regular basis.

Zucchini

I like to pick zucchini when they are about 6" long; gently twist the fruit from the plant. Inevitably a few zucchinis miss being harvested and grow to be big. These are good for grating and cooking in muffins and cakes or for zucchini base-ball! Some people like to freeze grated zucchini and use it for baking later in the winter.

Available Foods

In My Garden	In My Freezer	At the Grocery
Lettuce	Pesto	Tomatoes
Endive	Rhubarb	Cucumbers
Green Onions	Strawberries	Radishes
Shell Peas	Raspberries	Lettuce
Snow Peas		Mushrooms
Sugar Snap Peas		Cauliflower
Swiss Chard		Green Cabbage
Beets		Apples
Beet Greens		
Garlic		
Dill		
Coriander		
Parsley		
Basil		
Green or Yellow Beans		
Tomatoes		
Peppers		
Cucumbers		
Zucchini		

A July harvest of basil, cucumbers, beets, lettuce, green onions, yellow zucchini, Hungarian Hot wax peppers, green beans, and parsley.

Menu Ideas for July include:

Green Salad with lettuce, cucumbers, and
   tomatoes
Caesar Salad
Spanish Endive Salad
Cobb Salad
Salade Niçoise
Fresh Cucumbers
Cucumber, Tomato, and Basil Salad
Spicy Chicken and Cucumber Salad
Cucumber Salad with yogurt or sour
   cream and fresh dill
Chilled Cucumber Soup
Steamed Green or Yellow Beans
Marinated Green Beans
Black Bean Salad
Beet Sandwiches
Beet and Parsley Salad with Goat Cheese

Beet Greens with bacon and onion
Beet and Potato or Pasta Salad
Potato Salad with green onions and dill
   pickles
New Potatoes with butter and fresh dill
Greek Pasta Salad with Fresh Herbs
Pasta with garlic basil pesto
Sautéed Zucchini with garlic, onions, and
   tomatoes
Steamed Swiss Chard with butter and
   balsamic vinegar
Black Beans and Rice
Tortillas with refried beans, hot peppers,
   lettuce and tomatoes
Spaghetti Sauce with vegetables
Chicken or Tofu with a Coriander and
   Lemon Sauce

A Few Recipes

Beet and Potato or Pasta Salad

6 medium potatoes or 2 cups macaroni
3-4 hardboiled eggs
3-4 cooked beets
1 bunch green onions
1 bunch parsley
1 bunch dill
3-4 tbsp mayonnaise
1-2 tsp lemon juice
Salt and pepper

Cook the potatoes or noodles until tender. Drain and allow to cool; it is a good idea to rinse the noodles with cold water. Chop the potatoes into 1/2" chunks. Peel the eggs and chop into small chunks. Remove the skins from the beets and dice in 1/2" cubes. Clean and chop the green onions. Clean and stem the parsley and the dill and chop finely. Combine the potatoes or noodles with the remaining ingredients, add the mayonnaise and lemon juice, and season with salt and pepper. Serves 4.

Potato Salad with Green Onions and Dill Pickles

8 medium potatoes
4-6 green onions
3 medium sized dill pickles
1 bunch parsley
1 bunch dill
2-3 tbsp mayonnaise
1/4 cup pickle juice
Salt and pepper

Cook the potatoes until tender, then drain, and allow to cool. Cut into 1/2" pieces. Clean and chop the green onions. Clean, stem and finely chop the parsley and the dill. Dice the dill pickles. Combine the vegetables and the herbs in a bowl and add the mayonnaise and the pickle juice. Season with salt and pepper. Serves 4.

♥ Greek Pasta Salad with Fresh Herbs

4 cups penne or spiral noodles
1 bunch green onions
1 bunch parsley
1 bunch dill
1 bunch basil
1 cucumber
3-4 tomatoes
1/4 cup oil
2 tbsp balsamic vinegar
2 tbsp lemon juice

Cook and drain the pasta. Clean the green onions. Wash and stem the fresh herbs. Chop the green onions and the herbs until they are quite fine. Dice the cucumber and tomatoes. Combine the cooled pasta and the vegetables in a bowl and mix. Season with salt and pepper and dress with oil, balsamic vinegar, and lemon juice. This salad is also good with drained tuna and olives. Serves 4-6.

Beet and Parsley Salad with Goat Cheese

4 medium beets, cooked and cooled
1 large bunch parsley
250 g feta or other goat cheese
1/4 cup oil
2 tbsp balsamic vinegar
Salt and pepper

Peel the beets and cut into 1/2" cubes. Wash, stem, and finely chop the parsley, you should have about 1/2 cup. Combine the beets and the parsley and add the oil, balsamic vinegar, salt, and pepper. At the last minute, add the feta cheese and mix very lightly—otherwise everything will turn purple! Serves 4-6.

Salade Niçoise

1 head lettuce
2-3 tomatoes
8 anchovy fillets (optional)
1/2 cup green beans, steamed and cooled
4 hard boiled eggs
Salt and freshly ground pepper
1 can tuna, drained
2 potatoes, cooked and cooled
6 tbsp oil
2 tbsp red wine vinegar
1 tsp Dijon mustard

Wash and tear the lettuce into bite size pieces. Place in a large salad bowl. On top, arrange chopped tomatoes, cubed potatoes, chopped hard boiled eggs, tuna, and anchovy fillets. Mix the oil, red wine vinegar, and Dijon mustard and dress the salad. Serves 4-6.

♥ Tomato and Cucumber Salad

4-6 fresh tomatoes
2 cucumbers
1 bunch fresh basil
3 tbsp oil
2 tbsp red wine or balsamic vinegar
Salt and pepper

This is our favourite summer salad and we eat it regularly in late July and throughout August. Dice the tomatoes and cucumbers and place them in a bowl. Wash and stem the basil and chop it fairly finely. Add to the bowl along with the remaining ingredients. Let stand at least 15 minutes before serving. Crumble feta cheese on top for a delicious addition to of this salad. Serves 4.

Cucumbers with Yogurt or Sour Cream

2-3 cucumbers
1/2 tsp salt
1/2 cup yogurt or sour cream
2 cloves garlic, crushed and finely
    chopped and/or 1/4 cup finely
    chopped dill

Clean the cucumbers and remove the ends, rubbing to remove any bitterness. Slice the cucumbers thinly and place in a bowl. Add the remaining ingredients and stir. If desired, you can add 1 tsp of sugar. This recipe can also be used to make *Tzatziki*, a Greek cucumber dip. Slice the cucumbers lengthways and use a spoon to scoop out the seeds. Finely chop the cucumber and mix with yogurt and garlic. Serves 4-6.

♥ Spicy Chicken and Cucumber Salad

1 lb cooked chicken, cubed
2-3 cucumbers
1-2 medium hot peppers
2 tbsp olive oil
1/4 cup sesame seeds
3 tbsp soy or tamari sauce
2 tbsp oil
1 tsp sugar

Halve the cucumbers lengthways and scoop out the seeds. Cut the cucumber into thin strips, about 4" long. Seed and finely chop the hot pepper. Over medium heat, sauté the hot pepper in oil, add the cucumber and chicken and sauté about 2 minutes. Let cool, then transfer to a bowl or plate. Toast the sesame seeds in a dry pan until just golden. Remove from the heat, toss with chicken mixture. Combine the remaining ingredients and drizzle over the salad. Serves 4. (Adapted from *Basic Asian* by C. Schinharl, S. Dickhaut, and K Lane)

Chilled Cucumber Soup

2 medium cucumbers
6 green onions
1 clove garlic
2 tbsp butter
2 tbsp flour
2 cups chicken or vegetable broth
1 bunch dill
1 cup yogurt or sour cream
2 tbsp lemon juice

Cut the ends off the cucumbers and rub to remove any bitterness. Halve lengthways and if there are a lot of seeds, scoop some out. Cut the cucumber into small chunks. Clean and chop the green onions and the garlic. In a large saucepan, add the butter and sauté the cucumber, green onion, and garlic over medium heat for about 5 minutes. Add the flour and cook another few minutes, stirring to keep it from sticking. Gradually add the broth and simmer for about 5 minutes. Remove from heat and purée in a food processor or with a hand blender, and then allow to cool. Clean and stem the dill and chop it finely. Add the dill, yogurt or sour cream, and lemon juice to the soup and chill for several hours or overnight. Serves 4.

Marinated Green Bean Salad

2-3 cups green or yellow beans
2-3 green onions, chopped
1/2 cup oil
3 tbsp white wine vinegar
Salt and pepper

Blanch the beans until just tender by plunging into boiling water for 2 minutes and then transferring to cold water. Drain the beans and cut in 2-3" segments. Finely chop the green onions. Place beans and green onions in a bowl. Mix the oil and vinegar and pour over the beans. Season with salt and pepper and marinate for about one hour. Serves 4.

Sautéed Zucchini with Garlic, Onions, and Tomatoes

3 tbsp oil
3 cloves garlic, finely chopped
2 medium onions
3-4 zucchini
3-4 tomatoes
Salt and pepper

Peel the onions and slice thinly. Slice the zucchini and cut the tomatoes into wedges. In a cast iron pan, add the oil and sauté the garlic and onions over low heat for about 10 minutes. Add the zucchini and tomatoes and cook another few minutes. Season with salt and pepper. Serves 4.

Black Beans and Rice

2 onions
4-5 cloves garlic
2-3 medium hot peppers
2 tbsp oil
3 cups cooked black beans
3-4 cups Swiss chard
1 bunch fresh coriander
1 bunch fresh basil
2 tsp dried cumin
1 tsp dried coriander

Finely chop the onions, garlic, and peppers, then sauté in a large pot with oil. Add the black beans. Cook for about 10 minutes, stirring occasionally. Meanwhile, wash the Swiss chard and remove the tougher parts of the stems, then coarsely chop. Wash, stem, and finely chop the coriander and basil. Add the Swiss chard, fresh herbs, cumin, and coriander to the pot. There should be some moisture from the vegetables, but you may need to add a bit of water so that the Swiss chard can cook. Cover and simmer another 5 or 10 minutes. Season with salt and pepper and serve with rice, corn chips, and salsa. Serves 4.

❤ Fresh Coriander and Lemon Sauce

1 onion
1-3 medium hot peppers
4-5 cloves garlic
2 inches fresh ginger
3 cups fresh coriander leaves
1 cup chicken or vegetable stock
2 tbsp oil
1 tsp dried coriander
2 tsp dried cumin
2 tbsp lemon juice
Salt and pepper

Finely chop the onion and hot peppers. Peel the ginger and garlic and grate both on the fine side of a kitchen grater. Finely chop the coriander leaves. In a large pan, sauté the onion and peppers in oil over medium heat. After a few minutes, add the grated garlic and ginger and cook 2 or 3 minutes longer. Add the chopped coriander, stock, dried herbs, and lemon juice and simmer for about 5 minutes. Season with salt and pepper. This sauce is delicious served with rice and chicken or tofu. Serves 4. (Adapted from *Indian Cookery*, by Madhur Jaffrey).

Food for Thought
Making Food Choices

Any discussion of the environmental consequences of our food systems inevitably leads to a discussion of our own personal food choices. In my experience, this is very tricky territory, full of passionately held convictions and equally passionate misconceptions.

When I first began to think about food and its connection to environmental issues, I knew only one word—organic, that is food grown without chemical fertilizers, pesticides, or herbicides. Frances Moore Lappé's classic book **Diet for a Small Planet** brought to my attention the considerable waste, pollution, and cruelty associated with the factory farming of livestock. I began to think about eating less meat and buying meat that was either organic or from small, local farmers. As my journey continued, I became aware of a host of other issues and ideas: fair trade, social justice in the developing world, global warming, food miles, and support for local agriculture, to name just a few. All of these issues can be overwhelming when one enters the grocery store. It is important to find balance and perspective when making choices about food.

Deciding what and how to eat and where to shop is not a simple task. For the most part, I have switched my thinking from the term 'organic' to the term 'ecological' when I consider my food choices. For me, the word ecological balances how a food is grown with where it is grown and then considers the level of processing and packaging inherent in that food. My least complicated decisions involve food from my own garden—local, organic, seasonal, and definitely fair trade. Equally straightforward are decisions concerning food that is both local and organic. In my area that includes some vegetables and fruits, eggs, honey, and organic meats. Then there is what I call food that is gently farmed—vegetables, fruits, eggs, and meat from small, local farmers. It is my experience that a great many of these small farmers have not embraced chemical agriculture, both because it is too expensive and because they are comfortable with their own traditional methods of farming. They may buy conventional feed for their animals or occasionally spray their produce when there is a pest, but there isn't the ubiquitous use of chemicals, hormones and antibiotics associated with industrial farming.

Then come the dilemmas—do I buy organically grown apples from B.C. or do I buy conventional Product of Ontario apples from my grocery store? Do we eat potatoes all year round or do we enjoy rice and pasta that have been shipped the average 1500-2500 kilometres? I prefer olive oil to canola oil but organic olive oil is very expensive. Lime is one of my favourite flavours but I am still waiting for the introduction of local Ontario limes! There are no easy answers to any of these questions. As much as possible, I will buy North American organic produce over local, 'chemical' produce, partly because I don't want to eat a host of chemicals but also because I hope this will help to increase demand and thereby stimulate local production and availability.

As awareness surrounding local eating increases, there is definitely a need to look at issues of availability. Availability often depends upon economies of scale and in many parts of Canada there simply is not a well developed local agricultural sector. In their book ***The One Hundred Mile Diet***, Alisa Smith and J.B. MacKinnon of Vancouver experienced this lack of availability when they decided to eat only foods that came from within 100 miles of their home for one year. The couple estimated that this type of diet uses seventeen times less petroleum than the average imported food diet[1]. Living in Vancouver, this meant no sugar, pasta, bread, or rice. After collectively losing fifteen pounds in six weeks, they decided they would eat organic grains from Alberta and Saskatchewan. They did not store any food over the winter and by March there was absolutely no local produce in their supermarkets. They found themselves surviving on local fish, shellfish, and honey—delicious but expensive!

I think the Hundred Mile Diet is a very valuable exercise in raising awareness; however it only deals with what foods are available in today's markets. To contemplate a more local diet for things like grains, dairy products, meats, and processed goods we must look at what was once possible. Fifty years ago, North America was dotted with small dairies, mills, granaries, abattoirs, and fisheries. These have disappeared with big business and big government. It is entirely feasible to grow wheat, mill it, and produce '100

Mile Bread' but it seldom happens because the facilities have been lost.

In my own kitchen, I try to be aware of what has travelled a long distance and work to find local sources, but if this is not possible I must decide to either eliminate the food from my diet or live with it. When one looks at greenhouse gas emissions per calorie of food, the numbers for the air transport of fruit and vegetables are astronomical. I believe that this is one area where I can make significant changes without drastically limiting my diet. If we add eggs, honey, maple syrup, meat, and some grains to the list, we are probably well on our way to an impressively local diet. The rest will take time and perhaps it is not even necessary if we deal with the more significant problems.

One of the biggest questions facing most people who tackle the ethics of their food choices is whether or not to eat meat. It is important to look at this issue from many different angles. All too often, the comparison between eating a pound of hamburger and a pound of soybeans is greatly oversimplified, and of course, the soybeans win hands down. There is no question that the feedlot cow consumes huge quantities of water and chemically farmed grains—six to seven times more nutrients than it ever provides in protein.[2] It also produces huge amounts of manure that pollute our waterways. Similarly, industrially farmed soybeans are grown with chemical fertilizers, herbicides, and pesticides that are made from fossil fuels. These chemicals pollute waterways, kill fish and wildlife, and destroy millions of beneficial insects. The tractors, combine harvesters, and other equipment necessary to get these soybeans in from the field run on fossil fuels. In growing these soybeans, soil is compacted, biodiversity is lost, and the carbon storage abilities of our grasslands are destroyed.[3] These crops also consume large amounts of water through irrigation. Whether it is beef, soybeans, corn, or chicken, organic or conventional, large scale industrial farming, both conventional and organic is polluting and uses similar amounts of fossil fuels per pound of food.

In contrast, the pound of hamburger that comes from the small farmer with grass-fed cattle that do not overgraze their pastures is an environmentally benign source of protein. These cows efficiently convert grass to protein, often on land that is too rugged or rocky for crops. Manure decomposing in fields or on properly managed compost piles is far superior to chemical fertilizers; it not only adds nutrients to the soil, it also rebuilds the soil by adding organic matter and increasing its ability to store carbon. Similarly, a field of handworked soybeans is a very ecological thing, but it involves an incredible amount of human labour. When one considers the production of grains and legumes without the use of either fossil fuels or animal labour, it becomes questionable as to whether the soybeans are more efficient than the grass-fed cow in producing good quality protein.

In my mind, the small-scale mixed farm is our best model for ecological sustainability. This type of farm depends upon the co-operative efforts of humans, animals, and nature; some of the work is definitely made easier through the use of fossil fuels but it does not depend upon them. There are many organic farmers who are rediscovering (and many small and conventional farmers who never forgot) the simple and efficient ways that animals contribute to farming. Horses and oxen provide transportation; chickens, geese, and ducks devour insects and grubs; and one of the easiest ways to turn a grassy field into a well worked, well manured, and weed-free pasture is to let a few pigs spend some time in it. I have also read some pretty convincing arguments that a draft horse is a far better long-term investment than a tractor. By its very nature, the small, mixed farm produces vegetables, grains, legumes, and meats. If we want to reduce our use of fossil fuels in agriculture, there is definitely a place for both animal power and animal manures and this implies that there is a place for meat in the North American diet. This is not to endorse a heavy consumption of meat or the so-called 'typical' North American diet. Less than 1% of U.S. beef is grass fed and industrial meat production is highly polluting and often ignores the welfare of the animals.[4]

John Jeavons of **Ecology Action Research Farm** in California gives us some idea of what farming without animals might look like. He has estimated that our North American diet requires from 15,000 to 30,000 square feet of growing space, with the meat eaters using the most land. Jeavons has worked for thirty years to figure out just how much land it takes to grow the food that he needs and has come up with approximately 4000 square feet for a vegan diet of wheat, millet, dry beans, corn, and vegetable crops. There is no oil for cooking in this diet and it lacks Vitamin B12. Jeavons uses intensive farming methods, close plantings, composting, and he recycles all human waste. This recycling of human waste is essential if we want to forego animal manures—a fact that is almost always ignored in the whole discussion. A 4000-square-foot garden translates into ten wide beds, each one hundred feet long, which is a significant amount of work, especially if one also has a day job.

Michael Pollan is a professor of journalism and an award-winning author who lives in Berkeley, California. His books deal with the intersection of human society and the natural world. Pollan's latest book, **The Omnivore's Dilemma** looks at the relationship between the American public and food and discusses the relative merits of vegetarian and omnivorous diets. Pollan argues that:

- Humans need to eat a variety of foods to get all the nutrients they need and that our teeth, jaws, and digestive tracts are designed for both vegetable and meat consumption.
- This varied diet gave humans an evolutionary advantage allowing for survival in many different climates and types of ecosystems.
- It also meant that early humans, unlike for example cattle, which have only one food choice to make, had to figure out very complex diets. This figuring-out process relied upon systems of recognition, knowledge, and communication, which over time evolved into sophisticated cultural traditions concerning food. Many of these traditions, though initially derived through trial and error, were essential in adapting our nutritional requirements to widely differing climates and environments.
- Unlike the rest of the world, North America has never had a stable national cuisine. Because of this, we are subject to all sorts of food fads and constantly changing scientific and nutritional rules that govern our eating habits. He cites the 'no-carbohydrate' phase and the fast food industry's incredible ability to market all sorts of foods that have little or no nutritional value as examples of North American vulnerability and gullibility.

Pollan supports the domestication of animals and the ecological production of meat. He believes that our original relationships with animals were reciprocal relationships but that they have evolved into relationships of dominance, exploitation, and cruelty. Our mistreatment of animals affects us not only physically (i.e. through disease) but also spiritually and this mistreatment is reflective of the level of dysfunction in our society.

If we really begin to think about a diet that is based upon a sustainable model of agriculture we must realize that the earth, and every micro and macro system within it, has the potential to be a self-sustaining, non-depleting entity based entirely upon the idea of respectful and reciprocal relationships. Such a system would be one that is essentially a closed loop whereby very little leaves the system. Production, consumption, decay, and regeneration all must take place within an ecologically sustainable framework. In order to function relatively independently of fossil fuels these entities must be small, and therefore far more personal than our current global models. Somehow these small systems (communities) and the interactions that occur within them should have the potential to create a far more functional and humane society than the one we live in today. It is in this way that I see sustainability and environmentalism as very directly related to issues of equality and democracy.

If we look at so-called modern agriculture, many of the synergistic relationships between plants and animals that have allowed agriculture to flourish for thousands of years, and that exist in almost all ecosystems throughout the world, have been lost or declared obsolete. There are far too many places where depletion far outstrips regeneration. Most of us are so far removed from the people and places that produce our food that we are completely unaware of the kinds of environmental and human damage these industrial and commercial food systems create. Equally disturbing is our lack of understanding of the ways in which our lifestyles contribute to the unsustainable society in which we all live. By moving towards a smaller, community-based system of agriculture we can begin to understanding the context in which our food is grown and the consequences of the various methods of production.

Sources and Further Information

Cooper, Arnie, *Lost in the Supermarket: Michael Pollan on how the food industry has changed the way we eat*, in The Sun, Chapel Hill, North Carolina, May, 2006, p. 4.

D'Adamo, Peter J., *Eat Right for your Type*, G.P. Putman and Sons, New York, 1996.

Jeavons, John, at www.ecologyactionresearchgarden

Pollan, Michael, *The Anxiety of Eating,* in The Sun, Chapel Hill, North Carolina, May, 2006, p. 14.

Pollan, Michael, *The Omnivore's Dilemma: A Natural History of Four Meals*, Thompson Gale, Detroit, 2006.

Roberts, Wayne, *Green Eggs and Ham,* in Alternatives Magazine, University of Waterloo Press, Waterloo, Ontario, Spring, 2002, p.13.

Smith, A. and McKinnon, J.B., *The Hundred Mile Diet*, in The Utne Reader, LENS Publishing Co., Minneapolis, MN, Nov/Dec 2005, p. 97.

Endnotes

1   Smith, A. and MacKinnon, J.B., *The Hundred Mile Diet*, in The Utne Reader, LENS Publishing Co., Minneapolis, MN, Nov/Dec 2005, p. 97.

2   Roberts, Wayne, *Green Eggs and Ham*, in Alternatives Magazine, University of Waterloo Press, Spring 2002, p.13

3   Cooper, Arnie, *Lost in the Supermarket*, in The Sun, Chapel Hill, North Carolina, May 2006, p.8.

4   Cooper, Arnie, *Lost in the Supermarket*, in The Sun, Chapel Hill, North Carolina, May, 2006, p. 8.

AUGUST AND SEPTEMBER

When one tugs at a single thread in nature,
One finds it attached to the rest of the world.
— John Muir (1838 – 1914) *American naturalist and founder of the Sierra Club*

In the Garden

I have grouped August and September together because there is really very little to do in the garden in either of these months and also because the harvest is essentially the same. This is a good thing because I find that by this time my energy and enthusiasm for gardening has waned considerably. For many years I would tell myself in the spring that I would be a better late summer gardener but it never seems to happen, so I have decided that maybe it is okay to be thinking of other things!

A late summer planting of spinach seen in mid-September. The cooler weather makes for a really healthy crop that can be harvested into November.

I do manage one last push and plant the seedlings that were started in mid-July. Because the light levels are decreasing so rapidly at this time of year, it is crucial that these seedlings go into the garden during the first week of August. If they are planted at the right time they will mature and hold their quality well into October and often into November—too late and they will not reach their full size, too early and they will grow past their full size and optimum quality. These vegetables go into a section of the garden that was planted in May so the area must be cleaned up, and if possible, spread with a layer of compost before it is dug. Spinach and salad greens can be seeded directly into the garden anytime in August for harvesting in September. A final planting of

salad greens can be done around September 5 to 7. It will mature in late September and hold its quality well into October. As always, the salad greens should be covered with a section of floating row cover to protect them from flea beetles.

By the end of August the carrots and parsnips should be thinned to their final spacing. Both vegetables do much of their growing in September and early October as there is usually a more consistent supply of rain. Don't worry if your carrots are not overly sweet, their flavour will develop after they have had a few hard frosts.

Throughout September, any vegetable plants that are finished should be pulled and composted.

Winter Storage Vegetables

If you have not grown a winter storage garden but would like to store vegetables for the winter, you should begin to think about organizing an order with a farmer or local food store. If you planted a winter storage garden you will want to assess your harvest, and perhaps supplement what you have grown if you feel it is not enough to get you through the winter. It is nice if you can establish a relationship with a grower who will supply your winter vegetables on a regular basis. I currently have a very small garden so I order my vegetables in late September or early October. I try to wait until late October to pick everything up, both because my root cellar is colder at that time and because carrots taste far better if they have had a few hard frosts before they are harvested. The following is a list of the vegetables that I order for our family of four:

- 1 to 1 1/2 bushels onions
- 1 1/2 to 2 bushels carrots
- 1 1/2 to 3 bushels potatoes
- 1/2 bushel beets
- 1/2 bushel parsnips
- 1/2 bushel leeks (if possible with the roots still attached)
- 6-8 rutabagas
- 8-12 cabbages, both red and green
- 30-40 bulbs garlic
- 15-18 winter squash (Butternut, Buttercup, pie pumpkins, and Delicata store well)
- 4-5 bushels winter apples such as Empire, Idared, Spartan, or Northern Spy (These I get from a store that is supplied by a small, local orchard).

AUGUST/SEPTEMBER GARDEN SUMMARY

- ☐ Dig, compost, and mark out your August/September beds.
- ☐ Continue thinning carrots and parsnips.
- ☐ Pull and compost any plants that are finished.
- ☐ Decide what winter storage vegetables you will need.

In the Summer Gardens

- In early August, transplant lettuce, endive, spinach, and green onions. Spinach can also be direct seeded.
- In early September, direct seed salad greens.

Building a Simple Cold Storage

It is hard to eat seasonally in the winter months without some sort of area for cold storage. If you are building a new home you may be able to incorporate a design into your building plans, otherwise you will have to improvise with what you have. Depending on your situation this can result in something that works very well or something that is reasonably good.

The best root cellars are built into the ground outside of one's house, preferably into a hill. They have a dirt floor, a small door for access at the front, and soil around the walls and over the roof. If you live in the country and have the time and the space, building one of these structures may be a viable option. Many books give instructions for a buried space with an insulated trap door, but in my experience ice and snow eventually get to be significant problems and these types of structures can become inaccessible. ***Root Cellaring*** by Mike and Nancy Bubel is a very thorough and well researched book, which I found at my local library, with many different design instructions.

I have made two root cellars and both started with finding the coldest spot in an unfinished basement. My current root cellar is in an old cistern in my basement that has a small opening for a door. Look for an area that is as far away from the furnace as possible, preferably on a north wall. If possible, try to take advantage of existing walls or structures. A space that is between thirty and sixty square feet should be large enough for a medium-sized family. If you are really lucky you will have a dirt floor though it is more likely that your floor will be concrete.

Root cellars have several basic requirements. The first is that they are cool—between 2°C and 7°C is ideal.

- Begin by partitioning off a space and insulating it from the rest of the basement and from the floor above.
- In terms of insulation, 2 x 4" walls are suitable, 2 x 6" are even better.
- Do not forget to insulate the root cellar side of your access door.
- If possible, the installation of some ducting is useful in the spring and fall as it can bring cooler night air into the root cellar. Six-inch ducting can be fitted into a small outside window or you can arrange for a duct to be inserted through the foundation. You must be able to close the opening in the winter to prevent your cold storage area from

freezing. (Note: I have never had ducting; there have been times when I wished that I did but my root cellar still functions well without it).

- The duct should have a low-energy fan positioned within it. This fan can be controlled manually or by two thermostats attached to a wall outside of the root cellar. One thermostat reads the temperature in the root cellar; the other reads the outside temperature. When the root cellar goes above 9°C and the outside air is below 9°C, the fan is activated.[1]

The second basic requirement for a root cellar is that it is dark. This should not be a problem in a closed-off space, however if there is an outside window you will have to block out the light. Even small amounts of light can cause vegetables to sprout so be diligent about this.

The final requirements are adequate humidity and air circulation.

- Root cellars that are built into the ground and sit on dirt floors often have a humidity level of more than 90%.
- Few basements have that kind of humidity and generally it isn't a problem. For one thing, a lower humidity means that your root cellar's natural air circulation is probably good enough to prevent the growth of mould on your vegetables.
- If you do have a very humid basement you might see signs of mould on your produce. If this happens you will need to increase the air circulation by adding a vent or taking advantage of a small window.
- Moisture is necessary to prevent your

produce from drying out. It is particularly important for root crops such as carrots, beets, and parsnips. You can bring humidity to these crops by storing them in damp sand—this is discussed in the next chapter. Baskets of potatoes, rutabaga, and cabbage can be covered with damp sheets or burlap bags. You can also add moisture to the air by sprinkling water on the floor or by covering the floor in damp shavings or sawdust.

There are three temperature zones in a root cellar.

- The coldest is on the floor and this is where potatoes, rutabaga, carrots, parsnips, beets, and leeks should be kept. It is a good idea to put a few boards under your storage baskets so they do not sit directly on the floor.
- The second temperature zone is located above the floor and this is where I have some shelves. Here I keep my cabbages and my apples. Apples must be stored above potatoes because they emit ethylene gas and this will cause your potatoes to sprout. Many people also store their jars of canned fruits and vegetables on these shelves
- Finally the warmest part of a root cellar is near the ceiling. It is here that I hang mesh bags of onions and garlic.

Many people ask me about mice. I have a few in my basement but they do not seem to get into my produce. I also have a cat that keeps the area around my house relatively mouse free and I send her into the basement once or twice during the winter. If you have a mouse problem I would suggest you set traps or borrow a cat—it is not a good idea to use poison around food.

Do not be discouraged if you feel your root cellar options are less than perfect. I am constantly amazed at the quality of my produce and I have a fairly dry area with no outside ducting. In a regular year, most of my produce stores well into February or March and I still have excellent carrots, onions, garlic, and cabbages in late April.

Harvesting and Eating

August and September is the time to really enjoy local produce. Corn, broccoli, peppers, tomatoes, zucchini, cucumbers, squash, onions, and potatoes are all readily available at farmer's markets and roadside stands. We also try to enjoy as much local fruit as possible since this is the best time for plums, peaches, cantaloupe, pears, and early apples. Most of the fruit we enjoy fresh, however I have included a recipe for poached pears that is truly wonderful. In my area wild blueberries are available at many small roadside stands. They freeze well, without any preparation, and are great in pancakes, muffins, cooked cereals, and smoothies throughout the winter. If you are really serious about storing fruit for the winter you can buy large quantities of peaches, plums, and pears and can them in a light sugar syrup—consult a canning book.

Freezing tip—Corn is easy to freeze. Bring a large pot of water to boil, drop in the cobs of corn, and allow the water to come back to a boil. Boil for 2 minutes, remove the corn, plunge into a sink of cold water, and then drain. To remove the kernels, stand the cob on end on a cutting board and run a knife under the kernels, from top to bottom. Place in freezer bags and freeze.

Harvesting and Storage Techniques

Potatoes

Potatoes are ready to be harvested when the green leafy tops of the plants have died down and the plants look like they are dead. This is usually sometime in September. Storage potatoes should have developed a slightly thicker skin than new potatoes, so dig up one plant and use your thumb to test the skin. If the skin rubs off easily, wait another few weeks to harvest. It is best to dig potatoes on a cloudy day because they should dry without sun. I prefer to use a garden fork and carefully dig about one foot away from the plant, gradually working my way around it. Once dug, leave the potatoes on the soil for a few hours to dry. Then carefully sort them and put any damaged potatoes in a pile to be used first. Do not rub off the dirt, just put the potatoes in half-bushel baskets or strong cardboard boxes and bring them into your basement or cold cellar. They need to be stored in total darkness so it may be necessary to cover the baskets with newspaper or cardboard.

Onions and Garlic

Onions and garlic can be harvested once their tops have dried up and gone brown. They should be pulled from the soil, turned root side up, and left in the garden to dry for two or three, preferably sunny days. Then they can be moved to the kitchen for immediate use or cured for storage. To cure, find a shady spot and lay the bulbs out so that they are off the ground but also have some air circulation. I use an old wooden pallet and leave the bulbs out for about two weeks. If the spot is sunny you can cover the bulbs with a light cotton sheet, held down by some rocks. Store both onions and garlic in some sort of mesh bag or open basket— again because they need the air circulation. Restaurants often have large onion sacks to give away and the smaller sacks work well for garlic.

Squash

Winter squash should be harvested before the first fall frost because if they are touched by frost they will not store well. Cut them from the vines, leaving 2-4" of stem, and bring them into a warm, airy spot to cure for about two weeks before storing them. A porch works well or they can cure outside if you make sure to bring them in when there is a danger of frost. You can rub off any dirt when they are dry but do not wash them. Be careful not to carry them by their stems or bruise them as all these things diminish their storage capabilities.

Squash stores best in a cool, dark place with low humidity. An unheated closet is ideal although if you have a dry root cellar it will keep on shelves that are nearer to the ceiling as it is warmer there than at the floor. Some squash will keep well into spring but others will begin to soften or go mouldy; check them often and cook any that are looking suspect. If you need to cook several at once, they are easily frozen in meal-sized chunks on a cookie tray and then placed in freezer bags.

Peppers

Sweet peppers are easy to freeze. Take out the seeds and cut the peppers into 1/2" cubes, place on cookie sheets, and bag when frozen. They do not have the texture of fresh peppers but they do add flavour to sauces and soups.

Tomatoes

Tomatoes are at their best in August and should be enjoyed as much as possible. Although tomatoes will continue to ripen into September, their flavour isn't quite the same as it is in the heat of summer. I often buy a bushel of local tomatoes in August to preserve for the winter. Some of these I cook up and bottle in one-quart Mason jars and others I freeze. I find the easiest way to freeze tomatoes is to wash them and place the whole tomatoes on baking trays. When frozen, transfer to freezer bags. The skins peel off when they are defrosted and they are easy to use. Tomatoes can also be dried in your oven for a winter taste sensation. Wash the tomatoes and cut them in half, or if they are really large in several slices. Place on a glass baking dish (metal tends to burn the tomatoes) and dry in the oven for about 2 hours at 150°F/ 65° C.

Tomato tip: Often there are still many unripe tomatoes on the vine in September. You can help them to ripen by doing a drastic pruning and removing as many branches as possible. This allows more sun to reach the fruit, speeding up the ripening process.

Salad Greens

The salad greens that were planted in July can be cut in August. After they have been harvested once or twice I like to let this planting of greens continue to grow. With a bit of thinning they will grow into larger plants that can be harvested in the fall and used in soups, stews, stir-fries, and curries.

- Kale is a surprisingly delicious and nutritious fall vegetable. I gradually thin the kale plants until they are 12-16" apart.
- Tatsoi is actually a type of baby pak choi and the small greens will mature into beautiful rosettes that are wonderful in stir-fries. They should be thinned so that they are 9-12" apart.
- Arugula will mature into a spicy green that is great cooked and can be used much like spinach in soups, lasagna, or *spanokopita*. It only needs a light thinning so aim for a final spacing of 4-6".

A rosette if Tatsoi that has grown from thinning a section of salad greens.

To thin, allow the plants to grow to about 6-8" in height. Then go through the bed and gradually thin as much as you can without causing too much root disturbance. Give the remaining plants a few days to re-establish themselves and then repeat the process several times over a period of a week or two. The thinning does not have to be perfect. If there are two or three plants growing close together, one will outstrip its neighbours and grow to maturity. As these greens get larger they no longer need the floating row cover to protect them from flea beetles.

Vegetable Juice — This is a delicious way to use up extra produce. In a food processor, purée 2-3 dozen tomatoes and 3-4 onions and place in a large stock pot. Add any combination of puréed green and/or hot peppers, parsley, carrots, zucchini, beets, basil, salad greens, and spinach and anything else you think might work. Simmer for 30 minutes. Strain through a coarse sieve or colander to remove the larger pulp. Return to the pot and add 2 tbsp salt, 2 tbsp vinegar and 4 tbsp sugar. Simmer another 5 minutes and can in Mason jars or allow to cool and serve. If you have a juicer you can coarsely chop the vegetables, cook them, and then juice them.

Available Foods

In My Garden	In My Freezer	At the Grocery
Salad Greens	Tomatoes	Tomatoes
Lettuce	Pesto	Green and yellow beans
Spinach	Corn	Lettuce
Green Onions	Rhubarb	Cucumbers
Swiss Chard	Strawberries	Beets
Beets	Raspberries	Sprouts
Dill	Blueberries	Carrots
Coriander		Peppers
Basil		Corn
Parsley		Mushrooms
Yellow and green beans		Cabbage
Cucumbers		Broccoli
Zucchini		Cauliflower
Tomatoes		Potatoes
Peppers		Onions
Onions		Plums
Garlic		Peaches
Carrots		Apples
Potatoes		Cantaloupe
		Pears

Menu Ideas for August and September include:

Cucumbers with sour cream or yogurt and dill

Cucumber, Tomato, and Basil Salad

Danish Cucumber Salad

Greek Salad with lettuce, cucumbers, green peppers, and tomatoes

Salade Niçoise

Spinach and Mushroom Salad

Broccoli and Carrot Salad

Sliced Tomatoes with fresh garlic

Fresh Tomato Salsa

Fresh Tomato Soup

Gazpacho

Roasted Tomatoes

Steamed Green Beans

Marinated Green Beans

Grilled Roasted Vegetable and Cheese Sandwiches

Tortillas with refried beans, hot peppers, tomatoes, and lettuce

Sautéed Swiss Chard with onions and garlic

Black Beans and Rice with garlic, hot peppers, onions, Swiss chard, basil, and coriander

Pasta with garlic, onions, hot peppers, tomatoes, and zucchini

Sautéed Zucchini with onions, garlic, tomatoes, and/or hot peppers, and/or basil

Chicken Soup or Stew with tomatoes, hot peppers, and corn

Stir-Fry with peppers, hot peppers, onions, garlic, and zucchini

Black Bean Salad with green onions, hot-peppers, corn, basil, and coriander

New Potatoes with butter and fresh dill

Potato and Green Bean Salad

Summer Salad with arugula, tomatoes, and cucumber

Tabouleh—a Middle Eastern Salad with tomatoes and parsley

Steamed Beets

Beet Sandwiches

Potato and Beet Salad

Corn on the cob

Corn Pancakes

Tomato and Corn Salad

Poached Pears with ginger and lemon— a nice way to use fresh pears

A Few Recipes

Fresh Tomato Salsa

4 ripe tomatoes, diced
1 green pepper, diced
1 medium onion, finely chopped
2 cloves garlic, finely chopped
2 medium hot peppers
1 bunch fresh coriander
1 tbsp oil
Juice of 1 lime – 1-2 tbsp
Salt and pepper

Wash and stem the coriander and chop it finely. Put all the vegetables in a bowl; add the oil, lime juice, salt, and pepper. Marinate about 2 hours before serving. Serves 4.

Gazpacho

6-8 tomatoes, peeled and coarsely
    chopped
1 cucumber, peeled and chopped
3 green onions, finely chopped
1 green pepper, seeded and chopped
2 cloves garlic, finely chopped
1 medium hot pepper, seeded and
chopped (optional)
4 tbsp oil
1 tbsp red wine vinegar
1/2 tsp salt
1/4 tsp ground pepper
Dash Tabasco sauce

Mix all the ingredients well. For a smoother soup, purée in the food processor. Cover and refrigerate until very cold, at least 2 hours. Serves 4.

♥ Sliced Tomatoes with Fresh Garlic

8-10 ripe tomatoes
4-6 cloves garlic, minced

Wash the tomatoes and slice them around the middle, the slices should be about 1/4" thick. Arrange them on one or two plates so that they are in a single layer. Sprinkle the tomato slices with the chopped garlic, aiming for an even distribution. This dish is part of traditional Spanish appetizer plates called *Tapas* and is wonderful with many different meals. Serves 4-6.

♥ Fresh Tomato Soup

1 medium onion, minced
2 stalks celery, minced
1 tbsp oil
1 bunch fresh basil
8-10 fresh tomatoes, diced
2-3 cups chicken or vegetable stock
2 tbsp cornstarch

In a saucepan, heat the olive oil and sauté the onion and celery over medium heat for about 5 minutes. Add the tomatoes and stock and simmer for 5-10 minutes. If you wish you can purée the soup with a hand blender. In a separate container, dissolve the cornstarch in 1/2 cup of water and add about half of this to the soup. Allow it to thicken, adding more of the cornstarch and water if you want a thicker soup. Season soup with salt, pepper, and finely chopped basil. Serves 4.

Roasted Tomatoes

10-12 medium tomatoes
2 tbsp oil
2 cloves garlic, finely chopped
1 small bunch parsley
Salt and pepper

Preheat oven to 400°F (200°C). Wash the tomatoes and cut them in half around the middle. Place the tomatoes, cut side up, in a 9" x 13" glass baking dish. Mix with oil and garlic and season with salt and pepper. Place a small amount of this mixture on each tomato half. Roast in the oven for about 45 minutes, or until the tomatoes are starting to shrivel. Serves 6-8.

Chicken Soup with Tomatoes, Hot Peppers, and Corn

4-6 cups chicken stock
2 medium onions, chopped
2 hot peppers, finely chopped
6-10 tomatoes
3 cobs corn or 1 1/2 cups corn kernels
1 small bunch basil
1 small bunch parsley
Juice of 1 lime
Salt and pepper

Cut the tomatoes into quarters. Remove the corn kernels from the cob by running a sharp knife down the length of the cob, working your way around the cob. Wash and stem the basil and the parsley and chop them both finely. Put all the ingredients into a pot with the chicken stock. Bring to a boil and simmer for about 20 minutes, mashing the tomatoes slightly with a spoon. Season with lime juice, salt, and pepper. Serves 4-6.

Potato and Green Bean Salad

3 medium potatoes, cooked and cooled
1 cup green beans
1 – 1 1/2 cups cooked beans (navy, kidney, black eyed peas or a mix)
4 green onions, finely chopped
1 hot pepper, finely chopped
1 small bunch mint, chopped
1/3 cup oil
2 tbsp lemon juice
1/4 tsp chili powder
1 tsp honey
Salt and pepper

Cut the potatoes into small cubes. Lightly steam the green beans, and then cut into 1" pieces. Combine all the ingredients in a bowl and blend until mixed. Season with salt and pepper. Serves 4-6. Later in the summer you can add tomatoes to this salad.

Tomato and Corn Salad

4 medium tomatoes, diced
3 cobs of corn
4-6 green onions, finely chopped
1/4 tsp hot pepper, finely chopped
1 small bunch basil
2 tbsp oil
1 tbsp balsamic vinegar

Blanch the corn by boiling it in water for 2-3 minutes, cooling in cold water, and then draining it. Cut the kernels from the cob using a sharp knife. Wash and stem the basil and chop it finely. Place the tomatoes, corn, onion, hot pepper, and basil in a bowl and mix well. Add the oil, vinegar, salt, and pepper. Let stand for about 1 hour before serving. Serves 4-6. (Adapted from *Nourishing Traditions* by Sally Fallon)

Corn Pancakes

2 cups cooked corn kernels
1 ¼ cup flour
1 tsp baking powder
1 egg
1 1/2 cups milk or water
1 hot pepper, minced (optional)

Mix flour and baking powder. In a 2-cup measure, combine the egg and milk or water. Add to dry ingredients and mix well. Stir in the corn kernels and optional hot pepper. Drop in large spoonfuls onto a lightly greased pan and cook as you would regular pancakes. Delicious with maple syrup. Serves 4.

♥ Broccoli and Carrot Salad

1 medium head broccoli
2 medium carrots, grated
1/2 cup sunflower seeds
1/3 cup plain yogurt
1/3 cup mayonnaise
2 tsp lemon juice
Salt and pepper

I don't usually grow broccoli but this recipe from my friend, Carlina is just too good not to include. Cut the broccoli stems from the rest of the head, trim off the ends and the tough outer layer, and grate as you would carrots. Finely chop the head of the broccoli. Combine all the ingredients in a bowl and mix well. Serves 4-6.

Danish Cucumber Salad

3-4 cucumbers
1 cup water
3 tbsp lemon juice
1-2 tsp sugar

Slice the cucumbers very thinly—the slicer found on the side of a kitchen grater works well. Mix the water, lemon juice, and sugar and pour over the cucumbers. Let stand for 1 hour. Serves 4-6.

♥ Grilled Roasted Vegetable and Cheese Sandwiches

2 red peppers
1 zucchini
1-2 medium onions
3 tbsp oil
3-4 tbsp red wine vinegar
1 clove garlic, finely chopped
1 small bunch basil
4 slices light rye bread or 1 baguette
1 cup arugula
1/2 cup grated cheese
Salt and pepper

Preheat oven to 400°F (200°C). Slice the peppers, zucchini, and onions. Place them in a 9" x 13" glass baking dish along with the chopped garlic. Drizzle with oil and red wine vinegar and mix so that the vegetables are coated. Bake for 25 minutes or until the vegetables are tender. Slice the baguette in half lengthways. Arrange the slices of bread or the baguette on a cookie sheet. Layer the bread with the greens, spoon the roasted vegetables on top, and season with salt and pepper. Top it off with a few basil leaves and some grated cheese. Place under the broiler until the cheese is melted. Serves 4.

Sautéed Swiss Chard with Onions, Garlic, and Tomatoes

1 large bunch Swiss chard
2 onions
3-4 cloves garlic, finely chopped
6-8 tomatoes
3 tbsp oil
Salt and pepper

Wash the Swiss chard, remove the tougher parts of the stem, and coarsely chop the remainder. Peel the onions and slice them in wedges like the segments of an orange. Cut the tomatoes in quarters. In a large frying pan, heat the oil and sauté the onions and garlic over medium heat for about 5 minutes. Add the Swiss chard and tomatoes, cook for another 10-15 minutes, stirring often to blend the vegetables. Season with salt and pepper. Serves 4.

Summer Salad with Arugula, Tomatoes, and Cucumber

4 cups arugula
1 bunch green onions
1 small cucumber
2-3 tomatoes
2 tbsp fresh dill
1 tbsp lemon juice
3 tbsp oil

Wash the vegetables. Chop the green onions, cucumber, and tomatoes. Finely chop the dill. Place the arugula in a salad bowl and top with the chopped vegetables and dill. Toss with lemon juice and oil. Serves 4.

Tabouleh

1 cup bulgur
1 small bunch mint
1 1/2 cup boiling water
1 huge bunch parsley
1/4 cup lemon juice
1 bunch green onions
1/4 cup oil
3-4 tomatoes
2 cloves garlic
Salt and pepper

Combine the bulgur and boiling water in a large bowl. Cover and let stand 15-20 minutes. Add lemon juice and oil and mix well. Just before serving, clean and chop the garlic, mint, parsley, green onions, and tomatoes and add to the salad. Season with salt and pepper. Serves 6.

Poached Pears with Ginger and Lemon

8 slightly underripe pears
2 cups water
1/2 cup sugar
1/2 inch fresh ginger, peeled and finely chopped
1-2 tsp zested lemon rind
Juice of half a lemon

Cut the pears in quarters, then carefully peel them and remove the cores. In a large saucepan, combine the remaining ingredients and bring to a boil. Simmer for about five minutes, then add the pears and simmer until just soft. This will take from 5 to 15 minutes depending on how ripe your pears are. Place the whole mixture in a bowl and allow to cool. Serve with plain yogurt or whipped cream. Serves 4-6.

Food for Thought
Agriculture and Oil

Our modern way of life, both the good and the bad, has evolved almost entirely as a result of the availability of cheap oil, natural gas, and coal. The discovery of oil in the late nineteenth century launched a revolution in technology that has c ompletely transformed our lives and our society. Perhaps because oil was so cheap, or perhaps because it brought such instant and easy wealth, this transformation has resulted in a society that is extremely wasteful and an economy that is overly dependent upon excess material consumption.[2]

The face of agriculture has been completely changed by the discovery of fossil fuels. Nitrogen, an element essential for vegetative growth, was traditionally replenished through the application of both human and animal manures, as well as through the planting of green manure crops that absorb and trap atmospheric nitrogen in the soil. In 1909, two German chemists, Fritz Haber and Carl Bosch, came up with a method of fixing atmospheric nitrogen by combining it with hydrogen to make ammonia. This ammonia synthesis was initially fuelled by coal and later by natural gas and oil. It has had the effect of essentially doubling the amount of available nitrogen in the biosphere.[3] Today inorganic nitrogen fertilizers account for half of agricultural nitrogen input. This has led to a dramatic increase in food production in the twentieth century, closely paralleled by an equally dramatic rise in human population. It has also resulted in serious pollution problems with nitrogen runoff from fertilizers ending up in lakes, streams, and rivers. I think it is worth considering that science never asked why this nitrogen deficiency existed in the first place. For me, the answer lies in the fact that our society disposes of human waste rather than finding safe ways to return it to the land. We do not observe the principles of a closed loop system and this has resulted in serious depletion of our soils and a need for artificial fertilizers.

Agricultural machinery, manufactured with fossil fuels and running on gasoline and diesel fuel has enabled farmers to grow more food on more land with greater speed. Traditionally, about one third of all agricultural land was used to grow food for oxen and horses; this land is now available for food production.[4] Fewer farmers are needed to grow the same amount of food and farms have become larger, full of very expensive machinery, and increasingly corporate-owned. The introduction of oil-based herbicides and pesticides in the 1960s resulted in even higher yields and a host of environmental problems. Subsistence farming has become less and less viable and in the last fifty years many rural communities have disappeared.[5] Add to the picture oil-fuelled processing and packaging operations and storage and distribution systems and it is easy to understand how it takes ten calories of fossil fuel energy to produce just one calorie of food. Somehow, a whole series of what seemed like progressive and energy saving innovations have led to today's energy intensive food system.

But even as environmentalists and citizens focus on agriculture's excessive dependency upon fossil fuels, there is a whole other group of experts who are sending out a different set of warning flags—that of a rapidly approaching and steep decline in the availability of both oil and natural gas. 'Peak Oil' is as much of buzzword today as 'global warming' and 'climate change' were a decade ago. And perhaps, in what may be the ultimate irony, one could very well take care of the other. There are many who believe that our lifestyles will soon radically change because we will no longer have the oil to fuel them. If this is so, Mother Earth may once again be able to breathe. The overriding question will be: *how do we as humans adapt to the changes?*

The idea that our supply of oil might one day dwindle is not something that we have paid a great deal of attention to. M. King Hubbert was a respected American geophysicist who worked for the United States Geological Survey and Shell Oil. As early as 1956, Hubbert predicted that American oil production would peak sometime in the early 1970s. Few people took him seriously until the oil crisis of 1970-71 when oil prices went from $3 to $10 a barrel and the U.S. public got its first inkling that American oil production might be limited. Fortunately, there was still the Middle East, which contains 60% of all the recoverable oil reserves in the world. Geologists predicted that Middle East oil production would peak sometime in the first decade of the twenty-first

century and many believe that it is in fact peaking now.[6] If this is true, we may be facing serious supply and price issues within the next five to ten years.

One must understand the nature of peak oil in order to see why there really is cause for concern. A graph of oil production over time does not look like a gentle hill, with a smooth upward curve, a long plateau at the top, and an equally gentle downward slope. Instead, it looks more like a termite mound: the uphill side is steep, the top is small and rounded, and the downhill side is also very steep. What this means is that before the end of the twenty-first century we may have oil production levels that are similar to those of the early twentieth century—i.e. almost minimal. When one looks at a graph of oil well production, it follows a similarly steep up and down curve.[7] When a well is first drilled, the lighter, better quality oil comes out first and fastest. About half way through the reserve, the rate of extraction peaks and then falls dramatically. The remaining oil is heavier, the pressure in the well is lower, and often water, carbon dioxide, or natural gas must be pumped into the well to push the oil out. This heavier oil is also of poorer quality and requires more energy to refine. Similarly, the first wells drilled in a field have the greatest pressure but as more wells are drilled, the oil table and the pressure go down and the energy needed for extraction goes up, as of course does the cost. The first wells drilled in the 1930s and 40s yielded about 250-300 barrels of oil per foot of drilling; today we see production levels of about ten barrels of oil per foot of drilling.[8]

Not everyone accepts the idea of an impending oil shortage. Professor Mark Jaccard is an energy economist at Simon Fraser University in British Columbia who has written a book entitled ***Sustainable Fossil Fuels: The Unusual Suspect in the Quest for Clean and Enduring Energy.*** Jaccard argues that the so called "Hubbert's Peak" refers only to oil under natural pressure that easily gushes from an oil well. It does not include unconventional sources of oil, such as the tar sands, arctic oil, oil derived from coal, or oil that is extracted with the addition of pressure to the well. Jaccard believes that all of these methods are affordable at costs of less than $75 per barrel and that current reserves can last hundreds of years.[9] The challenge then is to clean up the burning of fossil fuels, focus on conservation, and develop alternative and renewable energy sources. In terms of the environment, Jaccard argues that there must be regulations and taxes to protect our water, land, and air. The atmosphere cannot be seen as a free waste receptacle and we must consider removing CO_2 from the atmosphere through a process of carbon capture and storage.[10] This can be accomplished through a system of pipelines that return CO_2 to empty oil wells where it is injected into the ground, a process that many argue is as safe as current natural gas usage.

No one can really predict which scenario will ultimately be proven true, but in the meantime we might want to consider our options. An analysis of alternative energy sources produces mixed results:

- Coal reserves are huge but coal is both inefficient and polluting.
- Nuclear power is very expensive and many consider it unsafe. It is estimated that the U.S. would have to increase its nuclear capacity by about 500-fold just to meet its transportation needs.
- Government and scientists seem to be in agreement that natural gas reserves are in decline.[11]
- Increasing coal and nuclear power capabilities will require enormous amounts of energy to build the necessary infrastructure. If the price of oil doubles or triples, they become even less affordable.

Renewable energy sources provide some hope and many experts feel they will grow dramatically over the next few decades.

- On a large scale, it is generally accepted that mega wind, tidal, hydro, or geothermal installations will not meet our current energy demands, primarily because they tend to be intermittent and inconveniently located.[12]
- Micro-hydro lacks the environmental problems of mega-hydro and has been developed in rural communities in Holland, Sri Lanka, and Zimbabwe. Many small towns and villages in North America, including where I live, have small dams and turbines that once provided electricity to the community. One long-time Sydenham resident described how the water at the dam was used to power several mills during the day and diverted to the turbine in the evenings for residential use. Electricity was also available on Monday mornings so that those fortunate enough to have an electric washing

machine could do their laundry.

～ Passive and active solar systems and small windmills are becoming more affordable and could considerably reduce our residential dependence on oil. It is interesting to note that China is currently the world's largest producer of windmills.

Analysis of so-called clean fuels such as ethanol, biodiesel, and hydrogen indicate that these fuels require more energy to produce than they actually provide. For example, one acre of corn will yield 328 gallons of ethanol but it takes about one thousand gallons of oil to plant, grow, harvest, and refine that acre of corn. This represents a net energy loss of 41%.[13] There are currently fourteen million hectares of U.S. farmland planted in crops for biofuel; India has the same amount, and Brazil plans to plant 120 million hectares in biofuel crops. The trend towards diverting land from food production to biofuel crop production is extremely alarming and will only result in more poor people going hungry so that those in the developing world can continue to drive their cars.

It is hard to imagine what agriculture might look like without oil but Cuba can provide some very valuable insights and expertise. In many ways, this small island with a population of 11.4 million is a local and organic foodie's dream. An economic crisis in the early 1990s resulted in a 50% drop in agricultural production and severe food shortages. Prior to the crisis, Cuba had already invested considerable resources into agricultural research, land reform, and a well educated population.[14]

Through a system of both private and co-operative state farms, all on government-owned land that is leased for free, Cubans grow approximately 80% of the fresh produce they consume.[15]. These farms use on the average only 5% of the energy that North American agriculture uses. The Cuban government has provided massive resources to farmers and they are currently in the top tier of state salaries. Large farming co-operatives of five or more acres are found throughout Cuban cities. One small city boasts thirteen such farms that supply consumers, local schools, hospitals, and daycare facilities. Since transportation fuel and electricity for refrigeration are both expensive and unreliable, most food is both local and seasonal. The food is also organic as agricultural chemicals are largely unavailable—though even if they were it is doubtful that consumers would want the pollution in their cities. Not everyone may like the sound of such a rigorous system of food production but it is well worth noting that Cuba leads nearly every developing country in human development and is currently the only country in the World Wildlife Fund's 2006 Living Planet Report to come even close to meeting targets for sustainable living and development.[16]

Decreased oil supplies and sharp price increases will affect much more than agriculture. The most obvious consequence is that almost everything we buy and do will get more expensive. Many believe our economy will go through a long series of recessions and that we will no longer have economic growth. Others see widespread political upheavals and more than fifty years of resource wars in the Middle East. One would hope that we have the potential to be the authors of this story and find far more positive and innovative outcomes—a cleaner, less wasteful society, a strengthening of community, and vibrant local food systems.

Sources and Further Information

Cockrall-King, Jennifer, *Why don't we have gardens like this?* in Macleans Magazine, Toronto, September 3, 2007, page 60.

Greene, Gregory, *The End of Suburbia: Oil Depletion and the Collapse of the American Dream*, Electric Wallpaper Films, 2004.

Heinberg, Richard, *The Party's Over: Oil, War and the Fate of Industrial Societies*, New Society Publishers, Gabriola Island, B.C., 2004.

Jaccard, Mark, *Sustainable Fossil Fuels: An Unusual Suspect in the Quest for Clean and Enduring Energy*, Ideas, CBC Radio, August, 2007.

Pfeiffer, Dale Allen, *Eating Fossil Fuels*, New Society Publishers, Gabriola Island, B.C., 2006

Ruppert, M.C., *Crossing the Rubicon: The Decline of the American Empire at the End of the Age of Oil*, New Society Publishers, Gabriola Island, B.C., 2003.

Endnotes

1 Raymond, Dick, *The Joy of Gardening*, Garden Way Publishing, 1982, page 190.

2 Heinberg, Richard, *The Party's Over*, New Society Publishers, Gabriola Island, B.C., 2003, p. 41.

3 Ibid, p.63

4 Ibid, p.64

5 Ibid, p. 65

6 Ibid

7 Ibid

8 Heinberg, Richard, *The Party's Over*, New Society Publishers, Gabriola Island, B.C., 2003, p. 109.

9 Jaccard, Mark, *Sustainable Fossil Fuels: The Unusual Suspect in the Quest for Clean and Enduring Energy*, Ideas, CBC Radio, August, 2007.

10 Ibid

11 Heinberg, Richard, *The Party's Over*, New Society Publishers, Gabriola Island, B.C., 2003, p. 136.

12 Ibid, p. 154.

13 Ibid, p. 156.

14 Pfeiffer, Dale Allen, *Eating Fossil Fuels,* New Society Publishers, Gabriola Island, B.C., 2006, page 57

15 Cockrall-King, Jennifer, *Why don't we have gardens like this?* in Maclean's Magazine, Toronto, September 3, 2007, page 60.

16 Ibid, page 60.

The greatest gift of the garden
Is the restoration of the five senses.

— Hanna Rion (1875 – 1924), *American landscape artist*

In the Garden

Again, it seemed to make sense to group the months of October and November together—the fall garden does not change much and many plants can be harvested well into November, sometimes even into December, if the overnight temperatures don't dip too low. I am always amazed by how much produce I have in my small garden. This year there is spinach, endive, salad greens, green onions, beets, dill, coriander, parsley, kale, and Swiss chard—enough to keep us well fed for a few months! Don't forget that

Red Russian Kale in November

the endive plants need to be tied up and blanched sometime in October. I usually do three or four at a time so that the harvest can be spread over a few weeks.

The first hard frost usually comes with the full moon in October—this moon is called the Harvest Moon. If your tomatoes, peppers, and basil are still growing, this frost usually finishes them off. Be aware of the forecast and try to harvest any of these vegetables that still remain. The larger green tomatoes are worth saving. They will often ripen on a sunny windowsill or they can be fried when they are green. Peppers will keep for several weeks in the fridge. Hot peppers will continue to ripen in an open container at room temperature, and many will dry nicely for winter use.

The rest of the garden will tolerate a considerable amount of frost; it can seem quite frozen in the morning and still look amazingly good by lunch time. If it is going to be really cold (-4°C to -8°C; 17°F to 28°F), a layer of floating row cover or a small cold frame will often protect many or all of your salad vegetables, beets, green onions, kale, and Swiss chard. Kale and Swiss chard will survive even colder nights if they are covered. In this way you can extend your harvest well into November and possibly into December.

In the winter storage garden, potatoes, onions, garlic, and winter squash should have been harvested in September. Of the remaining vegetables, beets and cabbage can tolerate some frost but should not freeze hard so they should probably be harvested in early October. Leeks, carrots, parsnips, and rutabagas can all tolerate hard frosts and can be left in the ground until late October. Detailed instructions for harvesting and storage are given later in this chapter.

After the first killing frost, the cucumber, zucchini, squash, pepper, and tomato plants should be pulled and put on the compost. Other than this I do not clean up the garden in the fall; in fact, I leave it alone on purpose. The reason for this is that usually a few of the fall vegetables survive the winter and come up again in early April. When there is nothing else growing, a bit of kale, spinach, garlic, or green onion is a wonderful sight. Anything that does not survive will either decompose over the winter or can be composted in the spring.

Planting Garlic

Sometime in October, I plant 40 to 50 cloves of garlic in my summer garden. They will come up in early April and will be the first green garlic of the year. The cloves can be planted in any free space and next year's garden planned so that the area does not interfere with April's bed. If you want to grow full-sized garlic for next year then you must plant another section with 60 to 70 bulbs, either in a winter storage garden or in an area that will not be needed for your summer garden. To plant garlic:

- Dig the area and if possible add some compost or well rotted manure.
- Break your garlic bulbs into individual cloves and lay them all out on the soil.
- For green garlic, allow a spacing of 3-4" between cloves, both down and across the bed.
- For garlic bulbs, make six or seven rows across the bed and space the cloves 6-8" apart within these rows.
- Push the cloves into the ground, the root side down and the pointy side up—they should be 1-2" deep.
- Cover the area with a 4-6" layer of straw to protect the garlic during the winter.

Garlic can be ordered from a seed company or bought from a local grower. If you don't have time to find anything else you can even plant the grocery store garlic that comes from China—it will grow though it may not be as well suited to your climate as more local varieties.

The Final Harvest

Continue to pay attention to the forecast and if it is going to be really cold (below -8°C to -10°C, 17°F to 14°F), try to harvest everything that you can from the summer gardens. This usually consists of kale, Swiss chard, beets, tatsoi, green onions, and perhaps some lettuce or salad greens. These will keep in the fridge for several weeks, extending the green vegetable supply even further. Well covered kale and Swiss chard will survive temperatures below -10°C (14°F) so it is up to you if you want to leave some in the garden for another few weeks. Again, I try to make sure that I leave five or six bunches of green onions in the ground to eat the next spring.

2007 Vegetable Countdown

- October 12: Harvested tomatoes, peppers, and basil
- November 17: Ate our last spinach salad
- November 22: Harvested lettuce, endive, arugula, and parsley
- November 25: Ate our last endive salad; parsley and salad greens froze
- December 1: Had dinner with a friend who served a salad with lettuce harvested from her cold frame
- December 3: Harvested kale, Swiss chard, and green onions
- December 5: Heavy snow and -12°C (unusually early) - no more garden!
- December 18: ate our last Swiss chard and kale
- January 9: January thaw, harvested a large bunch of Swiss chard that was still alive and well under an old cotton sheet.

Overwintering Vegetables

Planting vegetables specifically to survive the winter and grow again in the spring is called overwintering. I think this idea has some potential and one day I would like to do some experimenting. There are varieties of spinach and lettuce that are specifically meant for overwintering. They should be seeded in August or September and allowed to grow into the fall without being harvested; many people recommend planting them in a cold frame. As the weather gets colder, they should be mulched with a gradually increasing thickness of straw. In the spring the straw should be removed gradually as the weather warms up. If successful, there will be a plant, partly grown from last year, now growing again from an already established root system.

Turning the Compost

There is one fairly major job that I like to do in the fall and that is to turn the compost. Compost does not have to be turned—a single pile can be added to for years and left when full. It will eventually decompose and make good compost. However, I want to use some compost every year so I prefer to work with two compost bins: an actively accumulating pile (Bin #1) and an actively decomposing pile (Bin #2). In order to keep my system going, the compost needs some work every year. Before you begin, if at all possible, it really helps to have a bale of straw and 12 to 18 pails of manure to add to the compost as it is turned. I usually work at this job over a few weeks and collect my manure, six to eight pails at a time, from a nearby riding stable. This is my method:

STEP 1: Empty Bin #2. This is the bin that contains compost from last year and it should be nice and black by now. Spread this compost on the garden—I dump small piles wherever there is some free space as there are still a lot of plants in my garden. (Note: often larger items such as corncobs do not fully decompose: they will do no harm in the garden or they can be set aside and returned to the active compost pile—Bin #1). If this is your first year of gardening, Bin #2 should be empty so Step #1 is pretty easy!

STEP 2: This is the turning process. Take your garden fork and move 6-12" of compost from the top of Bin #1 and spread it over the bottom of the now empty Bin #2. Add a 3-4" layer of straw and top this off with one or two pails of manure. Then add more compost from Bin #1, followed by more straw, and more manure. Continue in this way until Bin #1 is empty.

STEP 3: This part requires no work. Let Bin #2 sit over the winter and throughout the next summer. It should be ready to use by next fall. The process of decomposition can be speeded up by watering the compost, aerating it, fluffing it up, or even turning it a third time. I have avoided all of this extra work and have always been pleased with the quality of my compost.

STEP 4: Fill the empty Bin #1 with new material until next fall when it will be turned.

Compost can be turned at any time but I find the fall works best for several reasons:
- Bin #1 is usually very full.
- Generally there is more rain in the fall, winter, and early spring so my newly turned compost can take advantage of this.
- I want to have finished compost for my garden when I plant in early April. But often the pile is still frozen in early spring and I can't get at the compost. I avoid this problem by emptying Bin #2 in the fall.
- The fall is not such a busy time.
- It is easy to find straw at gardening centres.

Equipment

It is really important to take some time to put away all of your tools and the floating row cover before winter. The row cover will not survive more than a year or two if it is left in the garden. It should be spread out on a sunny day, allowed to dry, and then folded and stored. I prefer to store it in an outside shed because it will have some soil on it and I don't want any crawly creatures making their way into my basement. All of the watering equipment must be disconnected and stored in a dry place. It may be necessary to shut off the outside water pipe so that it doesn't freeze and burst. Any plastic pails and rain barrels should be emptied of water and put away—it is easy to put this off and then before you know it, the water freezes solid and your nice rain barrel splits down the side (I am ashamed to say that I have done this more than once!). The seedling trays and pots should be gathered up and put away along with your tools. If some of your tools are rusty, a light sanding and a coat of mineral or vegetable oil on the metal will help to prevent further rusting.

Other than that—**YOU'RE ALL DONE.** Give yourself a big hug, be proud of all that you have learned and grown, and don't spend one single minute berating yourself for the things you didn't get right—there is always next year!!

Thinking ahead: It is a good idea to buy a few bags of composted sheep manure and a bag of soil-less mix for next year's transplants. They are much easier to find now than in March, when they are often covered in snow or ice.

OCTOBER GARDEN SUMMARY

- ☐ Watch the weather and protect your plants as necessary.
- ☐ Harvest as much as possible before that final, hard freeze.
- ☐ Harvest beets, cabbage, carrots, parsnips, leeks, and rutabagas for winter storage.
- ☐ Spread compost on your garden and turn your new compost pile.
- ☐ Put away tools, watering equipment, and floating row cover.

In the Summer Gardens

- Plant garlic to be harvested as green garlic early next spring. Mulch with straw

In the Winter Garden

- Plant garlic to be harvested as full-sized garlic bulbs next summer. Mulch with straw.

Harvesting and Eating

The fall months are the last kick at the can for fresh greenery until spring. All of the vegetables that were planted in the summer gardens in August should now be mature and should hold their quality over the fall season.

- You can **bring the garden inside** by planting **parsley** and **basil** in a large pot and placing it in a sunny spot in your kitchen. **Chives** and **garlic chives** can also be planted in pots but they must first freeze outside before you bring them in—try bringing the pots in sometime in January for a nice treat.

- **Tomatoes** ripen on the windowsill until early November. We eat them in salads and also make some fried green tomatoes.

- **Hot Peppers** that were picked in October sit in a bowl on my counter. They will dry slowly and can be used throughout the winter.

- As much as possible we eat a lot of **spinach, lettuce, endive,** and **salad greens** in October.

- There are **tatsoi** and **arugula** plants from a July planting of salad greens that have grown to full size—they are wonderful in stir-fries as well as in soups, stews, and curries. Mature arugula has a wonderful flavour and is delicious added to egg dishes, pastas, and soups.

- **Parsley** and **green onions** can survive many frosts and I try not to forget to use either of these vegetables.

- By late November there is only **Swiss chard** and **kale** left in the garden. My family really likes kale in a cream sauce or in a soup. Swiss chard needs a bit more disguising, but it seems to go over well in casseroles or lasagne.

- November is **carrot** month in our family—they are at their sweetest and crunchiest and we try to enjoy them as much as possible before we start into the other storage vegetables. As the weather gets colder, our meals begin to change towards some hearty fall soups and stews but there is always a bowl of fresh carrots for lunches, snacks, and suppers.

- I find that **leeks** and **beets** are the shortest-lived of all my storage vegetables; I do my best to use them up in November, December, and early January.

John Wise of Wiseacre Farms in Centreville, Ontario has supplied me with wonderful winter vegetables since I moved to my small village lot ten years ago.

✎ The **apples** in my root cellar are also at their best before Christmas and I encourage my family to eat as many as they like.

✎ Finally, I buy a few bags of **cranberries**, which I store in my freezer.

Freezing Tip: Swiss chard, spinach, and arugula are easy to freeze. Harvest the plants and wash them thoroughly. Remove the coarser stems and steam the leaves for about five minutes. Drain and chop the leaves and then place in freezer bags. They can all be used like frozen spinach and are nice in soups, lasagna, and spanokopita.

Winter Storage Techniques

Whether growing a winter storage garden or buying a supply of vegetables from a local farmer, your produce should be in cold storage by early November. If the weather is mild, you should delay harvesting or picking up your vegetables until it is colder as they will not store well in a warm root cellar. If this is not possible, consider keeping them in a shed or unheated garage until your storage area is cold enough. Similarly, if the weather is unseasonably cold, you may want to move the process forward a few weeks. Getting storage vegetables from a farmer and then storing them in the root cellar will probably take the better part of one day but then there is nothing else to be done until spring.

The better the quality of your produce, the more likely it is to store well. Sort through your vegetables and put anything that is damaged into separate containers to be used first. Check your produce regularly and use up or throw out anything that is starting to deteriorate.

Once a year you should completely empty your root cellar, sweep out all the cobwebs, and air out your storage baskets.

Sand

Many root vegetables are stored in damp sand. I get my sand from places that sell topsoil and gravel. The sand is usually in an open pile, which means it is moist—I bring my own shovel and five or six smaller pails, which I fill for about $1 a pail. Be careful that the sand is not overly wet as this can damage your vegetables and encourage them to rot. I do not recommend bagged sand from hardware stores because it is dry and also because it is often washed with some sort of chemical.

Beets

Beets can withstand a few light frosts but they should not freeze hard before they are harvested (below -4°C, 24°F if they are uncovered). Pull the plants from the garden and rub off any excess dirt. Cut the tops off, about 1" above the crown but do not cut off the roots from the beets. Cutting into beets at either end will cause them to bleed during cooking and will considerably affect their flavour.

I store my beets in a small plastic pail, layered with damp sand (see directions under carrots). Beets need cold

temperatures or they will begin to sprout, so if your the weather is still mild or if your storage area is not ideal, you might want to store a large bag in the fridge. Either way they keep well for two to three months.

Cabbage

Sometime in October you must harvest your cabbage—again, the plants should not have had a hard frost. To harvest, take a strong knife and cut the stem, slightly below the cabbage itself. Then remove the loose outer leaves. Cabbages can be stored in open bushel baskets or on shelves that have some air circulation. They should be stored on or near the floor of your root cellar. Often the outer leaves will go mouldy, but they can be peeled off and the cabbage underneath is still perfectly fine. I have had cabbage keep until April in my root cellar and if I then put it in my fridge it will last into May. The denser and firmer a cabbage is, the longer it will keep, so try to eat the looser wrapped heads first.

Carrots

Carrots will tolerate many frosts; in fact you should to wait to harvest them because the frosts make them sweeter. You can harvest all of your carrots at once, in late October or early November, or you can leave some in the ground and cover them with a layer of straw. These can be dug until the ground really freezes, sometime in December. When digging carrots, remove any excess dirt but do not let them dry or cure—they should go straight into your storage containers.

To store carrots, first cut off the top 1" of each carrot, otherwise it will start to sprout. Find a comfortable place to do this because it can be hard on the back if there is a bushel or more to do. Carrots store best in damp sand but one or two bushels of carrots requires a great deal of sand, which is heavy to lug up and down the basement stairs. To reduce the amount of sand needed, I divide my carrots in thirds—one-third for short-term storage (sometime into January) and the remaining two-thirds for long-term storage into May.

- I place the short-term storage carrots in a breathable bag (again I use a feed bag) on the floor of the root cellar. They will lose some moisture but they are easily 'reconstituted.' I bring up about a dozen at a time, clean them, cut them in half lengthways, and place them in a bowl of cold water overnight. By morning they are crisp and sweet.

- I try to save the larger carrots for long-term storage; these I store in seven-gallon plastic pails. At the bottom of each pail I place a 2-3" layer of damp sand, followed by a single, tightly packed layer of carrots, then another layer of sand, a layer of carrots, and so on, finishing with a layer of sand. The pails go on the floor of the root cellar. I place a sheet of heavy cardboard over the pails so that the sand retains its moisture. I usually have six or seven of these pails of carrots and they keep amazingly well into May.

Parsnips

If you grew parsnips for winter storage you must decide whether to harvest them now or in the spring. I prefer to harvest them in the spring, mainly because I have such a variety of foods in the fall and the spring menu is pretty lean by comparison. You can also do a bit of both - you can store some of your crop in your cold storage, cutting off the tops 1' below the crown and storing in damp sand (see directions under carrots) and you can cover the remaining crop with a thick layer (12-18") of straw. To protect the parsnips from freezing, this straw should extend outwards about two to three feet from the sides of the bed.

Leeks

Leeks are like kale; they are happy to stay in the garden into November. When you do decide to bring them in, harvest them root and all—shake off some soil but leave a reasonable amount. Place the leeks, root side down, into a seven-gallon plastic pail. You can put some damp sand in the bottom of the pail and bury the roots in this sand or you can just put the roots in as they are. Leeks keep well for about two months—the outer leaves dry out quickly and by the end of January most of the leek is dry.

Cleaning leeks: Leeks from the garden are usually much dirtier than their store-bought counterparts and they need to be cleaned thoroughly. Begin by cutting off the roots and peeling away the dry outer leaves. Trim the leeks, keeping the white part and as much of the light green part as possible. Slice each leek lengthways through the middle and then cut into 1/2" slices. Place these slices in a large bowl of cold water, separating the layers as much as possible. The dirt will sink to the bottom of the bowl and the leeks can be lifted out of the water.

An apple corer is an amazing timesaving device that peels, cores, and slices an apple in seconds. It costs about $30. Picture courtesy of Lee Valley Tools

Apples

Around the middle of October, I buy several bushels of apples for the winter. I try to buy one or two bushels of early apples such as Cortlands, Macintosh, or Mutsu as well as two to four of storage apples such as Idareds, Spartans, Empires, and/or Northern Spy. These I store in liquor store boxes that are divided into twelve sections. I punch holes on all four sides of the boxes and gently place the apples in each section. The holes allow for some air circulation, the dividers keep the apples separate so that one bad apple does not spoil the whole batch, and the box keeps the apples dark and somewhat insulated. ***The boxes go in my root cellar, somewhere above the potatoes because they give off ethylene gas which will cause the potatoes to sprout.*** I find they keep well into early February; after that I enjoy them as applesauce and in pies, crisps, and compotes.

Rutabagas

Rutabagas should have several hard frosts before they are harvested. Pull the plants and cut the leaves off slightly above the top. There is no need to trim the roots. They can be stored washed or unwashed. Rutabagas tend to lose moisture and shrivel in storage; to avoid this they can be stored in damp sand or in strong plastic bags that have had a few holes poked into them. They do best on the floor of the root cellar or on a low shelf.

Available Foods

In My Garden	In My Freezer	In My Root Cellar	At the Grocery
Salad Greens	Tomatoes	Carrots	Tomatoes
Lettuce	Corn	Cabbage	Cucumbers
Endive	Swiss Chard	Onions	Sprouts
Spinach	Pesto	Garlic	Carrots
Beets	Rhubarb	Beets	Onion
Green Onions	Strawberries	Potatoes	Cabbage
Swiss Chard	Raspberries	Turnip	Mushrooms
Kale	Blueberries	Leeks	Squash
Tatsoi	Cranberries	Squash (in a closet)	Potatoes
Parsley			Apples
Dill			Lettuce*
Coriander			Beets*
Hot Peppers			Green Beans*
Tomatoes			Broccoli*
			Cauliflower*
			Pears*
			Cantaloupe*

*not available in November

Leek and Potato Soup with Carrot, Beet, and Apple Salad, and Sunflower Seed Spread

Menu Ideas for the Fall include:

Caesar Salad
Spanish Endive Salad
Cobb Salad
Spinach and Mushroom Salad
Cooked Beets
Beet Sandwiches
Grated Carrot, Beet, and Apple Salad
Beet Borscht
Fried Green Tomatoes
Sautéed Swiss Chard with onions and
  garlic
Swiss Chard and Rice Casserole
Spanokopita
Steamed Kale with Balsamic Vinegar
Creamed Kale
Kale and Potato Soup
Sunflower Seed Spread with puréed kale
  and parsley
Soup or Stew with kale, onions, garlic, and
  tomatoes
Any kind of Stir-Fry or Fried Rice with

greens, onions, carrots, and herbs
Beans and Rice with hot peppers, toma-
  toes, and greens
Fresh Carrots
Grated Carrot and Parsley Salad
Coleslaw (recipes in January section)
Leek and Potato Soup
Mustard and Leek sauce
Mushroom and Leek Quiche
Leek and Mushroom Casserole
Stews or Curries with leeks, carrots, cab-
  bage, turnip, and/or potatoes
Baked Spaghetti Squash
Spaghetti Squash with tomatoes, onions,
  garlic, and herbs
Garlic Mashed Potatoes
Oven Roasted Potatoes
Pumpkin Soup
Pumpkin Pie
Pumpkin Muffins
Apple Pie and Apple Crisp
  (recipes in January section)

A Few Recipes

Carrot, Beet, and Apple Salad

2 medium beets
3 medium carrots
2 large apples
1/4 cup raisins (optional)
1/2 cup sunflower seeds
2 tbsp lemon juice
2 tbsp oil
1/2 cup plain yogurt (optional)
Salt and pepper

Clean and peel the beets and the carrots. Using a food processor or a hand grater, grate the beets and carrots. Quarter and core the apples and chop them finely. Place everything in a bowl, with the raisins and sunflower seeds. Dress with oil and lemon juice and add yogurt if desired. Let stand several hours so the raisins can soften. You can also leave out the raisins and sunflower seeds and dress the salad with olive oil, cider vinegar, and a bit of maple syrup. Serves 4.

Carrot and Parsley Salad

4 medium carrots, grated
1 large bunch parsley, finely chopped
1 bunch green onions, finely chopped
1/4 cup oil
2 tbsp cider vinegar or lemon juice
Salt and pepper

Combine all the ingredients in a bowl and mix well. This salad is also nice with 1/2 cup each of raisins, chopped nuts, and/or sunflower seeds. Serves 4.

♥ Sunflower Seed Spread with Kale and Parsley

1 cup sunflower seeds, soaked in water for about 4 hours
1 clove garlic
4 tbsp oil
Juice of l lemon—about 3 tbsp
1 tbsp tamari sauce
1 cup parsley, washed and stemmed
1 cup kale, washed and stemmed
Salt and pepper

Drain the sunflower seeds. Coarsely chop the kale. Place all the ingredients in a food processor. (It is easier if you put the kale at the bottom.) Purée until blended. Makes a great dip for vegetables or a spread for bread and crackers. Serves 4-6.

Beet Borscht

2 tbsp butter
1-2 onions, chopped
4 medium potatoes
1 tsp caraway seed
1 tsp dill weed
2-3 beets
2 carrots
1 1/2 tbsp cider vinegar
2 cups chopped cabbage
1 1/2 tbsp honey
1 tsp salt
1 cup tomato sauce or juice

Cook the beets in 4 cups of water. Save the cooking water. Remove the beets, allow them to cool, then peel and dice them. Peel and chop the potatoes and carrots. In a large pot, sauté the onions, potatoes, and carrots in butter. Add the

cabbage, the water from the beets, caraway seeds, and salt and cook, covered, until the
vegetables are tender, about 20 minutes. Add the chopped beets, the dill, cider vinegar, honey, and tomato sauce and extra water if needed. Simmer 10 minutes and correct the seasoning. Serves 6.

Mixed Vegetable Borscht

2 tbsp butter
3-4 beets, peeled and shredded
4 leeks, cleaned and chopped
2 large carrots, cleaned and grated
2 cloves garlic, minced
2 potatoes, chopped
2 tbsp tomato paste
7 cups stock
2 bay leaves
2 cups shredded cabbage
3 cups kidney or romano beans
4 tbsp red wine vinegar
1 tsp sugar
Salt and pepper

In a large soup pot, melt the butter and sauté the beets, leeks, carrots, garlic, and potato for about 10 minutes. Add the tomato paste, bay leaves, and stock and simmer 20 minutes. Add the remaining ingredients and simmer another 10 - 15 minutes. Serves 6.

Fried Green Tomatoes

4 large green tomatoes
Salt and pepper

Slice the tomatoes so that they are 1/4 - 1/2" thick. Season with salt and pepper. Fry in butter over medium heat for several minutes, turning once. Other options include dipping the tomato slices in an egg and milk mixture, then dredging them in flour before frying. Or thinly slice one onion, fry it in butter with 1 tsp curry powder, and then add tomato slices. Serves 4.

♥ Swiss Chard and Rice Casserole

1 large bunch Swiss chard
1 cup uncooked white rice
1-2 onions
2 cups tomato sauce
1 pound tofu or ground beef
2 1/2 cups boiling water
Salt and pepper

Preheat oven to 375°F (190°C). Wash the chard, remove the tougher stems, and coarsely chop. Chop the onions. Place the rice, onions, and Swiss chard in a large covered casserole dish. Add the tomato sauce, crumbled tofu or ground beef, and the water. Stir to mix the ingredients. Cover and bake for about 1 hour or until the rice is soft. Check the casserole after about 45 minutes and add a bit more water if the rice is still crunchy. Season with salt and pepper. It is surprising how many children like this casserole. It is good as is or with sour cream or grated cheese on top. Serves 4-6.

Spanakopita

1 large onion
4 cloves garlic
1 bunch Swiss chard or arugula
2 tbsp oil
1/2 pound feta cheese
1 pound cottage cheese
4 eggs
1 tsp oregano
1 tsp basil
Salt and pepper
1/4 cup butter
12-18 sheets Phyllo pastry,

Peel and chop the onion and garlic. Wash the chard or arugula, remove the tougher stems, and chop finely (you should have 3-4 cups). In a large saucepan, sauté the onion and garlic in oil. Add the Swiss chard or arugula and cover the pan with a lid. Sauté over low heat for 5-10 minutes until the greens are cooked, stirring occasionally so nothing burns. Place the feta cheese, cottage cheese, eggs, cooked vegetables, and seasonings in a food processor and blend until smooth.

Preheat oven to 375°F (190°C). Melt the butter in a small pot. Using a pastry brush, lightly butter a 9" x 13" baking pan. Add a layer of phyllo pastry, cut to the size of the pan, and brush with butter. Add another layer of phyllo pastry, and brush with butter. Repeat this process, using 6-9 sheets of phyllo pastry. Add the contents of the food processor. Top with another 6-9 sheets of phyllo pastry, each brushed with butter. Bake for 45 minutes until golden brown. Serves 4-6.

Steamed Kale with Balsamic Vinegar

1 bunch kale (the smaller leaves are more
    tender)
Balsamic vinegar
Butter
Salt and pepper

Wash the kale and remove the tougher stems. Coarsely chop the kale and place it in a saucepan with about 2" of water in the bottom. Cover the pot and steam the kale until soft, about 10-15 minutes. Drain and serve, then pass around the balsamic vinegar and butter. Each person can drizzle a small amount of balsamic vinegar on their kale and add butter, as well as salt and pepper if they wish. Serves 4.

Kale and Potato Soup

2 onions, chopped
2 medium carrots
1 large bunch kale
4-6 cloves garlic, minced
2 tbsp oil
4 medium potatoes
1/8 - 1/4 tsp finely chopped hot pepper
1/2 lb spicy sausage and/or 2 cups cooked
    dried beans
4 cups stock

Peel the potatoes and carrots and cut into small chunks. Clean the kale, discard the tougher stems, and chop finely. In a large soup pot, add the oil and sauté the onions and garlic over medium heat for 5 minutes. Add the potatoes, carrots, hot pepper, and kale and cover with water or stock. Cook until the vegetables are tender, about 15 minutes, then add sausage and/or cooked beans and simmer another 15 minutes. Add more water if necessary and season with salt and pepper. Serves 6-8

♥ Creamed Kale (a traditional Danish recipe)

1 pound kale
4 tbsp butter
4 tbsp flour
2 cups milk or 1 cup milk and 1 cup cream
Salt and pepper

Wash the kale, remove the tougher stems, and chop into medium-sized pieces. Place in a saucepan with about 2" of water, cover, and cook over medium heat until soft, about 10-15 minutes. Put in a sieve and drain well.

In a heavy saucepan melt the butter over low heat. Stir in the flour and cook for several minutes. Gradually add the milk and possibly cream, blending to form a smooth sauce. Simmer for a few minutes, stirring constantly. Add the drained kale, season with salt and pepper, and continue cooking another 1 or 2 minutes. This dish is also good with several leeks, sliced thinly and sautéed in butter, added to the white sauce. Serves 6.

♥ Leek and Potato Soup

4-6 large leeks
4 medium potatoes
4 slices bacon, cut into 1/2" chunks or 2
    tbsp butter
4 cups stock
Salt and pepper

Clean and slice the leeks. Peel the potatoes and cut into small cubes. In a large pot, lightly cook the bacon or melt the butter, and then add the potatoes and the drained leeks. Sauté for 5 minutes, cover with stock, and simmer until vegetables are tender, about 30 minutes. Using a potato masher, a hand blender or a food processor, purée the soup to the desired consistency. Season with salt and pepper. For a creamier soup, cook vegetables in 2 cups stock and add 2 cups milk or light cream after puréeing. Heat through. Serves 4-6.

♥ Mustard and Leek Sauce

3 cloves garlic, chopped
3 cups leeks, sliced thinly
3 tbsp butter
2 cups stock
1/2 cup white wine
3-4 tbsp Dijon mustard
Juice and zest of 1/2 lemon
Salt and pepper

In a sauce pan, melt the butter over medium heat. Sauté the garlic and leeks until soft, about 5 minutes. Add the stock, white wine, mustard, and lemon juice and zest and simmer another 5 or 10 minutes. Season with salt and pepper, and simmer 2 or 3 minutes. Serve with rice and braised chicken. Serves 4. (This recipe also works well with 2 or 3 medium onions, coarsely chopped instead of the leeks).

Mushroom and Leek Quiche

2 9" pie shells
3 cups thinly sliced leeks
2 cups mushrooms, sliced
2 tbsp butter
4 eggs
1 1/2 cups milk (or half milk and half yogurt)
2 cups grated cheese
Salt and pepper

Preheat oven to 400°F (200°C). In a cast iron pan, sauté the leeks and mushrooms in butter until cooked. While they are cooking, bake the pie shells for 5 minutes. Remove from the oven and lower the temperature to 375°F (190°C). In a separate bowl, beat together the eggs, milk, salt, and pepper. When the vegetables are soft, put them in the pie shells. Top with grated cheese and pour the milk mixture over. Bake for 30 to 35 minutes until firm. Serves 4-6 with leftovers for lunch.

♥ Leek and Mushroom Casserole

Cooked noodles or rice
3 cups sliced mushrooms
3 cups sliced leeks
3 tbsp butter
3 tbsp flour
3 cups stock
1 tsp dill
Salt and pepper

Sauté the mushrooms and leeks in butter for about 5-10 minutes. Add the flour and stir to blend well. Gradually stir in the stock, blending to make a smooth sauce. Season with dill, salt, and pepper. Stir the sauce into cooked noodles or rice and if desired add cooked chicken, canned salmon, grated cheese, or cubed tofu. Serves 4-6.

Baked Spaghetti Squash

1 spaghetti squash
3 tbsp butter
2 tbsp brown sugar (optional)
Salt and pepper

Preheat oven to 350°F (175°C). Bake the whole spaghetti squash for about 1 hour or until a fork goes in easily. Cut in half, remove the seeds, and scoop out the spaghetti-like flesh. Place in a bowl, add butter and brown sugar, and mix well. Season with salt and pepper. Serves 6-8.

Spaghetti Squash with Onions, Garlic, and Tomatoes

3-4 cups cooked spaghetti squash
4 cloves garlic, minced
1 onion, finely chopped
2 cups chopped tomatoes
2 tbsp oil
1 tsp oregano
1 tsp basil
1 small bunch parsley, chopped
1/8 - 1/4 tsp finely chopped hot pepper
Salt and pepper

Sauté the onion and garlic in oil over medium heat until soft. Add the chopped tomatoes, hot pepper, and herbs and simmer for 5-10 minutes. Stir in the spaghetti squash, heat through and serve. Top with grated cheese if desired. Serves 4-6.

Garlic Mashed Potatoes

1 bulb garlic
8-10 medium potatoes, cooked and
    mashed
1 cup milk
3-4 tbsp butter
Salt and pepper

Roast the garlic in a 350°F (175°C) oven until soft, about 20 minutes. When cool use your fingers to squeeze the soft garlic into a bowl. Add to the potatoes along with the milk and the butter, blending well. Season with salt and pepper. Serves 6.

Oven Roasted Potatoes

12 medium potatoes, peeled and cut into
    1-2" pieces
1/3 cup oil
1/2 tsp each thyme, oregano, salt, and
pepper

Preheat oven to 350°F (175°C). Place all the ingredients in a 9x13" baking pan, mix well, and bake until potatoes are tender, about 1 hour. Serves 6.

Pumpkin Soup

2 tbsp butter
1 onion, chopped
2 tbsp flour
2 cups stock
2 cups cooked pumpkin purée*
2 cups milk
1/2 tsp thyme
1/4 tsp nutmeg
Fresh parsley

Melt the butter in a large saucepan. Sauté the onion until soft. Blend in the flour and cook for 5 minutes. Add the stock, pumpkin, milk, thyme, and nutmeg and cook until thick, stirring constantly. Garnish with lots of fresh parsley. Serves 4.

* See the next page for cooked pumpkin purée.

Pumpkin Pie

2 cups cooked pumpkin purée*
1 1/2 cups light cream
1/2 cup brown sugar
1/2 tsp ginger
1/4 tsp cloves
11 tsp cinnamon
/4 tsp nutmeg
1/4 tsp allspice
1/2 tsp salt
3 eggs
1 cup mincemeat (optional)
1 9" pie shell

Preheat oven to 400°F (200°C). Using a potato masher, whisk, or food processor combine the pumpkin, cream, sugar, spices, and eggs. Line the pie shell with a layer of mincemeat. Pour the pumpkin mixture on top. Bake for 15 minutes, then lower the temperature to 350°F (175°C) and bake for another 45 minutes. Serves 6-8.

Pumpkin Muffins

2 cups flour
2 tsp baking powder
1 tsp cinnamon
1/2 tsp ginger
1/2 tsp nutmeg
1/2 cup brown sugar or honey
1 1/2 cups cooked pumpkin purée*
1/4 cup melted butter
3 eggs
1/2 cup sunflower seeds (optional)

Preheat oven to 350°F (175°C). Combine the dry ingredients in a bowl. In another bowl combine the pumpkin, melted butter, and eggs. Add the wet ingredients and the sunflower seeds to the flour and spices. Mix until just blended. Pour into greased muffin tins. Bake for 25 minutes. Makes 1 dozen muffins.

*Pumpkin Purée

Baking method: Preheat oven to 350°F (175°C). Place the whole pumpkin on a baking sheet and bake until easily pierced with a fork. Cut in half, remove the seeds, and scoop out the pulp. Purée using a potato masher or a food processor, adding water if necessary.

Boiling Method: Cut the pumpkin in half and scoop out the seeds. Cut into large chunks and remove the peel. Cut into 3-4" chunks and place in a pot with 2-3" of water on the bottom. Steam until soft, about 20-25 minutes. Drain and purée using a potato masher or a food processor.

Food for Thought

Community Action Projects Involving Gardens

It is relatively easy to describe and identify the environmental or health benefits of having a garden, but there are also many important yet perhaps less obviously tangible reasons for growing one's own food. For many, gardens are an important source of emotional and spiritual relaxation, islands of tranquility and refuge in an all too busy and noisy world. Gardening can be an extremely meditative experience where one can gain very important insights and understandings that perhaps are not evident outside of Nature. In my own experience, the opportunity to work in a garden allowed me to connect with nature and to discover a different kind of knowing, one that was perhaps once an inherent part of human consciousness. The processes, balances, and constraints that operate within nature and that ultimately govern my own existence expressed themselves over and over again through my garden and this has contributed in very significant ways to my development as a person.

There is also the experience of harvesting and eating one's own food. Food is fundamental to our daily lives. Through food, Nature converts energy from the sun, air, and earth into something that nourishes us. When one stops and really thinks about this process, it is nothing less than magical. When we grow our own food, we are directly experiencing this manifestation of Nature's role in our lives. It is through these kinds of interactions with the natural world that we begin to realize the full extent to which the Earth nurtures us. We experience first hand the ways in which nature works and the ways in which all things are connected. This kind of understanding is essential if we are to shift our own world view to the kind of Earth-centered philosophy that is so necessary if we are to achieve environmental sustainability and ensure our own survival.

One of the most powerful aspects of a garden is its incredible ability to nourish us, not only physically, but emotionally and spiritually as well. A garden is a peaceful place in which to work or putter to one's own inner rhythm while contemplating life and day-to-day events. For many a garden is an accepting place where a person can find expression and accomplishment without criticism. There are many who have used gardens and growing as a means to bring healing to those who feel disenfranchised or who are marginalized within our society. Since gardens abound with parallels to life, they provide an experiential and meaningful form of education, where simple but important lessons can be observed and pondered. Seniors meet for gardening programs; horticultural therapy is a recognized profession; and there are many interesting programs that connect youth with food. On the following pages, I profile three innovative programs that build community through gardening.

The Food Project

The Food Project farms twenty-one acres of conservation land and a total of two acres of inner-city land in and around Dorchester, about fifteen miles west of Boston. The project began in 1991 with a farmer named Ward Cheney who wanted to "practice care for land and community" by growing and distributing food to Boston's hungry. With a small initial grant and a staff of two, Cheney set about creating the Food Project, which today boasts a staff of sixteen, a paid summer crew of sixty suburban and inner city teens, and more than 1000 adult volunteers. Together they grow and harvest more than 150,000 pounds of food a year; half of this is sold at two low-cost city markets and the other half is donated to local food banks, soup kitchens, and homeless shelters. The volunteers and staff also contribute about 2,500 hours of time to these same soup kitchens and shelters. Food Project initiatives focus on all aspects of the food system and this has led to the creation of several small food businesses, a Community Supported Agriculture operation, a free community lunch program, and an Environmental Protection Agency-sponsored environmental awareness program. The Food Project also works with about 150 inner city families, largely African American or Cape Verdean, who have backyard vegetable gardens and want advice or extra help. These initiatives foster a sense of pride and community spirit in the inner-city neighbourhoods that they serve.

For the teens participating in the project there are many benefits. Many speak of working side by side with teens from different cultural and social backgrounds. For some there is a greater awareness of the issues surrounding poverty, race, and community. For others it is the first time they have had to do hard physical work. There is a real sense of connection to the work that takes place. If it is done well then there is a successful harvest; where work is neglected or poorly done, the harvest reflects this. The program provides education about environmental and social issues through a series of workshops and discussion groups and the youth are expected to actively share this knowledge with their communities. Teens are also members of the Board of Directors and are encouraged to contribute to its leadership and organization. Since its inception fifteen years ago, The Food Project has worked to establish reciprocal and respectful relationships with all those whom it serves and has brought lasting and positive change to the workings of Boston's inner city food systems.

Foodshare

Operating out of a large warehouse on the fringe of industrial land and surrounded by freeways, FoodShare Toronto runs a variety of programs that address issues of poverty and food security in the city of Toronto.

· Its largest program, ***The Good Food Box***, delivers a monthly box of wholesale priced fruit and vegetables to low-income families. The program started in 1985 with 45 customers—today volunteers pack more than 4000 boxes a month with produce that is either grown by FoodShare Toronto or purchased directly through a network of local farmers.

· ***The Urban Agriculture Program*** operates beehives, a sprouting operation, and several urban gardens, including a joint garden with the Centre for Addiction and Mental Health on Queen Street. Most of the produce from these gardens is distributed through the Good Food Box program.

· For residents of ***the Centre for Addiction and Mental Health***, the garden work is a unique form of therapy that allows them to build self-esteem and to earn a small paycheque. Other benefits include improved social skills, a greater awareness of nutrition, and practice working with other people.

· FoodShare Toronto also operates a ***fully equipped industrial kitchen*** that can be rented to individuals wishing to learn the ropes before opening their own businesses as well as a catering operation where participants learn to prepare meals for other volunteers and for private and corporate functions.

Focus on Food is FoodShare's latest initiative. This project is a Youth Services Project funded through Human Resources Development Canada. The program employs approximately 16 young people, many with multiple barriers and many on the verge of homelessness, in all aspects of FoodShare's operations. The intent is to help participants develop a focus and improve their self-esteem. Focus on Food also works to provide participants with employable skills, not only gardening skills, but also time and people management skills developed through working co-operatively with volunteers and participants from all walks of life. For many troubled young people, Focus on Food provides "meaningful work in a non-judgmental environment." Working with residents of the Centre for Addiction and Mental Health, youth must develop both patience and tolerance. Preparing soil, planting seeds, and nurturing plants bring a feeling of hope and teach valuable lessons in planning and care.

Focus on Food proudly boasts many success stories, from a university dropout who was living on the streets and addicted to heroin who is now back at university, to a young immigrant who was expelled from high school and is now back attending college, to a young woman recovering from cancer who, after participating in all aspects of FoodShare's operations, decided that she wanted to open her own bakery. FoodShare is a multidimensional program that advocates for a more equitable food system while bringing healing and discovery to those who pass through its programs.

The Edible Schoolyard

Martin Luther King Jr. Middle School, in Berkeley, California, is the site for a wonderful and comprehensive project called The Edible Schoolyard. Gardeners, staff, students, and parents envisioned the project in 1994, and in 1995 they restored a two-acre parking lot adjacent to the school. With the help of a garden manager they planted an acre of beds with seasonal produce, grains, herbs, vines, berries, and flowers. The remaining acre contains an outdoor classroom (called the Ramada), a tool shed, seed propagation tables, a chicken coop, and pizza oven, as well as a variety of fruit trees.

Students participate in all aspects of the garden, including preparing beds, planting seeds, tending crops, and harvesting produce. There is also a kitchen where students and teachers prepare and enjoy the food they have harvested. Through hands-on activities, students learn about concepts related to the cycles of food production and the principles of ecology.

All grades participate in the garden but for Grades 6 through 8, both the garden and the kitchen are integral parts of the science and humanities curricula. Teachers and garden staff teach eleven classes of 90 minutes each in the garden every week. Volunteers come on a weekly basis so they can work with a specific class and get to know the students. Key concepts of community, sustainability, diversity, responsibility, networks, systems, and cycles are linked to the work done in the Edible Schoolyard. It was the decision of school staff to integrate the Edible Schoolyard activities into the regular classroom education because it was felt that it would enrich students' overall educational experience. Specific lessons that meet the California Standards are developed in conjunction with the garden; these include composting, vermiculture, plant structure and function, and ecology. The garden also gives teachers and students the opportunity to interact in a setting that is quite different from the traditional classroom and teachers are able to gain insight into different aspects of a child's abilities and potential. The program helps students to appreciate the value of nature and of meaningful, physical work while fostering a sense of co-operation and collective responsibility within the school.

The Edible Schoolyard program works in conjunction with the nearby Center for Ecoliteracy to teach principals of ecology, sustainability, and conservation. The garden provides an example of a managed ecosystem and is an ideal way to teach principles of ecology and systems management. Central to the sustainability of natural ecosystems is the principle of zero waste and of recycling and reusing all elements of that ecosystem. Students gain an understanding of their roles and responsibilities in a sustainable community. It is hoped that by understanding the principles of organization that ecosystems have developed to sustain life students will be better able to create and maintain sustainable communities in the future.

Sources and Further Information

Simmons, Katrina, *FoodShare's Focus on Food, fertile ground for change* in EcoFarm and Garden, Volume 5, #1, Winter, 2002, Ottawa.

www.edibleschoolyard.org

www.foodshare.net

www.WhatKidsCanDo.org/The Food Project

DECEMBER

A garden really lives only insofar
As it is an expression of faith,
The embodiment of hope,
And a song of praise.

— Russell Page (1905 – 1985), *British landscape artist and garden designer*

In the Garden

December is a time for rest, reflection, and renewal. Your garden has a natural rhythm to it that, for all of our technology, we really can't change. It has worked hard all summer and must now take time to rest before Spring and another season of growing. As we find connections to nature, we also can begin to find meaning in these rhythms. So I hope that for you too, December is a time to rest, to enjoy the quiet of nature, to feel warmth and contentment in your life, and to find pleasure in your accomplishments. In reflection, I wish you many happy hours mulling over your experiences and thinking about all the new ideas and skills that have found their way into your life as you have embraced this idea that is gardening. Aside from the physical accomplishment of growing your own food, there is the beauty of spending time outside and of being intimately connected to that which nourishes you. And finally, in renewal, I hope that you have that wonderful feeling of excitement and enthusiasm for the next year that for me is so much a part of my relationship with my garden. I wish you a very peaceful and happy December.

A Few Holiday Recipes

Roasted Vegetables
3-4 parsnips
3-4 medium carrots
1 sweet potato
1/2 lb mushrooms
2 red onions
4 cloves garlic, chopped
1/3 cup oil
Salt and pepper

Preheat oven to 350°F (175°C). Peel the parsnips and carrots and slice into 1/4" slices. Peel the sweet potato and cut into 1" cubes. Clean the mushrooms and cut the larger ones in half. Cut the onion into thick wedges. Combine all of the ingredients in a 9x13" baking pan and bake for 1 hour or until vegetables are tender. Serves 6-8.

Scalloped Potatoes
6-8 medium potatoes
1 onion, thinly sliced
2 cups milk, soymilk, and/or cream
Salt and pepper

Preheat oven 375°F (175°C). Clean the potatoes and peel if you wish. Cut into 1/8" slices. Layer the potato and onion slices in a 9x13" baking pan, add the milk, salt, and pepper and stir lightly. Bake for 45 minutes or until potatoes are soft. Serves 6.

Potato Leek Pie

2 9" pie crusts
5 cups thinly sliced leeks
3 tbsp butter
3 cups mashed potatoes
1 pound cottage cheese
1 cup feta cheese, crumbled
2 eggs
Salt and pepper

Preheat oven to 400°F (200°C). Bake the pie crusts for 10 minutes. Sauté the leeks in butter over medium heat until soft. Combine the cottage cheese and the mashed potatoes and beat until smooth. Add the feta cheese, eggs, salt, and pepper. Place half the leeks in each pie crust and top with half the potato mixture. Reduce the oven temperature to 350°F and bake another 45 minutes. Top with grated Parmesan cheese if desired. Serves 6-8.

Baked Squash, Onions, and Apples

6 cups squash, peeled and cut into 1" cubes
3-4 medium onions, cut in wedges
3 apples, cored and cut in wedges
3 tbsp butter
Salt and pepper

Preheat oven to 375°F (190°C). Combine all the ingredients in a casserole dish. Cover and bake for 45-50 minutes or until squash is soft. Season with salt and pepper. Serves 6-8. For a nice soup, purée the leftovers and add some stock and/or light cream.

Wild Rice, Cranberry, and Hazelnut Stuffing

1/2 cup wild rice
1/2 cup brown rice
1 tsp parsley
1/2 cup hazelnuts, coarsely chopped
1/2 cup dried cranberries
2 carrots, peeled and grated
1 onion, finely chopped
3 cups water or stock
1/2 tsp thyme
Salt and pepper

Rinse the wild rice and cook in stock or water for 15 minutes. Add the brown rice and simmer until both are tender. Drain any excess moisture. Combine the rice and all of the remaining ingredients. This stuffing is delicious in chicken or turkey (make a double batch) and with baked squash, either alone or topped with grated cheese. Serves 6.

Cranberry Apple Strudel

6 apples
3/4 cup chopped almonds
1 cup dried cranberries
1/3 cup melted butter
Honey or sugar to taste
6-12 sheets phyllo pastry

Preheat oven to 350°F (175°C). Core and slice the apples. Combine the apples, cranberries, almonds, and sweetener to taste. In a 9x13" baking pan place one sheet of phyllo pastry, spread with melted butter, and continue in this way until there are 6-9 layers of buttered pastry. Add the apple mixture. Top with 6-9 layers of phyllo spread with melted butter. Sprinkle with sugar or drizzle with honey. Bake for 45 minutes. Serves 6-8.

Cranberry Upside-down Cake

2 cups cranberries
1/2 cup walnuts
3/4 cup sugar or honey
1 1/2 cups flour
2 tsp baking powder
2 eggs
1/4 cup melted butter
3/4 cup milk
1 tsp grated orange rind

Preheat oven to 350°F (175°C). Butter a 9" square baking pan. Combine the walnuts, cranberries, and 1/4 cup sugar or honey and place in the bottom of the pan. In a bowl, mix together the remaining sugar or honey, flour, baking powder and orange rind. Combine the butter, eggs, and milk. Stir the wet ingredients into the dry ingredients, mix until blended, and spoon over top of the cranberry mixture. Bake for 40 minutes. Serves 6.

Cranberry Muffins

1 1/2 cups flour
2 eggs
1/2 cup sugar or honey
1/4 cup melted butter
1 tbsp baking powder
1 cup milk
1 cup cranberries

Preheat oven to 350°F (175°C). In a large bowl combine the flour, baking powder, and cranberries. Add the remaining ingredients and stir until just blended. Spoon into greased muffin tins and bake for 20-25 minutes. Makes 1 dozen muffins.

Food for Thought
The Road Ahead

It has been almost four years since I wrote an article for Earth Day that was published in my local newspaper. That article inspired me to begin work on this book and is now the introduction to *From Seed to Table*. Its basic message is that by doing even small things that are constructive and positive, we begin to change ourselves and the parameters that govern the world around us, and in doing so we strengthen both ourselves and our communities. Eventually many small changes coalesce and bring about fundamental shifts in society.

Much has changed in these four years and much has remained the same. Local food initiatives are blossoming and the issue even made the front cover of *Time* magazine. In 2007, the United Nations declared that organic agriculture has the greatest potential for feeding the developing world. Throughout the world, there is a call for serious action to reduce greenhouse gas emissions and, according to the polls, Canadians cite climate change and the environment as their most pressing concerns. On the depressing side, those same polls indicate that only 50% of Canadians are willing to make any changes in their lives when it comes to reducing greenhouse gas emissions and the Canadian government continues to spend far more time talking than doing in this area. Farming in Canada is in crisis, with income levels below the poverty line for many small farmers. In 2005, the average conventional farm showed a loss of $10,000 before government subsidies.[1]

In December of 2007, the United Nations Conference on Climate Change was held in Bali, Indonesia. The purpose of this conference was to map out an agenda for upcoming negotiations that will lead to an agreement to succeed Kyoto, which runs out in 2012. The conference has provided some hope for environmentalists, with a general consensus among developed nations and scientists that greenhouse gas emissions must be reduced by somewhere between 25-40% by the year 2020 if we are to have any hope of dealing with climate change. But Canada emerged as the black sheep of the industrialized world at this conference, taking a serious beating from the international community and environmental activists, as well as from our own scientists. Increasingly, we are seen as a country with zero credibility, unwilling to take any kind of serious action, and fundamentally uncooperative in our policies. Of 56 industrialized countries, Canada ranks 53 out of 56 for pollution trends and environmental policy, ahead of only Australia, Saudi Arabia, and the United States. Canada and the United States were the only two countries not to ratify Kyoto and Canada's position at the Bali conference has repeatedly been described as nothing short of obstructionist. The prime minister, Stephen Harper, made it clear that Canada would not sign any agreement unless all major emitters signed and would not take on binding reduction targets without their also being applied to developing countries. We are at odds with the European Union and the rest of the developing world who feel that an agreement must be reached, even if it does not have the support of all countries, and they also feel that industrialized countries must take the lead when it comes to emissions reductions.

On the agricultural front, I have spent twenty some years watching as government policy in Canada and the U.S. has undermined our food systems. These policies have allowed large corporations to sell and plant poorly tested genetically modified crops while increasing their use of polluting chemicals. Consumers have been denied the right to choose through government's failure to implement mandatory labelling of foods and biotech companies have managed to defy any kind of moral imperative to take responsibility for the damage done by their technologies. The kind of corporate maneuvering and farmer harassment and intimidation that has occurred as GM foods have been introduced, patented, and promoted is nothing less than shameful. There have been some encouraging developments in recent years—increasingly new patents are being rejected because of insufficient environmental assessment and, in 2007, the U.S. Patent and Trademark Office rejected four Monsanto patents because the company was using them to "harass, intimidate, sue, and bankrupt farmers."

Waiting for governments to make environmentally responsible changes has never been my forte—and these issues reinforce my basic perception that action must come on the personal level. I believe that the fight for an ecological and just food system is a David versus Goliath battle and one that will not be won through legislation and government leadership. It will be won through consumer action and consumer choice. This has been evident in Europe where biotechnology met with strong consumer resistance. In France, riots at major port cities succeeded in denying entry to ships loaded with U.S. imports of genetically modified grains while in England activists destroyed acres of GM test plots. This kind of consumer action has sent a strong message to both government and industry, resulting in many positive changes. France has announced a moratorium (albeit short) on the planting of GM crops, many major European food stores refuse to carry genetically modified foods, and Britain is actively promoting food with a low carbon footprint.

Canadians are beginning to find their voice in both the local and the environmental food movements. There are many encouraging initiatives, media attention is high, and public awareness is growing daily. Our commitment to our communities and to our environment must be connected to our actions as consumers. If we are strong and committed, our government and its policies will eventually reflect our value systems.

Life is about connections. Living simply and ecologically is about our connection to the planet and to all those who live on it. In my life, opting out of industrial agriculture and what I call "unbridled capitalism" has been my way of saying no to the social and environmental damage that these two are responsible for throughout the world. I strongly believe that when enough of us do this, we create a space where something far healthier can enter.

Eating locally is about our connection to our community and to the land around us. A strong, vibrant community with a healthy agricultural base is a wonderful place in which to live. Local food movements have the potential to build such communities. They also provide far more room for choice in terms of the environmental and social practices associated with the foods we buy. We should not underestimate the value of this choice, nor let it slip away through a lack of consumer support.

Growing food is about our connection to the earth and to the power that is our Universe. As we grow our own food, we must observe principles of care, value, and balance. We must care for the soil so that it can produce plants that are healthy and disease resistant. We learn that the labour and time that we give in order to feed ourselves has very little monetary value and yet it is invaluable. But perhaps most importantly, through doing this simple and basic work, we learn about balance. There must be balance with the micro-organisms that live in the soil, balance between what we take from the garden and what we return to it, and balance between what we grow and what we eat. As we work in the garden we begin to balance the work of the mind with the work of the body. When we take these values into our own lives we find peace and spiritual nourishment. When we take these values into our communities we begin to create a world in which there is room for ideas of social justice, equality, democracy, and peace. It is from this kind of place that lasting and positive change can come.

Endnotes

1   Wallace, Janet, *The Value of Organic* in The Canadian Organic Grower, published by Canadian Organic Growers, Ottawa, Winter, 2007, page 5.

Additional Sources and References

Gardening Books

Batholomew, Mel, *Square Foot Gardening,* Rodale Press, Pennsylvania, 2005.

Coleman, Eliot, The *New Organic Grower,* Chelsea Green Books, White River Junction, Vermont,1995.

Ellis, B and Bradley, M., *The Organic Gardener's Handbook of Natural Insect and Disease Control,* Rodale Press, Pennsylvania, 1992.

Jason, Dan, *Greening the Garden: A Guide to Sustainable Growing,* New Society Publishers, Gabriola Island, B.C., 1991.

Jason, Dan, *The Whole Organic Food Book,* Raincoast Books, Vancouver, 2001.

Proulx, Annie, *The Fine Art of Salad Gardening,* Rodale Press, Pennsylvania, 1985.

Raymond, Dick, *The Joy of Gardening*, Storey Publishing, North Adams, Massachusetts, 1982

Cookbooks & Food Books

Bubel, Nancy and Mike, *Root Cellaring: The Simple, No-Processing Way to Store Fruits and Vegetables,* Rodale Press, Pennsylvania, 1979.

De Green, P. and Newbury, V., *The Chez Piggy Cookbook,* Firefly Books, Toronto, 1998.

Jaffrey, Madhur, *Indian Cookery,* BBC Books, London, 1993.

Harrowsmith Kitchens, *The Harrowsmith Cookbook, Volume #1,* Camden House Press, Ontario, 1991.

Midkiff, Ken, *The Meat You Eat: How Corporate Farming Has Endangered America's Food Supply St.* Martin's Press, New York, 2004

Peterson, Lee, *A Field Guide to Edible Wild Plants,* Houghton Mifflin, Boston, 1977.

Roberts, Wayne; MacRae, Rod and Stahlbrand, Lori, *Real Food For a Change,* Random House, 1999.

Schinharl, Cornelia. et al, *Basic Asian: Everything You Need for Yin and Yang in the Kitchen,* Silverback Books, England, 2003.

Farming & Environmental Issues

Berry, Wendell, The *Gift of Good Land: Further Essays Cultural and Agricultural,* North Point Press, San Francisco, 1989.

Cadbury, Deborah, *Altering Eden: The Feminization of Nature,* St. Martin's Press, New York, 1999.

Lappé, F.M. and Anna, *Hope's Edge: The Next Diet for a Small Planet,* Jeremy Tarcher/Putnam, New York, 2002.

Shiva, Vandana, Stolen *Harvest: The Hijacking of the Global Food Supply,* South End Press, Boston, 1997

Shiva, Vandana, *Staying Alive: Women, Ecology and Development,* Zed Books, London, 1997

Magazines, Newsletters and Organizations

Alternatives Journal, published by the Faculty of Environmental Studies, University of Waterloo, Waterloo, Ontario, N2L 3G1 (*www.alternativesjournal.ca*)

Eco-Farm and Garden, published by Canadian Organic Growers, 323 Chapel St, Ottawa, Ont., K1N 7Z2 (*www.cog.ca*)

ETC Group (Action Group on Erosion, Technology, and Concentration, formerly Rural Advancement Foundation International) Organisation devoted to "the conservation and sustainable
advancement of cultural and ecological diversity and human rights." (*www.etcgroup.org*)

La Via Campesina, an international peasant farmers movement, (*www.viacampesina.org*)

Organic Gardening, Emmaus, PA., 18099 (*www.organicgardening.com*)

Rural Vermont, a grassroots farm organization which publishes an interesting newsletter, (*www.ruralvermont.org*)

Seeds of Diversity Canada, P.O. Box 36, Station Q, Toronto, Ont., M4T 2L7 (*www.seeds.ca*)

Small Farm Canada, Southern Tip Publishing Inc., 4623 William Head Rd, Victoria, B.C., V9C 3Y7 (*www.smallfarmcanada.ca*)

The Ram's Horn, published by Brewster and Cathleen Kneen, Sorrento, B.C. (*www.ramshorn. ca*)

The Union Farmer Monthly, published by the National Farmer's Union, Saskatoon, Sask, (*www.nfu.ca*)